Islam: An Introduction

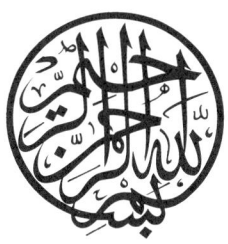

ISLAM
AN INTRODUCTION

Yusuf al-Qaradawi

Translated by
Syed Bashir Ahmad Kashmiri

IBT
Islamic Book Trust
Kuala Lumpur

Published 2010
First reprint 2010

Published by
Islamic Book Trust
607 Mutiara Majestic
Jalan Othman
46000 Petaling Jaya
Selangor, Malaysia
www.ibtbooks.com

Islamic Book Trust is affiliated with The Other Press.

Perpustakaan Negara Malaysia Cataloguing-in-Publication Data

Qaradawi, Yusuf, 1926-
Islam : an introduction / Yusuf Al-Qaradawi ; translated from Arabic : Syed Bashir Ahmad Kashmiri.
Includes index
ISBN 978-967-5062-36-0
ISBN 978-967-5062-35-3 (pbk)
1. Islam. 2. Islam--Doctrines I. Syed Bashir Ahmad Kasmiri
II. Title.
297

This book is a translation based on the author's original work in Arabic, *Madkhal li-Maʿrifah al-Islām.*

Printed by
Vinlin Press Sdn. Bhd.
No. 2, Jalan Meranti Permai 1
Meranti Permai Industrial Park
Batu 15, Jalan Puchong
47100 Puchong, Selangor, Malaysia.

Contents

Note from the Publisher

This work by one of the most influential Muslim scholars of this century comes at a time when a host of Islamic terminology has been thrust into the current media coverage about Islam and Muslims. The rise of what is known in the West as 'political Islam', Islamic finance and greater interest about the moral system of Muslim societies has brought with it many challenges. One of these challenges is to explain Islam in a way that will undress the many intellectual disguises behind which Islamic tenets have been misinterpreted both by Muslims and non-Muslims for their own selfish ends.

In his inimitable style, Shaykh Yusuf al-Qaradawi's *Madkhal li-Ma'rifah al-Islām* (*lit.* "An Introduction to Knowing Islam"), first published in 1996, attempts to explain Islamic concepts and decipher their meaning in the context of contemporary debates. Divided into five chapters, much of Qaradawi's explanation of Islamic concepts is compared with current issues and perspectives on Islam. This work is not an attempt to preach to the reader, rather, it aims to fill the gaps in one's understanding of the Islamic worldview, breaking away from the usual arrangement of Islamic topics that is found in many introductory books on Islam.

Translating from Arabic into English is no easy task, especially when the work is penned by a prolific scholar such as Qaradawi whose writings have had a huge influence in contemporary debates involving Islam and Muslims. As such, Syed Bashir Ahmad Kashmiri is to be commended for taking up this challenge, showing a commitment to complete the work long before we were able to settle on the final revision. As the translation underwent several revisions, the result is not an exact reproduction of the original. The nature of the English language is such that paraphrasing thoughts is unavoidable in order to get the intended message across to the English-thinking minds. Despite this, we hope we have done justice to the original work in our effort to present Qaradawi's thought in simple language to the ordinary reader. The publication of this work also partly fulfils our ongoing programme to introduce works by traditional Muslim scholars who are savvy about modern day issues.

Islamic Book Trust,
Kuala Lumpur.

Translator's Preface

Translating religious texts is a unique exercise. It is sometimes claimed that a translation amounts to a betrayal of the original text. This cannot be truer about religious texts, wherein a slight remissness can result in digression, making something wicked into devout.

Islam being a meticulous system encompassing every aspect of the individual as well as social life, it becomes all the more important to convey the intended message accurately, especially when the source text is characterised with rhetorical eloquence. In this case, the Arabic syntax and expression make the source text more intricate.

Shaykh Yusuf al-Qaradawi's style is eloquent. His thoughts are conveyed in an explanatory manner, and his ideas traverse in such a way that whole paragraphs are comprised of single sentences.

Translating *Madkhal li-Ma'rifah al-Islām* by interpreting the intended meanings and then conveying it using my own expression would have been smoother for English readers who have not read the original Arabic text. Yet, it would not have done justice to the sophistication of Qaradawi's work. To preserve his style and delivery and also to conserve the flavour of the original, I have attempted to adhere to the author's style, and not resorted to omission of texts in order to remove repetitive expression.

Certainly mine is not a literal translation of the source text, but I believe that it is imperative to remain faithful to the author and not to overdo the translation or to rewrite the original and thus deprive the reader of relishing the essence of Qaradawi's message. I have also not adopted the standard rule for translating Arabic-Islamic terminology into English. Rather, I have tried to be as close as possible to the meaning in its specific context. Lastly, in giving the meaning of the Qur'anic verses, I have borrowed from the work of the late 'Abdullah Yūsuf 'Alī.

Dr Syed Bashir Ahmad Kashmiri
Assistant Professor of Translation and Interpretation
University of Nizwa, Oman.

Foreword

Praise be to Allah, Who suffices. Peace be upon His Messenger, whom He chose, especially upon Muḥammad (ṣ)—the seal of the prophets—upon his family, upon his Companions, and upon all those who shall follow them rightly till the Day of Judgement.

This book is intended to be a window to the world of Islam, a gateway to acquaint those who are unfamiliar with it, or for those whose knowledge of Islam is insufficient or distorted. It is also intended to be a reminder and an affirmation to those who do have a sufficient knowledge of Islam; 'for surely, remembrance benefits the faithful'. It is an introduction to the fundamental constituents of Islam, of its general characteristics, of its major goals and of its untainted sources, as well as being a narrative for the need of religion in general and for Islam in particular.

It is in this light that this book has been divided into the following chapters:

Chapter 1: The Need for Religion: Its necessity for the intellect, the self and the nature of an individual; and society's need for a purpose and a set of guiding principles.

Chapter 2: The Essentials of Islam: Its constituent parts such as belief, worship, morals and legislation.

Chapter 3: The Characteristics of Islam: Godliness, humanness, comprehensiveness, moderation and its accommodating nature (in Sharīʻah).

Chapter 4: The Objectives of Islam: The development of a righteous human being, a righteous family, a righteous society, a righteous nation, a righteous state, and the 'Call' for the benefit of humanity.

Chapter 5: The Sources of Islam: The Qur'an and the Sunnah (i.e., the prophetic tradition as an elucidation and explanation of the Qur'an).

In describing these important aspects of Islam, I have referred to my previous writings such as: *Al-Īmān wal Hayāt* (Faith and Life), *Al-'Ibādah fil Islām* (Worship in Islam), *Al-Khaṣā'iṣ al-'Āmah lil-Islām* (General Chracteristics of Islam), *Al-Marja'iyyah al-'Ulyah lil-Qur'ān wal Sunnah* (Supreme Authority of the Qur'an and the Sunnah) and *Bayyināt al-Ḥal al-Islāmī* (The Clear Signs of the Islamic Solution) and among others.

Whoever wishes to acquire a wider knowledge of the subjects that appear in this book should refer to the details found in the books mentioned above.

I sincerely hope that all that I have written herein will be sufficient for a modern day Muslim, so that they may become familiar with the great realities attached to the Islamic faith and that this book equips them with the right amount of Islamic knowledge so desperately required for a Muslim of our times. This will enable them to acquaint themselves with the essence of their religion, in a manner that is free from fragmentation, dogmatism, distortion and parody, and one which is safe from the corruption of fanatical Muslims, from the deceptions of the liars and the interpretations of the ignorant.

The book shall also present a true picture of the basics of this religion to those non-Muslims who desire to understand Islam, the religion with which Allah chose to send His final book and with which He sent His final Messenger, as a mercy for the whole universe and as an evidence of authority for the whole of humankind.

My accomplishment is only contingent upon the mercy of Allah, in Whom I put all my trust and to Whom I always turn.

Ever a *faqīr* before his Lord,
Yusuf al-Qaradawi
Doha, Rajab 1416 H.

CHAPTER 1

The Need for Religion

THE MEANING OF RELIGION

Before we discuss the need for religion in general, and for Islam in particular, it is incumbent upon us to clarify the meaning of the word religion. We will not go into the detailed discussions surrounding the word religion as stated by linguists, historians of religion, or as discussed by philosophers of various beliefs. Rather, we will deal with the subject directly.

The subject of religion has been studied in detail by Muḥammad 'Abdullah Darrāz in his brilliant book *al-Dīn*. He has arrived at the following definition of religion, regardless of whether it is considered to be true or false or based on revelation or polytheism:

> Religion is the belief in an unseen Higher Power (or powers) which has a sensibility and a will of its own. This Greater Power has absolute dominion and providence over the affairs of man. It is the belief that one can call upon and seek refuge in this Sublime Essence in times of fear and longing

> or purely out of submissiveness and praise. In sum, religion is the belief in a "divine being which is worthy of worship and obedience." This is the case when we look at religion from a psychological perspective, in terms of religiosity. However, if the meaning has any external reality, we can say it is a set of abstract concepts which define that Divine Power and which outlines the way to worship It.[1]

This definition is encompassing of the word religion, even if the said religion is one established on polytheism or idolatry. This embracing definition is also the Qur'anic definition of religion, as shown by the following verses:

> *To you be your way, and to me mine.* [109:6]

> *If anyone desires a religion other than Islam (submission to Allah), never will it be accepted of him; and in the Hereafter He will be in the ranks of those who have lost (all spiritual good).* [3:85]

Islamic scholars, understood the term religion as "a divine scheme which encourages those with sound minds to make the correct choices regarding the present life and the Hereafter."

THE UNITY OF DIVINELY INSPIRED RELIGIONS

Scholars of religion have classified religion into two categories:

Divinely inspired religions or religions based on a revealed scripture

This is taken to mean those religions with a revealed scripture, containing guidance for mankind. For example, Judaism

---

1. p.52, *al-Dīn* (Dār al-Qalam, Kuwait).

is based on the Torah as was revealed to the prophet Moses, Christianity is based on the Bible as revealed to Jesus and Islam is based on the Qur'an as was revealed to the last Messenger, and the final prophet of God, Muḥammad (ṣ).

The difference between Islam and other revealed religions is the belief that God has protected the foundations of Islam and its sources from corruption by virtue of it being the final divinely inspired message sent to mankind. It is believed that these sources have not been subjected to any kind of distortion or change. On the other hand, the sources of other religions were not safeguarded and therefore were liable to distortion, alteration and, in some cases, were lost altogether.

Pagan traditions

These religions have their origins in the physical world rather than being divinely inspired revelations. They have more to do with human beings than God. In this category one could place Buddhism (as practised in China and Japan), Hinduism (as practised in India), Zoroastrianism as once practiced by the ancient Persians, and a host of other Asian and African religions. These religions are essentially either man-made or else were once religions with scriptures that were subsequently lost, leaving no trace, as in the case of Zoroastrianism.

Ultimately, all the divinely inspired religions are united in their fundamental beliefs despite the differing laws within them, which are relative to their time. This point has been elucidated and emphasised in the Qur'an:

> *The same religion has He established for you as that which He enjoined on Noah—that which We have sent by inspiration to*

> *thee—and that which We enjoined on Abraham, Moses, and Jesus: Namely, that ye should remain steadfast in religion, and make no divisions therein...* [42:13]

And in another passage God says:

> *...To each among you have We prescribed a Law and an Open Way...* [5:48]

The Qur'an has affirmed that the religion of God is one. It is based on this single religion that God has sent all His revelations and messengers. This religion, as He, the Exalted, states, is Islam:

> *The Religion before Allah is Islam (submission to His Will)...* [3:19]

Viewed in this light, all the messengers sent by God were Muslims and advocated the religion of Islam:

> *Abraham was not a Jew nor yet a Christian but he was true in faith and bowed his will to Allah's (which is Islam), and he joined not gods with Allah.* [3:67]

> *And this was the legacy that Abraham left to his sons, and so did Jacob; "Oh my sons! Allah has chosen the Faith for you; then die not except in the Faith of Islam."* [2:132]

In the Qur'an the prophet Moses calls on his people saying:

> *O my people! If ye do (really) believe in Allah, then in Him put your trust if ye submit (your will to His).* [10:84]

The disciples of Jesus said to him:

> *... We are Allah's helpers: We believe in Allah, and do you bear witness that we are Muslims.* [3:52]

The prophet Muḥammad (ṣ), known as the Seal of the Prophets, was sent with the revelation of Islam—the religion of all the previous messengers sent by God. He confirmed the religions and revelations that preceded him, corroborating all contained therein concerning the realities of religion and rectitude. Furthermore, the Qur'an was revealed to surpass those former revelations by way of correcting the linguistic distortions and misinterpretations of God's word. Also integral to the revelation of the Qur'an was the refinement of good character, which all of God's previous prophets promulgated until mankind had reached its peak of maturity, and its guidance was complete.

God, the Exalted, addresses his Messenger, Muḥammad (ṣ) saying:

> *To you We sent the Scripture in truth confirming the scripture that came before it and guarding it in safety; so judge between them by what Allah has revealed and follow not their vain desires diverging from the truth that has come to you...* [5:48]

Let us now move on to clarify the individual and collective need of human beings for religion in general, particularly for the revealed religions and especially for the seal of all religions, Islam.

MAN'S NEED FOR RELIGION

Man's general need for religion, and for Islam specifically, is not a secondary need but an essential need pertaining to the essence of life itself, to the secret of existence itself and to the deepest depths of man's being.

We shall now try to describe, as concisely as possible, the need for religion in man's life.

Need of the intellect to know greater realities of existence

Man's need for religious belief springs, primarily, from the desire to know himself, to know the macrocosm that surrounds him and to know the answers to those questions that have engaged the philosophers of the past who failed to reach a satisfying conclusion.

Since its inception, mankind has been plagued by questions pertaining to existence, demanding an answer. Such questions as: from where did I come? What will be my end? And why am I here? However much the needs of his daily life may distract him from these pressing inquiries, he will most surely stop one day to ask himself these timeless questions:

He will ask himself: where did I come from? Where did this universe around me come from? Did I come into existence on my own, or is there a creator who created me? If so, what is this Creator? What is my connection with It? Did this enormous world around me, with its earth and sky; with its animals, plants, inanimate bodies and surrounding planets, come into being of its own accord or was it the creation of an Intelligent Designer?

What is there after this life, after death? What will be the end of this short-lived journey to earth? Can it be that the story of life is simply one of "as wombs deliver [the new born], the earth devours [the dead]" and nothing else after that? How is it fair that the end of virtuous people, who sacrificed their lives for the sake of truth and decency, will be similar to the end of the iniquitous, who massacred others relentlessly according to their own evil and vain desires? Does this life end with death? Or is there another life wherein those who did evil are rewarded with the evil they did, and those who did good rewarded with goodness?

Why did man come into existence? Why, unlike any other living animal, has man been given the faculties of intellect, free-will and discernment? Why is it that all things in the heavens and the earth have been made subservient to man's needs? Is there a purpose to his existence? Does he have an aim in life? Or was man brought into existence merely to eat and drink like cattle and then to die, departing from this life as though he were an animal? If there is a purpose to his existence, what then is this purpose? How does he realise this purpose?

Man has been confronted with such perplexing questions throughout the ages, and has sought to find convincing answers to put his heart at rest. However, satisfactory answers to these questions can only be found by resorting to religion and by having recourse to an unsullied religious belief. It is religion, in the first instance, which makes man cognizant of the fact that he did not come into existence by chance and that he is not alone in this universe. Rather, it informs man that he is in fact a creation of an All-powerful Creator. This Creator is his cherisher, the one who created him in due proportion and gave him a balanced form; breathed into him something of His spirit; gave him the faculties of listening, seeing and feeling (in the heart); and bestowed upon man innumerable blessings, from the very moment when he was a mere embryo, lodged in the womb of his mother:

> *Have We not created you from a fluid (held) despicable?—The which We placed in a place of rest, firmly fixed, for a period (of gestation), determined (according to need)? For We do determine (according to need); for We are the best to determine (things).* [77:20-23]

Religion also informs man that this vast universe around him is neither indifferent to him, nor is it his rival. Just like him, the universe is also God's creation; it does not go on blindly on its course, nor does it follow its cosmic course arbitrarily; everything is fixed and precise; and every event and movement is calculated and measured. This is a bounty from God bestowed upon man, so that he may enjoy His blessings, benefit from His benedictions, reflect over His signs, and above all, that he may infer from all these signs that he surely has a Cherisher:

> *Who has created and further given order and proportion, Who has ordained laws, and granted guidance.* [87:2-3]

> *Behold! in the creation of the heavens and the earth, and the alternation of night and day—there are indeed Signs for men of understanding.* [3:190]

It is this belief which connects man with the macrocosm and to the Lord of existence itself. It ensures that he does not live withdrawn from the knowledge of himself and does not feel estranged from his surroundings.

Religion tells man what his fate shall be after death. It informs him that through death, one is not made completely extinct. It tells man that death is but a transitional phase to another stage of existence, the *barzakh* or the interval of the grave, after which there will be the resurrection, wherein every person will be recompensed for all his deeds. After this, he will reside in eternity in all that he had ever worked for. No one's deeds, whether male or female, will be in vain, nor shall any tyrant or arrogant person escape the grasp of divine justice:

> *On that Day will men proceed in companies sorted out to be shown the Deeds that they (had done). Then shall anyone who has done an atom's weight of good see it! And anyone who has done an atom's weight of evil shall see it.* [99:6-8]

It is in this conscious state that man shall reside in for eternity and realises that his creation is one destined for eternity and that death is merely a temporary vehicle which transports him from one abode to another.

It is religion which informs man of the questions: why is there a creation? Why all these bounties and blessings? It lets man know the purpose of his existence and his aim in life. It tells him that he has not been created in vain nor has he been left unguided; that he has been created to be the representative of God on the earth. It is through this knowledge that man has dominion over the earth and cultivates it according to God's will and preference, discovering therein hidden riches of various kinds and eating of all that is good on earth. He does this without transgressing the rights due to his fellow human beings and remains ever vigilant of the rights due to his Lord. The first debt that he owes to his Lord and Cherisher is that He alone should be worshipped and that nothing be associated with Him. Another right belonging to his Lord is that He be worshipped according to the law He has prescribed and revealed through His messengers, whom He sent to mankind as torchbearers, teachers, as bearers of glad tidings and warners. If man fulfils his duty in this life, which is fraught with trials and tribulations, he will be rewarded in the hereafter:

> *On the day when every soul will be confronted with all the good it has done...* [3:30]

Thus, one realises the secret of his existence and one is made aware of one's goal in life. This awakening is bestowed upon him by the Originator of the universe, the Provider of life and the Creator of man.

One who lives life with no religion, with no faith in God and the hereafter, is one most deprived. He sees himself as merely an animal, no different from the various animals that he sees moving and crawling along the surface of the earth. Like such animals who live life in futile pleasures and then die without realising the secret or purpose of their existence. Such a life is fruitless and worthless where one exists, but is ignorant of how one came to be and of who brought him into existence. Such an individual lives, but does not know why he lives. He dies, but does not know why he dies and knows not what there is after death. This person lives a life dogged by doubt and is blind concerning the aim of life, about the reality of life and death, about his origins and ultimate end. He is like those about whom God says:

> *Still less can their knowledge comprehend the Hereafter: nay they are in doubt and uncertainty thereof; nay they are blind thereunto!* [27:66]

How harsh is the life lived in the agony of doubt and confusion, in the darkness of ignorance concerning matters most important to man's existence. Matters concerning the reality of his own self, of the secret of his existence and the ultimate objective of his life. This person is surely one most abject, even if he is a wealthy person with mountains of gold, fine silk and one who enjoys much luxury and comfort in life. He may even be one who has excelled in his education and has gained the highest marks in academia. There is a big difference between a man who knows the real purpose of life and one who does not as the poet 'Umar Khayyām exclaimed in his state of confusion and doubt:

> I was made to wear the dress of life, never was I consulted;
> I wandered there vacillating between many thoughts!
> The day shall come when I will have to shed this attire
> And never will I know: why I came here and where I am going;

And yet another poet exclaims with conviction:

> Death is merely a journey;
> But a journey from a state of annihilation to the state of eternal abidance.

'Umar ibn 'Abd al-'Azīz once remarked: "We were created for eternity; and we shall be delivered from one abode to another."

Man's yearning for religion emanates, before everything, from the desire to know the reality of his self and to know the realities of a greater existence. One of the foremost of these realities is to know the existence of God, His unity and His perfect exaltedness. It is through knowledge of Him and faith in Him, the Most Exalted, that the mystery of existence itself begins to unfold, and the purpose of life becomes clearer to those who were once perplexed, and the way is plainly defined.

The need of human nature

So far we have mentioned man's need for religion based primarily on an intellectual level, but there are also man's emotional requirements. Man's make up is not made up of intelligence alone like that of an electronic computer. His complex constitution is one which consists of an intellect, emotions, and also consists of the soul. This is the sum of man's constitution. The nature of man is such that science and knowledge alone do not convince him nor does art and literature alone satiate his appetite for inquiry. His emptiness is not one which is easily fulfilled by futile pleasures. His self remains restless, his soul remains hungry and his intuitive nature remains quenchless, with an inexplicable feeling of emptiness and void until he finds faith in God. When man attains faith in God, anxiety is alleviated and replaced by contentment, unrest is replaced by tranquillity, and a sense of security prevails in the place of fear, and he feels that he has finally found himself.

The philosopher Auguste Sietec writes in his book *The Philosophy of Religions*:

> 'Why am I religious?' Whenever I put this question to myself, I find myself compelled to answer: 'I am religious, because I cannot find it in myself not to be. Religiosity is simply one of the essential subjective attributes of my nature'. People tell me that this sentiment is a remnant of my past, my upbringing or merely my temperament. I respond to them by

> saying, 'Many times have I remonstrated with myself, raising these very same objections, but these objections do nothing but retreat from the matter altogether instead of helping to solve it.'

It is no wonder then that this kind of belief (of religion being part of our essential nature) has been prevalent among most peoples, primitive or civilised, in every continent and both in the East and West. It has been found in every epoch, irrespective of the fact that the majority of people were not on the Straight Path *i.e.*, Islam.

The Greek historian Plutarch says: "History has shown us cities without castles, cities without palaces, cities without schools, but never has it shown us cities without places of worship..."

This is the reason why the Qur'an has said religion—in the sense of belief—is part of human nature itself:

> *So set you your face steadily and truly to the Faith: (establish) Allah's handiwork according to the pattern on which He has made mankind...* [30:30]

Man's need for psychological health and spiritual strength

Man's other need for religion stems from the hopes and pain endured throughout life. He needs an unmovable, strong pillar to rely on whenever he is struck by the tribulations of life. Such trials may come in the form of losing ones belongings, being faced with difficult circumstances, losing what one loves most, having to face what one hates most, not fulfilling ones hopes or being confronted with your worst fears. It is here that religious belief plays a vital role. It provides one with strength in times of weakness, hope in the hour of despair, inspiration in moments of fear, patience in times of suffering and endurance in times of anguish.

Belief in God, in His justice and mercy, in the fact one shall be compensated with rewards for the good acts one does in the House of Eternity, endows man with a psychological wellbeing and strengthens his spirit. It is through this knowledge that his being is infused with a sense of joy and optimism. His concept of existence is broadened and his perception of life is brightened. The hardships which he faces in this short life are made easy. He finds a sense of incomparable solace and tranquillity the like of which can never be obtained by way of knowledge, philosophy, wealth, offspring or by having dominion over the East and West. May God be pleased with 'Umar ibn al-Khaṭṭāb, who once said,

> Never did a trial befall me except that God accompanied it with four blessings: firstly, it was never a trial which impacted my faith in anyway; secondly, it was never as bad as it seemed; thirdly, when it arrived, I was never deprived of contentment; finally, I knew that God would reward me as a result of enduring it.[2]

The one who lives life without religion or faith always returns to religion in difficult times, when troubles bombard him in succession and when his sense of direction becomes obscured. He seeks guidance and he is guided, he calls on God and he receives an answer and when he asks for help, he is helped. His

2. See "Endurance of Privations" and "Strength" in my book *Faith and Life* (Beirut and Cairo).

faith provides him with an insurmountable assistance which is never ceases. The one who lives life without faith lives a life full of anxiety. This person is in intellectual disarray, has no sense of direction and has a divided self. Philosophers of ethics deem such a complex as the 'Raqāyak complex'. Raqāyak, as is narrated, was a murderer who assassinated a king. After being convicted, he was condemned to death. As a punishment, it is said that his hands and feet were tied to four strong horses facing four different directions. The tails of the horses were then set on fire and when the horses galloped swiftly in their respective directions, the limbs of his body were horrifically torn apart!

This violent analogy of limbs being torn apart can also be used to describe the divided self of a person who lives life with no religion. In fact some sagacious individuals believe that the latter is worse than the former. This is because, unlike the former, the latter is not over in an instant. A divided self is an affliction which can last for a very long time and a person may have to endure this all his life.

In view of this, those who live without firm belief are prone to anxiety, stress, nervous tension and mental disturbance. Such people, whenever the catastrophes of life hit them, collapse instantly under the pressure. They either quickly commit suicide or live a life with mental illness and depression. They are likened to that of the living dead of which an ancient Arab poet said:

> The dead are not those who are laid to rest;
> The dead are those living-dead;

The ones who live a life of melancholy;
The ones who are abject and have little hope.

This is what modern psychologists and psychiatrists have confirmed in their studies, backed by intellectuals and critics all over the world. The famous philosopher and historian Arnold Toynbee says:

> Religion is one of the indispensable human faculties. It suffices to say that lacking religion pushes a human being to a state of spiritual despondency. It drives him to seek spiritual consolation from those who possess nothing of that sort.[3]

Dr Carl Jung notes,

> In the past thirty years the reasons behind many of the sick patients who came to consult me was their lack of faith and their shaken beliefs, and they did not get better until they had fully regained their faith.[4]

The philosopher of pragmatism, William James, writes, "Certainly, the best treatment for anxiety and stress is nothing but faith." Dr Brail writes, "A truly religious person never suffers from psychiatric disorders." In his book, *How to Stop Worrying and Start Living*, the author Dale Carnegie writes:

> Psychiatrists know that strong faith and religious devotion suffice to defeat anxiety and nervous tension and to recover from diseases of that sort.

Dr Henry Link, in his book *The Return to Faith*, has written at length on this subject. In support of his views, he has used

3. Toynbee, *A Study of History*, Vol 3, p. 179.
4. Jung, *Modern Man in Search of a Soul*, 1933.

what he witnessed and discovered during his career as a practising psychiatrist.[5]

Society's need for moral incentives and order

There is another societal need for religion. This the need for moral incentives, incentives that will encourage members of a society to do good actions and to fulfil their duties even in the absence of an observer or someone who will reward them. There is the need for a moral code that will govern human relationships and oblige every individual to remain within their limits, so that one does not violate the rights of others, and society as whole, when pursuing ones own desires.

It cannot be said that the Law is enough to engender such regulations and moral incentives. The Law is not there to act as an incentive nor does it suffice as a regulator. It is always possible to escape the grasp of the Law and to pervert the course of justice. It is for this reason that true moral regulations and incentives are those which man fosters within himself and not ones which come from without. There is a need for this inner moral imperative and from this stems inner restraint impelled by ones 'conscience' or ones 'heart'. Call it what you may, it is a force that, if it happens to be virtuous, the whole being of man will as a result of it be virtuous, and if it turns out to be corrupt then all of ones actions will be corrupt.

Man has known, through observation, experiment and through the study of history that nothing can be as effective as religious belief when it comes to cultivating the conscience,

---

5. See "Between Science and Faith" in my *Faith and Life*, especially what has been written under the title "Psychiatry Marching along with Faith".

purifying ones morals, fostering incentives required for doing righteous deeds and deterring one from doing bad deeds. A British judge was so appalled by the heinous crimes being committed today despite the rapid advance of science and the spread of knowledge, and despite the sophistication of laws that he remarked, "Without morality there would be no Law; without faith there would be not morality."[6]

It is no wonder that even some atheists have acknowledged that life cannot be virtuous without religion, belief in God and in recompense in the Hereafter. Voltaire even said that, "If God did not exist, it would be necessary to invent Him." By this he meant that there would be a need to invent God for the people so that they could hope for his mercy, fear his punishment, seek his blessings, do good deeds, and refrain from doing bad deeds. Yet at another place, he says with sarcasm: "I never doubted the existence of God. If it wasn't for Him, my wife would have cheated on me and my servant would have stolen from me!"

The historian Plutarch also said, "to build a city without having land, is easier than building a state without a god."

Society's need for cooperation and cohesion

Religion plays a very significant role in the strengthening of bonds amongst people. This is most important considering that they are all the slaves and creation of one single Creator and that they are all the children of a single father. This is further complemented with what religion establishes between man in

6. See "Faith and Morals" in *Faith and Life*.

the form of brotherhood based on belief and faith. According to the Qur'an:

> *The Believers are but a single Brotherhood...* [49:10]

This brotherhood based on faith roots itself so firmly in the character and lives of the believers that one desires for ones brother what one desires for oneself. Indeed, he puts his brother before himself even though by this he may impoverish himself.

Professor Muḥammad 'Abdullah Darrāz writes in his book *Religion*:

> We do not need to enlighten anyone about the fact that a community cannot be established without the cooperation of its members. This cooperation is achieved through the Law which governs the community's relations and lays down the rights and responsibilities therein. This Law is indispensable for the ruler, who makes sure it is implemented, guarantees that its dignity is upheld at all costs, by everyone, and that its sanctity is never violated.

All these are established principles and any further discussion about this would be tedious.

But what exactly is the thing which prevents us from violating the sanctity of law?

What I wish to establish through this study is that there is no power on the face of the earth like that of religiosity when it comes to guaranteeing that the Law is venerated. It is through religiosity that society is held together, its stability ensured and rifts are healed therein.

The secret behind this is that man excels all other living creatures. In everything from his very movements, his innate disposition to his imaginings, he is controlled by something that is neither heard by his sense of hearing nor perceived by his sense of sight. It is not something obvious like being given something in ones hand or having something placed around ones neck. It does not run through his muscles, nerves nor does this thing flow in his veins. This thing is a human and spiritual abstraction known as conceptualisation and belief and man has forever been captivated by this dual ability of conceptualisation and belief.

People have gone astray from this concept and as a consequence have assumed that thought and conscience do not affect material and economic life, and instead have come to the flawed conclusion that it is ones material and economic standing which affects ones thought conscience. This Marxist assumption firstly demotes man from the station of an endowed dignified nature and confers upon him instead an animalistic character. Secondly, this representation of man inverts all the established facts and observations of man's behaviour individually and collectively throughout the ages. For people to opt for purely a materialistic life where no importance or attention is attached to the heart and soul they must, at the outset, convince themselves that their happiness lies in this present type of life. Man has always been guided by his beliefs, whether they be right or wrong. If his beliefs are sound then everything about him will be sound and if his beliefs are corrupt then everything about him will surely be corrupt.

For this reason man is driven by his innate sense of self and not by his exterior circumstances. Neither will the laws of society alone nor the power of governments suffice to establish a welfare state, where rights will be revered and duties fulfilled accordingly. Anyone who merely fulfils his duties out of fear of being punished, imprisoned or out of fear from suffering financial retribution, will disregard the Law as soon as he is convinced that he can evade it and escape its grasp.

It is erroneous to assume that the spread of science and culture alone can guarantee peace and prosperity instead of cultivating and refining good character. This is because knowledge is a two-edged sword which can be used for either construction or demolition. In order to ensure that it is used appropriately, there must be an ethical framework which guides it towards what will be most beneficial for humanity, which is constructive, as oppose to being simply a tool for spreading evil and vice. This framework is belief and faith.[7]

EXCERPTS FROM MUḤAMMAD 'ABDUH

In his outstanding book *Risālah al-Tawḥīd* (The Message of Monotheism), the great prodigy (of our times) Muḥammad 'Abduh has described various aspects of mankind's need for prophecy and divine guidance. He considers divine guidance tantamount to the importance of the mind to an individual. He goes as far to say that there is no way that human beings can go through life without divine guidance and this is why messengers were sent to them as bearers of glad tidings and warners.

---

7. Darrāz, *al-Dīn*, pp. 98-99.

...and there never was a people, without a warner having lived among them (in the past). [35:24]

He has emphasised this point in his interpretation of the first chapter of the holy Qur'an (Sūrah al-Fātiḥah—as reported in *Tafsīr al-Manār*), when describing the necessity of divine guidance for a people.

Show us the straight way. [1:6]

He has dealt with this subject again towards the end of his interpretation of verse 13 of Sūrah al-Nisā', after explaining the laws of inheritance.

Those are limits set by Allah: those who obey Allah and His Messenger will be admitted to Gardens with rivers flowing beneath, to abide therein (for ever)... [4:13]

He comments:

Obedience to the Messenger is nothing but obedience to Allah. This is because the Messenger commands us with what is revealed to him by Allah as being in our interest, leading to our welfare in this world and in the hereafter. Obedience to the Messenger is mentioned alongside the obedience to Allah, because some people in the pre, as well as post-Judaic period, believed, and persisted to believe after the advent of Islam as well, that man with his intellect and knowledge can through life without recourse to divine revelation. One such person has said that although he believed that the world had an Omniscient and prudent Creator, it was up to him to use his own intellect to discern good and to avoid evil. This is in actual fact and error on man's part. Had it been correct, mankind would not have been in need of divine messengers.

It has already been stated in our interpretation of Chapter 1 of the Qur'an (Sūrah al-Fātiḥah) that human beings, due to their specific nature, are in need of religious guidance. It is the fourth guide that Allah has conferred upon man after the guidance given through the various senses, conscience and intellect. Never in the history of mankind was intelligence sufficient as a guide for a nation or the sole vehicle of progress without being assisted by religion.[8]

ANSWERS TO THE OBJECTIONS RAISED BY ATHEISTS

Shaykh Rashīd Riḍā, the eminent disciple of Muḥammad 'Abduh, has annotated the commentary of his mentor, in *Tafsīr al-Manār,* in a detailed rebuttal to the objections raised by sceptics and atheists alike:

> Some disbelievers and atheists counter this assertion saying that they see lots of people who do not follow any religion. Such people are of high intellectual and literary standing; they do such good deeds that benefit them and as well as others, to the extent that an impartial intelligent person, free from religious intolerance, wishes that all of mankind was just like such people. Many philosophers have even striven to model whole nations on the morals and sophistication of such well-bred individuals.

My initial response to such a statement would be to view the guidance of communities of mankind in the past, such as tribes and whole nations, whether nomadic or urban, which emerged by way of cultivating a sense of humanity and philanthropy

8. *Tafsīr al-Manār.*

in community life. History has taught us that no enlightened civilization has ever advanced on the face of the earth except on the basis of religion. Even the pagan civilizations of old such as the ancient Egyptians, Chaldeans and the Greeks are no exception to this rule. The Qur'an tells us that never was there a people without a warner (from Allah) having lived among them (for their guidance).

By this we come to understand even those pagan religions have divine roots to them. It was later on that idolatry crept into the creed of these followers and gradually triumphed over the original message. Similarly, it crept into the beliefs of the followers after them, of which nothing but fragments and shards remain.

There is no other religion known to mankind, which has survived intact throughout the course of history, as Islam. This is despite the fact that history books have recorded the way in which paganism has overtly and covertly spread into many of those faiths professing to be related to Islam like the Nuṣayriyyah and other false sects, who were overwhelmed by interpretation or ignorance. Even today there are those who associate themselves with Islam, yet they do not know many of its common practices. Like those professing to be Muslims clashing with their Muslim neighbours with regards to the permissibility of eating beef in remote regions of India! Or like those who profess to be Muslim and yet are ignorant of the Islamic way of conducting marriages and burying the dead as in some parts of Russia and others. The one who knows these types of cases never rules out the possibility that ancient divine religions can easily change into pagan ones.

Following the example set by the divine messengers and complying with religious guidance is the foundation of every civilization. This is because it is only by way of moral progress that we can progress materially. According to the eminent sociologist and philosopher of our times, Herbert Spencer, the ethics and virtues of a nation which forms the backbone of a society are all grounded in religion and stem from it. Some scholars try to deny this fact saying instead that they are based on science and intellect. Nations that allow this kind of distortion are bound to fall into ethical chaos, the dire consequences of which can never be predicted nor can the damages of such thinking ever be calculated. This is just some of what 'Abduh's writings convey. Herbert Spencer told Muḥammad 'Abduh during a meeting: "In the last few years, the virtues of the English nation have weakened as the greed for material gain has strengthened."

As we are aware, despite the strength of its civilization and its rapid advancement, it is the English who have traditionally been known for their devoutness to religion out of all the nations in Europe. This is because religion served as the central pillar of its civilization, stabilising it through the spirit of its morals and virtues. Although European civilization is now far from the true spirit of Christianity, one which espouses a life of abstinence from wealth, power and the allures of the world, we see that if it was not for the fact that some of the morals of the Gospel had triumphed in Europe, it would have squandered its material wealth instead of regulating it through acts of piety and charity and its civilization would have ended swiftly. Hence, the person who said that the civilization farthest from religion is the one nearest to destruction, did not make such statement in vain, but with a sure knowledge and understanding of the rules that govern a society in mind.

This returns us to the comment made at the beginning by Rashīd Riḍā. Firstly, the existence of irreligious yet virtuous individuals does not nullify 'Abduh's claim that religion is the fourth source of guidance for mankind and that this guidance leads to social integrity in the world as well as to felicity in the hereafter.

Secondly, it cannot be said decisively that a certain atheist, who is intelligent and has a degree of moral rectitude, was brought up on atheism right from his childhood and as a result is in no need of religion because we know of no nation that rears its children on atheism. On the contrary, we know of some atheists who are considered high-ranking individuals within their circle, and who had an upbringing which was strictly religious and based on moral precepts found in religion. Atheism took a hold of them at some later stage in their lives when they plunged into philosophy that contradicted some principles of their childhood religion. Philosophy may change some of the beliefs and opinions of a person, but it does not contain anything that is repulsed by religious virtues and morals, or anything which deprives one of ones faculties and deep-rooted morality. On the contrary, atheism strips one of some religious values, like the value of being content with legitimate wealth. It fosters in one a desire to increase his wealth, even by illegitimate means, like swallowing up the rights due to others and by gambling. The only concern such a person may have is how to avoid being perceived as wretched by his peers, or how to avoid imprisonment. Such a person may also lose their moral standing by feeding their desires and permitting themselves to indulge in their lusts. As for the most cultured of them, they are unable to deter such people from corrupting the earth in terms of wasting its resources and destroying it for posterity. Nothing can deter them except a higher, more powerful force.

Had Europe not set up well organised institutions like the police force to protect the rights of people and provided an organised military which can be called into action when the cause arises, no one's land or wealth would have remained safe. Anarchy and chaos would have prevailed in their cities and towns. In days when such highly organised security forces were absent, it was religion which was observed through its morality and laws. What we gather from this is that the obedience to God and His messengers was necessary in order to achieve happiness in this world."[9]

HISTORICAL FACTS AND EVIDENCE

All the experiences and facts of history speak of the excellence of faith in life and its necessity for man. It is necessary for the individual if he is to live a life of tranquillity, happiness and purity. It is a requirement of society so that it may achieve stability and progress.

The great Egyptian thinker 'Abbās Maḥmūd al-'Aqqād said:

> The experiences throughout history have establish the excellence of religion in the all major movements in history. Never do we hear anyone say of religion that it is a thing which can be done away with altogether and that it

9. *Tafsīr al-Manār*, Vol. 4, pp. 428-431.

is something which one is able to reject or dispense with in ones dealings with society or those closest to him.

History has repeatedly shown us that among the various factors found in certain movements of the past there has never been a more greater and decisive factor than religion. This is besides various other factors in the common movements of the past which vary in strength according to its resemblance with religious belief which dictates the excellence of consciousness and the inner most feelings of a people.

This authority is not matched by tribalism, nationalism, tradition ethics or the Law. This is because all of the aforementioned is dependent on the conditional relationship between an individual and his country or between an individual and his society or between an individual and his race amidst the diversity of countries and nations in the world.

As for religion its recourse is to that bond between a person and the existence in its totality. Religion's province spans out to include everything in existence that is seen and unseen. Its domain includes all that is past or destined to be for an eternity which can never be measured wherein will be uncovered to man knowledge of the unseen. This is the province and function of religious belief at the very least even if religious people in the past have failed to comprehend it.

Further evidence of the excellence of religion is the fact that you are given the opportunity to compare it with other religious and irreligious societies and societies which do not hold to religion as firmly.

Similarly, we notice the excellence of religion when we compare an individual who believes in one of the comprehensive systems of belief to another with an inactive conscience and confused perception, living his life without a standard to adhere to or without an ideal to aspire towards.

For this reason, the dissimilarity between these two groups or two such individuals is like the dissimilarity between two trees, one firmly grounded and the other which is completely uprooted!

Often it so happens that we see confused people having a good deal of strength become more empowered when belief untangles their inner most self from its perplexed state"[10]

NO SUBSTITUTE FOR RELIGION

Some people may fancy the idea that religion can be replaced by modern science, while some may believe that it can be substituted with contemporary ideologies. Both these perceptions are erroneous.

Conclusive evidence has shown that nothing can surpass religion and take its place. Nor can anything else perform the huge role it plays in the life of man.

Science not a substitute for religion

Science in no way is a substitute for religion and faith. The domain of science is not the same as that of religion. By 'science', I mean here the Western concept of science and not the comprehensive Islamic concept of science. According to the Islamic concept of science, science encompasses knowledge of partial phenomenon of the universe as well as knowledge of the

10. *Ḥaqāiq al-Islām wa Abāṭīl Khuṣūmih* (Facts of Islam & Trivialities of its Enemies), pp.15-16.

key realities of greater existence. In other words, it encompasses worldly knowledge as well as religious knowledge. Science, here, does not mean matter and its properties alone. Rather, it means knowledge of the universe, life, man and its Creator.

Science, as conceived of by the West, does not qualify to substitute religion, because the sole purpose of Western science is to simplify the means of life for man, not to shed light on life's mysteries. Science assists man in solving the problems of life, but it does help him when it comes to solving the mystery of existence and its key questions.

This is the reason why we in our own times witness that the most scientifically and technologically advanced of countries have people who suffer from a spiritual vacuum, anxiety, ideological disarray, never ending feelings of insignificance, emptiness, dejection and estrangement. In response to the mechanisation and materialism of modern life, the youth in these advanced countries drift from one ideological vogue and craze to another, never finding a sound guidance to the Straight Path.

This is the hidden aspect of deviation, perversion and divergence which the whole world has seen in the behaviour of those bewildered youth who go by the name of hippies, who have become fed up with insignificance of life and as a result rebel against their own civilisation which brought them up.

Modern science is limited in its capacity, capability and scope. Science can provide the mankind with the means and tools, but it is beyond its capacity and specialisation to grant man with clear goals and purposes. How unfortunate is the man who accumulates means and yet is oblivious to the purpose of his own existence or to the value of his own life. The one who is only aware of the goals of the beasts of prey and of the goals simply of eating and mating. As far as any ideal befitting the many gifts, traits and dignity of man is concerned, then such a simplistic aim is most unbefitting to him.

Religion alone bestows upon man higher ideals pertaining to life and the greater purpose of existence. It grants him a task and a purpose therein. It gives value and worth to his life. It confers upon him moral values and lofty ideals, which hold him back from evil and motivate him towards the good in spite of any immediate material gains.

Science has reinforced the material nature of man, but it has weakened his spiritual nature to a pathetic level.

Science gave man the wings of birds with which to fly and ascend the heavens. It gave him the gills of a whale so that he could dive into the deepest of waters, yet it could not bestow upon him the heart of a human being!

When a human being lives life without a "human heart", the tools of science in his hands can easily turn into jaws and fangs to kill and terrify, and into shovels and land mines to destroy and devastate.

Tools of science turn into nuclear weapons, napalm bombs, poisonous gases, chemical and biological weapons, which spread an unimaginable degree of death and destruction when they are used.[11]

---

11. Please refer to the Arabic book of Dr Nabil Subhi, *Chemical and Biological Weapons* (al-Risalah Establishment, Beirut), to know what the enemies of humanity prepare for destroying the living beings by the authority of science and muscle of the scientists.

Certainly, science has enabled man to tread on the surface of the moon, but it has not been able to place its finger on the secret of his existence and the purpose behind his life!

With the help of science, man has discovered many *things*, but he has not been able to discover the reality of his own self. The science of the twentieth century has taken him to the moon, but it has not guided him to a place of bliss and tranquillity on the surface of the earth. From the moon, man gathered some stones and soil, but he did not find there what could release him from the suffering and anxiety found on his own planet.

Science allowed man to better his physical being, but it fell short of reforming his inner self. It has not been able to stress his 'Divine Essence', the perceptive and conscious facets of his being, which, when it is sound, man's whole being is sound and which, when it deteriorates, leads to the deterioration of his whole being. This inner essence is known as the *heart,* the *self* or the *soul.* Whatever one may call this, it is certainly the essence of man's being!

Science granted the twentieth-century man the tools with which to triumph over some of the forces of nature, but it did not give him the means to prevail over his own self; over his desires, his doubts, his anxiety, over his fears, confusion and the struggle against his inner self and society at large.

Modern medicine, like surgical procedures, has advanced greatly in this century alone. So far reaching has its advancement been that physicians have declared that science is capable of eradicating every disease, except that of death and old age. Despite this claim, diseases continue to proliferate, bifurcate and spread at an astonishing rate. From these many proliferating conditions, one can speak of "neurological and psychological illnesses", which demonstrates the dire 'contradiction' which the individual and the society are passing through. The core of this is that material knowledge, with all its diversity and discoveries, has not been able to grasp the reality of man, who knows even about matter and its laws but nothing about his own nature. No wonder, that this situation lead a great scientist like Alexis Carrel (Nobel Prize in Physiology or Medicine, 1912) to pen his famous book *Man, the Unknown.*

Hence, modern science tried to nurture all the material aspects of the human body, but it failed to nourish the human-self along with its contents of conscience, aspirations and will. This led to healthy bodies with strong muscles, but, on the flip side, the inner self of man was made to endure incurable troubles.

Statistics reveal that eighty percent of sick people in major American cities have been diagnosed with some form of disease as a result of psychological and nervous unrest.

Modern psychology affirms that among the root causes of psychological illnesses are hatred, malice, fear, fatigue, despondency, dismay, distrust, selfishness and paranoia. All these illnesses can be linked directly to a life which is deprived of faith in God.[12]

Philosophy not a substitute for religion

As elucidated by Alexis Carrel, René Jules Dubos and others, it is evident that human beings are that "unknown" sphere, the core of which modern science has not been able to probe, nor

12. See Wahiduddin Khan, *Islam and Modern Challenges*; and the chapter "Influence of Faith on the Life of an Individual" in my book *Faith and Life.*

has it ascertained its essence or penetrated its depths. Science has come to know of inanimate bodies and of matter and by analysis has discovered their laws, but it has been incapable of knowing man in his totality, because his composition and complexity are such that he is not fully known to anyone except to the One who created him.

Should He not know,—He that created? [67:14]

As long as science is ignorant of the nature of man, he cannot expect from it clear guidance, and for it to nurture him and accurately set out clear laws for him. It has become apparent now that science, or more specifically, its technological applications have become a threat to man's very existence and his environment.

The "man of philosophy" is not more fortunate than the "man of science", although it is philosophy that has been concerned with man ever since Socrates brought it down from the heavens to the earth and guided the human mind towards self-discovery through self-knowledge. Philosophy has never agreed on a single theory regarding man: is he soul or mere matter? Is he a mortal body or an immortal soul? Is he intellect or desire? Is he an angel or a demon? Is his disposition good or evil? Is he only as we perceive him as or is he actually a wolf in a sheep's disguise? Is his nature egocentric or altruistic? Is he by nature an individualistic or a social animal? Is he static or dynamic? Is nurturing him beneficial or futile? Is he free to chose or are his choices limited?

Philosophies have differed and contradicted in their responses to these questions. It is futile to expect something useful therein. Shaykh 'Abd al-Ḥalīm Maḥmūd, chancellor of al-Azhar University and professor of philosophy at its College of Theology, once said, "Philosophy does not have an opinion, because it expresses an opinion and contradicts it; it develops an idea and counters it as well."

That is how divine philosophy contradicts profane philosophy; the philosophy of idealism is contrary to the philosophy of realism; the philosophy of responsibility disagrees with the utilitarian philosophy and hedonism; besides many of the other inconsistencies in philosophical thought. One idea ascertains while the other negates, one builds and the other simply demolishes.

Consequently, philosophy alone cannot lead mankind or quench its thirst. It cannot develop for us a trustworthy system to rely and to establish life on this basis.

The philosophies farthest from the ability to guide mankind are the materialistic philosophies, which reject that the universe has a god, that the human being has a soul or that there is an after life. The frontrunner of these philosophies is Marxism, which is based on dialectic materialism, which has adopted the adage: God did not create man, rather it was man who created God.

Similarly, philosophies like the philosophy of the absurd, nihilism and the philosophy of doubt, all demolish and are not constructive. Such philosophies take away life instead of granting it.

According to Professor Muḥammad 'Abdullah Darrāz, the difference between philosophy and religion is that philosophical thought is placid and cold, while religion is a propelling, dynamic and inventive force. Whenever anything stands in the way of this force, it belittles it and steers it towards its course.

This is really the difference between philosophy and religion. The purpose of philosophy is knowledge, while the purpose of religion is faith; the pursuit of philosophy is for sterile thought, which forms pessimistic picture, while the pursuit of religion is instil in one a spirit and force of optimism. We do not say, as many people say, that philosophy speaks directly to the intellect, whereas religion is not at all convinced by the workings of the intellect alone until it is accompanied by the heart.

Hence, we can say that philosophy functions in only one segment of the human-self, whereas religion possesses it entirely. From this, the minute difference between philosophy and religion can be summarised as follows:

The purpose of philosophy is theory even in action. The purpose of religion, even in its scholastic aspect, is action. The highest claim of philosophy is that it informs us about truth and virtue. What are they? Where are they? After that, it is not concerned about our place with regards to the truth and virtue it has defined. As for religion, it introduces us to the truth. It tells us not only to know the truth, but also to believe in it, to love it and glorify it. It informs about our responsibility to support it and remain faithful to it. It is by accomplishing this fact that we begin to perfect ourselves.

Shaykh Darrāz then illustrates further by explaining that religion is the common man's (democratic) movement, whereas philosophy is a private (aristocratic) movement. Religion by its nature seeks to reach out and be inclusive, whereas philosophy inclines to solitude and is exclusive. A prophet of a religion lives in the middle of the masses, whereas a philosopher takes refuge in his ivory tower. If you come across a philosopher propagating his thought, it indicates that his status has changed and that his thought has transformed itself into a faith; whereas if you find a believer concerned only with his own self, it indicates that the fire of his faith has turned into mere ashes.

REFUTATION OF THE MARXISTS

Marxists claim that religion (being the opium of the masses) affects the faculty of man's reasoning in the same way drugs affect an individual's brain. It distracts one from thinking about one's stolen rights with wishful thinking of an after-life. It subjects one to the whims and desires of oppressors and tyrants all too willingly. It is an unacceptable claim.

In fact, the right religion does not intoxicate the people and does not distract them from claiming their rights in this world by way of keeping them solely preoccupied with seeking bliss in the life to come. The right religion does not allow oppression in any form, nor does it approve of corruption and deviation. If this claim was right in case of some religions, it does not hold true with regards to Islam.

Indeed Islam is the greatest revolution in human history. It is the revolution which espouses the liberty of every individual, freeing them from the bonds of servitude and from submission to anyone other than ones Creator. It is the revolution of thought, conscience and perception. It is a revolution of our reality and function in the world.

The mantra of this revolution is the grand declaration of monotheism *Lā ilāha illā Allāh* (there is no god, but God). Anyone who claims divinity for themselves, by word or by deed, is in fact false, has no substance and is not worthy of obedience.

All those who set themselves up as lords beside God should be vanquished forever and vanish from life altogether.

This is because people are created equal. No one should be allowed to enslave others (by claiming divinity) nor should people given the opportunity to tyrannise one another. If someone begins to oppress a people then other members of society should obstruct this tyrants path and stop his iniquities, or else they will be considered accomplices in the sin and be deserving of retribution from God.

The Holy Qur'an affirms this by saying:

> *And incline not to those who do wrong, or the Fire will seize you; and you have no protectors other than Allah, nor shall you be helped.* [11:113]

> *And fear tumult or oppression, which affects not in particular (only) those of you who do wrong: and know that Allah is strict in punishment.* [8:25]

The Messenger of Allah (ṣ) says,

> When people see an oppressor and do not seize his hands, this is when Allah will punish them collectively with punishment from Himself.[13]

He (the Prophet) makes it obligatory upon everyone spotting an abhorrent act (oppression or corruption or deviation) to strive to alter it by any means:

> Anyone spotting an abhorrent act, should change it with his hand; if he can't do so, he should change it with his tongue;

---

13. Narrated by Abū Dāwūd and Tirmidhī as authentic.

> and in case he can't do this, he should try to change it with (a wish in) his heart; this is the weakest (level) of faith.[14]

Changing something through one's heart, which represents the lowest level of faith, is not a negative state to be in. It is in fact an ember of hatred against corruption and abhorrent acts, which continues to glow and flares up inside the core of its bearer until it gets a chance to implement change by word and deed or by speech and action. In the short term, the smallest benefit of hating something in one's heart is the loathing of oppressors and corrupt individuals and shunning them altogether. It is a state which warns the faithful against mingling with such individuals by eating or drinking with them or by befriending them.

The Prophet (ṣ) considered the resistance against internal oppression and corruption as important as the resistance against external invasion and aggression; both were considered holy struggles for the sake of the divine. When asked: "Which type of struggle is the best?" He replied: "A truthful word in front of a powerful tyrant"[15]. He thus regarded this kind of struggle as the best and most noble of struggles.

Islam is a religion which encourages resistance against oppression even until death. It regards those who give their life for such a noble and just cause as a martyrs of the Divine cause. Such a martyr is ranked among the highest and most venerated of martyrs. The Prophet (ṣ) even said that such a martyr will be in the proximity of the greatest of all martyrs, Ḥamzah ibn 'Abd al-Muṭṭalib:

---

14. Narrated by Muslim and others
15. Narrated by al-Nasā'ī as authentic, and occurs in *al-Targhīb.*

> The greatest of all martyrs is Ḥamzah along with a man who stands up in front of a tyrannical ruler to enjoin (righteousness upon) him and to forbid him (from evil) and (as a result of this deed) is killed.[16]

Islam nurtures a sense of dignity and self-esteem in a Muslim's personality and makes it one of the primary characteristics and traits of faith:

> *...honour belongs to Allah and His Messenger, and to the Believers...* [63:8]

> *We have honoured the sons of Adam...* [17:70]

Islam has declared that no soul should resign themselves to a life of shame and disgrace. No one should be content with the shackles around his neck and feet without resisting such oppression with all their might even if it be through the act of migration for the sake of God:

> *When angels take the souls of those who die in sin against their souls, they say: "In what (plight) were you?" They reply: "Weak and oppressed were we in the earth." They say: "Was not the earth of Allah spacious enough for you to move yourselves away (from evil)?" Such men will find their abode in Hell,—What an evil refuge!"* [4:97]

The Messenger of Allah (ṣ) rejected resignation to the misfortunes of life in the name of destiny (*qadr*). He considered such thinking as being suggestive of shortcomings in the religion of Islam. Once, when he passed his judgement between two disputing persons, the condemned one, while walking

16. Narrated by al-Ḥākim and Ḍiyā' from Jābir.

away, grumbled, "Allah is sufficient to me; He is the Disposer of my affairs!" Hearing this, the Prophet (ṣ) retorted:

> Verily, Allah admonishes weak resignation so it is vital that you remain strong; then if you are overwhelmed (by hardship), you should say: Allah is sufficient to me; He is Disposer of my affairs.[17]

The Prophet (ṣ) abhorred the fact that man, instead of facing reality with wisdom and insight, tried to hide his weak resignation by simply saying, "Allah is sufficient to me; there is neither might nor power except from Allah." Mentioning and invoking Allah in such an empty manner is nothing but weak resignation on the part of an individual. This is why we find in his commandments and sayings such wisdom like:

> A strong believer is better and dearer to Allah than a weak believer... Take care of your interests; seek help from Allah and do not be unproductive.[18]

Among the invocations he taught his companions is this:

> O Allah! I seek refuge with You from distress and sorrow; I seek refuge with You from helplessness and laziness; I seek refuge with You from miserliness and cowardice; I seek refuge with You from being heavily in debt and from being overcome by people.[19]

This invocation teaches man to seek refuge with Allah from every kind of weakness which befalls him and which attempts to overpower him, subjugate and humiliate him.

---

17. Narrated by Abū Dāwūd, No. 3627.
18. Narrated by Muslim.
19. Narrated by Abū Dāwūd, No. 1555.

A similar supplication can be found in "The Prayer of Humility" (al-Qunūt), narrated by 'Abdullah ibn Mas'ūd:

> O Allah! We beg for Your assistance; we seek guidance from You alone; we ask forgiveness from You; we revert back to You; we believe in You and trust in You; we praise You for all goodness; we are grateful to You and are not ungrateful to You; we renounce and part with all those who are disobedient to You. O Allah, you alone worship do we worship; we pray to You, prostrate to you and hasten to You; we submit to You, anticipate Your Mercy and fear Your punishment; certainly your punishment is going to overtake those who reject faith.

So through this supplication we seek refuge with Allah from the weakness. So is it fair to say of such a religion, one which calls for resistance against injustice, weakness, resignation and submission, one which advocates truth, strength and freedom, is simply an opium for the masses and that it inebriates them with promises of bliss in a paradise, so that they remain silent about injustices in this world?

Perhaps Karl Marx can be excused for saying what he said, because of his ignorance of Islam and its stance against oppression, transgression and depravation. The scientific method should have obliged him not to issue such a generalisation of religion without first scrutinising and carrying out a comprehensive study of all the religions, or at least, all the major religions of the world and their impact on the civilizations of the past. If he was unable to carry out such a study then he should have passed judgement only regarding the religion he was most familiar with. This is a requisite of the scientific methodology and its analytical approach.

CHAPTER 2

The Essentials of Islam

THE CREED

The Islamic creed is the seal of all heavenly inspired systems of belief. It is substantiated and elucidated by the Holy Qur'an and the practice and examples of the Messenger of Allah (ṣ). It is embodied in the belief in Allah, in the Day of Judgement, in the angels, in the Book (*i.e.*, any of the divinely revealed scriptures such as Torah and Gospel, and in the belief of the prophets).

The Islamic creed is a creed which solves the mystery of existence. It explains to man the secret of life and death, and answers those three timeless questions: What is our origin? Where will we go? Why were we created at all? In fact, this belief is not an innovation of Islam, nor is it an invention of Prophet Muḥammad (ṣ). It is rather the same purified belief which all the prophets of Allah were sent with. It is the belief that was conveyed through all the previously revealed heavenly scriptures, before distortion and corruption took their hold and undermined them. It embodies the eternal realities regarding the Creator and His relationship with this universe. It informs him of those things perceivable to man and those hidden from him. It tells man about the essence of life, his role therein and his fate after life. These realities were taught by Adam to his children; declared by Noah to his nation; Hūd and Ṣāliḥ called ʻĀd and Thamūd to these realities; Abraham, Ishmael, Isaac and others professed these; these were affirmed by Moses in Torah, by David in Zabūr (Psalms) and by Jesus in the Bible.

It was Islam that refined this belief from extraneous blemishes and purified it from the outside influences that the passage of time had brought with it. It did so when the purity of this eternal belief had been tainted; when its monotheistic message had been distorted by such concepts as the Trinity, by notions of mediations and by taking up pagan gods besides the One and the only God. Islam came at a time when the purity of this belief had been denigrated through assimilation and personification; when human imperfections and limitations had been attributed to God, the Exalted and Almighty; when its perception of the universe, of life and of man had been distorted; when the relation with God, His revelation and the divine commandments had been damaged. Islam also presented this faith in a new way according to the message which the Divine Wisdom wished to convey, namely, that it was to be the final instalment of all the revealed scriptures and that it was to be the purpose and goal for all of mankind until the Day of Resurrection.

When the Islamic faith came, it sought to purify the concept of monotheism and absolute divinity from all that it had been tarnished with during the passing of time. It also purified the idea of prophethood and the Message from misconceptions.

It purified the belief of absolution from the illusions imputed to it by the ignorant. It purified belief from the misinterpretations made by extremists and from the plagiarism of charlatans.

The basic components of this faith are belief in Allah (the one and only God), belief in the Prophets and the belief in a Hereafter.

It can be summarised in the faith in Allah and the resurrection. Belief in Allah comprises faith in His existence, in His Presence and in His infallible nature.

Existence of God

Evidence has shown that behind this universe there is a Supreme Power which governs it, controls it and oversees it. This Supreme Power has been called "the First Cause", "the First Intelligence", and "the Unmoved Mover". The Holy Qur'an, however, and the heavenly books, named it with the comprehensive name of "Allah", which incorporates the attributes of beauty and grandeur.

This Supreme Power, or in other words, this Great Deity, cannot be comprehended fully by the human mind alone, nor can the human mind know its essence. How can it do so, when man has failed to grasp the essence of his own being and self? When he has failed to understand the reality of life and even many of the material realities of this universe like electromagnetic matter and many others? What humans have grasped is only the traces of these realities. How then can they aspire to know the divine being Allah, the Exalted, the Majestic?

> *That is Allah, your Lord! There is no god but He, the Creator of all things: then worship you Him: and He has power to dispose of all affairs. No vision can grasp Him, but His grasp is over all vision: He is above all comprehension, yet is acquainted with all things.* [6:102-103]

This God is not for a limited faction, nor is He the God of a particular people, nor of a certain region of the globe. In the words of the Qur'an, He is the Cherisher and Sustainer of the worlds, Lord of the heavens and of the earth, Lord of the East and the West.[1]

Let us listen to what the Qur'an narrates from the dialogue between Moses and Pharaoh, so that we can realise the comprehensiveness of His divinity.

> *Pharaoh said: "And what is the 'Lord and Cherisher of the worlds'?" (Moses) said: "The Lord and Cherisher of the heavens and the earth, and all between,—if you want to be quite sure." (Pharaoh) said to those around: "Did you not listen (to what he says)?" (Moses) said: "Your Lord and the Lord of your fathers from the beginning!" (Pharaoh) said: "Truly your messenger who has been sent to you is a veritable madman!" (Moses) said: "Lord of the East and the West, and all between! if you only had sense!"* [26:23-28]

The Qur'an has used a variety of approaches to substantiate the existence of Allah:

1. It directs the mind and intellect to those signs that are spread across the universe, bearing witness to the fact that there is a Wise Designer behind its creation. This, in fact, is

---

1. See for example Sūrah al-Fātiḥah: 2, al-Kahf: 14, al-Shu'arā': 28, and al-An'ām: 164.

the axiomatic norm of the mind which believes in causality naturally without the need for any instruction and evidence:

> *Behold! In the creation of the heavens and the earth; in the alternation of the night and the day; in the sailing of the ships through the ocean for the profit of mankind; in the rain which Allah sends down from the skies, and the life which He gives therewith to an earth that is dead; in the beasts of all kinds that He scatters through the earth; in the change of the winds, and the clouds which they trail like their slaves between the sky and the earth;—(here) indeed are Signs for a people that are wise.* [2:164]

This creation certainly must have a Creator and this system must have a controller:

> *(Were they created of nothing, or were they themselves the creators? Or did they create the heavens and the earth? Nay, they have no firm belief.)... (When this message was delivered), (Pharaoh) said: "Who, then, O Moses, is the Lord of you two?" He said: "Our Lord is He Who gave to each (created) thing its form and nature, and further, gave (it) guidance."* [52:35-36, 20:49-50]

2. This Creator touches and moves the intuitive nature of man, whereby he directly realises that he has a Powerful and Magnificent Lord who protects and guards him:

> *So set you your face steadily and truly to the Faith: (establish) Allah's handiwork according to the pattern on which He has made mankind: no change (let there be) in the work (wrought) by Allah: that is the standard Religion: but most among mankind understand not.* [30:30]

This intuitive nature may disappear in times of opulence or phases of enjoyment, but it re-emerges upon hardship and torment. It does not take long for the dross to melt away revealing the essence of the human self, one which naturally returns to its Lord for help and assistance:

> *He it is Who enables you to traverse through land and sea; so that you even board ships;—they sail with them with a favourable wind, and they rejoice thereat; then comes a stormy wind and the waves come to them from all sides, and they think they are being overwhelmed: they cry unto Allah, sincerely offering (their) duty unto Him saying, "If you do deliver us from this, we shall truly show our gratitude!".* [10:22]

This happens when man is suddenly confronted with the question about the origin of this universe and its Facilitator. At that moment, the intuitive self cannot withstand crying out suddenly "God!":

> *If indeed you ask them who has created the heavens and the earth and subjected the sun and the moon (to his Law), they will certainly reply, "Allah"...* [29:61]

> *Say: "Who is it that sustains you (in life) from the sky and from the earth? Or who is it that has power over hearing and sight? And who is it that brings out the living from the dead and the dead from the living? and who is it that rules and regulates all affairs?" They will soon say, "Allah". Say, "will you not then show piety (to Him)? Such is Allah, your real Cherisher and Sustainer: apart from truth, what (remains) but error? How then are you turned away?* [10:31-32]

3. The Qur'an cites from the long history of mankind explaining that the faith in Allah and His messengers has

always been the ark of salvation for the faithful, whereas belying Him and His messengers has always been the beginning of destruction and ruin. For example, while narrating the story of Noah, it says:

> *But they rejected him, and We delivered him, and those with him, in the Ark: but We overwhelmed in the flood those who rejected Our signs. They were indeed a blind people!* [7:64]

About Hūd it says:

> *We saved him and those who adhered to him. By Our Mercy, and We cut off the roots of those who rejected Our signs and did not believe.* [7:72]

Regarding prophet Ṣāliḥ and His people it says:

> *Now such were their houses—in utter ruin—because they practised wrong-doing. Verily in this is a Sign for people of knowledge. And We saved those who believed and practised righteousness.* [27:52-53]

While addressing His Messenger Muḥammad (ṣ), Allah says:

> *We did indeed send, before you, messengers to their (respective) peoples, and they came to them with Clear Signs: then, to those who transgressed, We meted out Retribution: and it was due from Us to aid those who believed. [30:47]*

Allah—the One and the Only God

Allah, the Exalted, is the One and the only God. He has no partners whatsoever. There is nothing comparable to Him, His essence, His attributes or to His actions.

> *Say: He is Allah, the One and Only; Allah, the Eternal, Absolute; He begets not, nor is He begotten; and there is none like unto Him.* [112]

> *And your Allah is One Allah: There is no god but He, Most Gracious, Most Merciful.* [2:163]

All the design and structure seen in the universe indicate that its originator and designer is One. Had there been more than one Intelligent Designer and Regulator, the system (of the universe) would have gone into disarray and its laws would have been disturbed. Allah, the Exalted, has rightly said:

> *If there were, in the heavens and the earth, other gods besides Allah, there would have been confusion in both! but glory to Allah, the Lord of the Throne: (High is He) above what they attribute to Him!* [21:22]

> *No son did Allah beget, nor is there any god along with Him: (if there were many gods), behold, each god would have taken away what he had created, and some would have lorded it over others! Glory to Allah! (He is free) from the (sort of) things they attribute to Him!* [23:91]

He, the Exalted, is one in His divinity; He is the lord of the heavens and the earth and of all who are therein; He created all things and ordered them in due proportion, and to everything He gave its nature and direction. No one from amongst His creation can claim to be the creator or the provider or to be the designer of even an iota in the heavens or in the earth.

> *It would neither suit them nor would they be able (to produce it).* [26:211]

He, the Exalted, is sole in His Lordship; none except He is worthy of worship; none except He should be sought in fear or hope. There is nothing worth fearing except when it is from Him; there is no humility except before Him; there is no desire except the desire for His mercy; there is no reliance except upon Him; there is no submission except to His authority. All human beings—be they prophets, nobles, monarchs or sultans—are slaves of Allah. They do not have authority in matters of harm, benefit, death, life or in matters of resurrection, even authority over themselves. Whosoever takes anyone (of the above mentioned) as a god or humbles himself or bows to anyone of them, unduly ascribes to them an exaggerated status and as a result degrades his own self.

Hence the call of Islam to all mankind, particularly to the People of the Book, has been:

> *Say: "O People of the Book! come to common terms as between us and you: That we worship none but Allah; that we associate no partners with him; that we erect not, from among ourselves, Lords and patrons other than Allah…"* [3:64]

Muḥammad (ṣ) has been described by the Qur'an as being "no more than a messenger: many were the messenger that passed away before him" (3:144). He too did not describe himself as being anything other than "a slave and Messenger of Allah".[2]

According to the Qur'an all the prophets were humans just like us. They were chosen by Allah to deliver His message to

---

2. In one authentic *ḥadīth*, he is reported to have said: "Do not extol me like the Christians did to Jesus the son of Mary; but call me a slave and Messenger of Allah."

His creation, to call them to His worship and to the belief in His unity.

Thus the quintessence of the Islamic creed was formulated in the magnificent expression of *Lā ilāha illā Allāh* (*i.e.*, there is no god but Allah). Amongst Muslims this is known by various names as *tawḥid* (belief in unity), as *ikhlāṣ* (sincerity) and as *taqwā* (God conciousness).

The expression *"Lā ilāha illā Allāh"* revolutionises the force against the idols of paganism and the tyrants of the earth. It was a revolt against all purported deities and gods taken (for worship) besides the One God, whether in the form of trees, stones or human beings.

Lā ilāha illā Allāh was a universal call for the freedom of man from the bondage of other men, nature, all living things and the whole creation of Allah. It was the title of a new order that was not designed by a ruler or envisaged by a philosopher. It was the system created by Allah, the One before Whom faces humble themselves, hearts submit and the One to Whose authority the minds surrender.

Lā ilāha illā Allāh was the annunciation of a new society contrary to the pagan societies before it, a society distinct in its belief and with a unique system, wherein there is no racism, nationalism nor any class system, because it belongs to Allah alone and does not owe allegiance to anything except to His exalted Self.

Pagan leaders and tyrants recognised how *Lā ilāha illā Allāh* was capable of destroying the thrones of their authority, eliminate their high-handedness and oppression, and would support those who had long been oppressed in rising against them. Hence they left no stone unturned in their attempts to combat this call and lurked on its every path, threatening and obstructing the faithful on the path of Allah, those who believed in Him, and seeking thereby in it something crooked.

The greatest tragedy of humanity has been that some of its members have been allocating to themselves, or have been allocated, God-like status on earth. People submit to them, show reverence to them, bow and prostrate in front of them, yield to them and humble themselves before them.

On the other hand, the monotheistic belief elevated the spirit of the faithful so that no mortal human could remain neither a deity, a semi-deity, one third of a deity, be the son of a deity nor be God incarnate.

No human being should prostrate before another, no one should bow to another human being, nor should anyone kiss the ground in front of another human being. In fact, such ideas of equality form the foundations of a sincere human brotherhood, freedom and are the essence of dignity itself. How can there be brotherhood between an adorer and a deity? Humans do not have freedom before a alleged false deity. There is no dignity for the one who bows to or prostrates in front of a created being similar to him, or who takes someone as an authority instead of Allah.

The Perfection of God

Alongside faith in the existence of God and His Oneness, it is essential to attribute to Him perfection according to His generosity:

> *He begets not, nor is He begotten; and there is none like unto Him.* [112:3-4]

> *...there is nothing whatever like unto Him, and He is the One that hears and sees (all things).* [42:11]

This is testified by the wonderful universe with its marvellous precision. Man's disposition has been guided towards His perfection and the divine revelations revealed to the prophets throughout the ages have elaborated on this point.

Allah, the Glorious and All-Knowing, is the One from which nothing is hidden:

> *With Him are the keys of the unseen, the treasures that none knows but He. He knows whatever there is on the earth and in the sea. Not a leaf does fall but with His knowledge: there is not a grain in the darkness (or depths) of the earth, nor anything fresh or dry (green or withered), but is (inscribed) in a Record clear (to those who can read).* [6:59]

He is the Omnipotent and All-Powerful and executes whatever command He wishes; nothing triumphs over Him; nothing subdues His will:

> *Say: "O Allah! Lord of Power (and Rule), You give power to whom You please, and You strip off power from whom You please: You endue with honour whom You please, and You bring low whom You please: In Your hand is all Good. Verily, over all things You have power.* [3:26]

Such is His might that nothing can prevent His will. He listens to the distressed (soul) when it calls on Him, and relieves its suffering. He gives life to the dead and buried. He repeats the process of creation; and for Him it is most easy:

> *Blessed be He in Whose hands is Dominion; and He over all things has Power.* [67:1]

He is the wise, Who does not create in vain nor does He leave anything purposeless. He does not ordain any law without wisdom; some people understand this while others remain ignorant. To this, the angels bore witness in the lofty heavens:

> *They said: "Glory to You, of knowledge we have none, save what You have taught us: In truth it is You Who are perfect in knowledge and wisdom."* [2:32]

The prophets of Allah, His friends (*awliyā'*) and the wise among His servants too bore witness to this:

> *Men who celebrate the praises of Allah, standing, sitting, and lying down on their sides, and contemplate the (wonders of) creation in the heavens and the earth, (with the thought): "Our Lord! not for naught have You created (all) this! Glory to You!...* [3:191] ·

He is the Most Merciful, whose mercy precedes His wrath and whose mercy encompasses everything just as his knowledge is embracing of all things in existence. This has been referred to in various places of the Qur'an:

> *Our Lord! Your Reach is over all things, in Mercy and Knowledge.* [40:7]

> *With My punishment I visit whom I will; but My mercy extends to all things.* [7:156]

The opening declaration before any chapter of the Qur'an begins with the words *Bismillāhi-rraḥmāni-rraḥīm* (In the name of Allah, Most Gracious, Most Merciful). The fact that He emphasises that His mercy is all-embracing, strengthens the hope of human hearts, even if they might have committed transgression or been sinful.

> *Say: "O my Servants who have transgressed against their souls! Despair not of the Mercy of Allah: for Allah forgives all sins: for He is Oft-Forgiving, Most Merciful.* [39:53]

God in Islam is not isolated from this universe and from all that exists in it. He is unlike the god of Aristotle, whom he named as the Prime Mover or the First Cause and portrayed as having attributes which are nothing but passive attributes connoting ineffectiveness, triviality, without any control or disposition. Such a god—as depicted by Aristotelian philosophy—knows nothing but his own self and is unaware of what happens in this enormous universe.

The god of Aristotle and of the Greek mythology did not create this universe from nothingness. According to them, the world has rather been eternal—neither having been originated nor created.

The god of Aristotle has no relation with this world or and is indifferent to it. He does not administer anything in it simply because he is unaware of what is going on therein (what goes into the earth or what emerges out of it; what comes down from the sky or all that which ascends to it). All Aristotle and his disciples claim about God is that He is neither the essence nor is He the sustainer; He neither has a beginning nor an end; He is neither a compound nor part of a compound; He is neither within the universe nor without; He is neither attached to it nor detached from it. These negative attributes of the Aristotelian god do not qualify him as the god who can be invoked with hope or who can be feared. With such a conception of god, people cannot have a strong bond with God—a bond which is founded on the basis of supervision, piety, trust, reliance, reverence and devotion.

Deposed from the universe, this god of Greek mythology—who found its way into modern European thought—is alien to Islam. The God in Islam is:

> *Who created the earth and the heavens on high. (Allah) Most Gracious is firmly established on the throne (of authority). To Him belongs what is in the heavens and on earth, and all between them, and all beneath the soil. If you pronounce the word aloud, (it is no matter): for verily He knows what is secret and what is yet more hidden. Allah! there is no god but He! To Him belong the most Beautiful Names.* [20:4-8]

> *Allah! There is no god but He—the Living, the Self-subsisting, Eternal. No slumber can seize Him nor sleep. His are all things in the heavens and on earth. Who is there can intercede in His presence except as He permits? He knows what (appears to His creatures as) before or after or behind them. Nor shall they compass aught of His knowledge except as He wills. His Throne does extend over the heavens and the earth, and He feels no fatigue in guarding and preserving them for He is the Most High, the Supreme (in glory).* [2:255]

God in Islam is the Creator of everything, the Provider of every living creature, the Planner of every affair. His knowledge encompasses everything; He takes account of every single thing; His mercy embraces all things; He created everything and made it in due proportion; He ordained laws and granted guidance; He hears and sees; He knows the secrets of all intimate discourse.

> *There is not a secret consultation between three, but He makes the fourth among them—nor between five but He makes the sixth—nor*

> *between fewer nor more, but He is in them, wheresoever they be: In the end will He tell them the truth of their conduct, on the Day of Judgement...* [58:7]

Creation and authority belong to Him; in His hands is the dominion of all things; He merges night into day; He merges day into night; He brings the living out of the dead, and He brings the dead out of the living; He gives sustenance to whom He pleases, without measure.

The entire universe with all its highs and lows, its disclosures and silences, its animate and inanimate bodies, its orbits and stars, is subject to the command of God, dictated by His laws, bears witness to His oneness and Grandeur. It is replete with the signs of His knowledge and wisdom, and glorifies and praises Him:

> *The seven heavens and the earth, and all beings therein, declare His glory: there is not a thing but celebrates His praise; And yet you understand not how they declare His glory! Verily He is Oft-Forbearing, Most Forgiving!* [17:44]

The glorification of Allah by the universe, its submission to Him, is a great reality, but many eyes are blind to it and many ears fail to hear it. Yet it has manifested itself to those who see with the eyes of their inner spiritual perception and listen to it with the hearing of their hearts. As a result, the latter group views the whole of existence as a sacred sanctuary with everything in it submitting in awe to Allah as it recites His praise, the Exalted in Might, the Most Wise, the Most Gracious and the All-Merciful.

> *Whatever beings there are in the heavens and the earth do prostrate themselves to Allah (acknowledging subjection)—with good-will*

or in spite of themselves: so do their shadows in the morning and evenings. [13:15]

See you not that to Allah bow down in worship all things that are in the heavens and on earth—the sun, the moon, the stars; the hills, the trees, the animals; and a great number among mankind?... [22:18]

Whatever is in the heavens and on earth—let it declare the Praises and Glory of Allah: for He is the Exalted in Might, the Wise. To Him belongs the dominion of the heavens and the earth: It is He Who gives Life and Death; and He has Power over all things. He is the First and the Last, the Evident and the Immanent: and He has full knowledge of all things. [57:1-3]

Belief in Prophethood

After believing in the perfect nature of God, in His wisdom, in His mercy, His patronage of the universe and organisation of the world, and His bestowing honour on man, faith in prophethood is inevitable. It is rather a natural offshoot of that basic belief. Allah would not have created man, made subservient to him whatever is in the universe and then left him floundering without guidance. It was only by the precision of His wisdom that He illuminated for man the path to success in the hereafter, just as He guided man with regards to the life of this world and provided for him spiritual as well as material provisions. It was also through His infinite wisdom that He sent revelation from the heavens to revive the hearts and minds of mankind, just as He sends down rain to revive the dead.

It would not have been wise to leave man at the mercy of his own self. Leaving the individual to struggle against his various capabilities and leaving society to struggle against its conflicting passions and interests. Indeed wisdom decided the opposite of this would happen. It ensured that messengers would be sent with clear signs and guidance for people, directing them to Allah and to instruct them in the establishment of justice between everyone.

For this reason, the Messengers of Allah condemned those who were surprised that Allah had sent them as His messengers to inform the people of His laws and prohibitions. For example, Noah said to his people:

> *...O my people! No wandering is there in my (mind): on the contrary, I am a messenger from the Lord and Cherisher of the worlds! I but fulfil towards you the duties of my Lord's mission: Sincere is my advice to you, and I know from Allah something that you know not. Do you wonder that there has come to you a message from your Lord, through a man of your own people, to warn you—so that you may fear Allah and haply receive His Mercy?* [7:61-63]

Hūd too told his nation something similar to Noah. In response to the denial of the message of Muḥammad (ṣ) by the pagans of Arabia, the Qur'an states:

> *Is it a matter of wonderment to men that We have sent Our inspiration to a man from among themselves?—that he should warn mankind (of their danger), and give the good news to the Believers that they have before their Lord the lofty rank of truth. (But) say the Unbelievers: "This is indeed an evident sorcerer!"* [10:2]

Being guided by divine revelation is just one of the highest levels of guidance conferred onto us by Allah.

The first level of guidance is the instinctive natural guidance. This was explained by some learned man upon being questioned: "When did you start comprehending things?" He said, "Ever since the time my mother gave birth to me; whenever I felt hungry, I instinctively drank milk from her breasts; Whenever I felt discomfort, I instinctively cried!"

This guidance is not limited to humans, but includes animals, birds and insects also. While making mention of the honeybee, the Qur'an has described it as being inspired as though by revelation:

> *And your Lord taught the Bee to build its cells in hills, on trees, and in (men's) habitations.* [16:68]

This guidance is rather spread across the universe: in plants which gain their nourishment from the nutrients in the soul in due proportion and amount; in planets that follow their orbit with precision, without any transgression and without contravening the fixed laws.

> *It is not permitted to the Sun to catch up the Moon, nor can the Night outstrip the Day: Each (just) swims along in (its own) orbit (according to Law).* [36:40]

This guidance is common for all creatures, whether considered to be superior or inferior. This is what is implied in Moses's reply to Pharaoh:

> *(Pharaoh) said: "Who, then, O Moses, is the Lord of you two?" He said: "Our Lord is He Who gave to each (created) thing its form and nature, and further, gave (it) guidance."* [20:49-50]

Furthermore, Allah states in the Qur'an:

> *Glorify the name of your Guardian—Lord Most High, Who has created, and further, given order and proportion; Who has ordained laws and granted guidance.* [87:1-3]

The second level of guidance is the guidance of the senses. These are the apparent senses of hearing, sight, smell and taste, and hidden senses, such as hunger, thirst, joy and grief. This level is higher than the previous. There is a sort of attentiveness and a type of realisation in it, although it cannot be faultless, as we see in case of a mirage taken by the viewer for real water; or in case of a shadow which is assumed to be still but is actually moving.

The third level of guidance is the guidance of intellect with its various faculties and powers. This is higher in degree than that of the senses. However, in judgement and derivation it often draws upon senses and thus becomes liable to error. For instance in the case where it makes a mistake by setting up a false proposition and thereby derives false conclusions. The intellect, in its higher functions, is an exclusive peculiarity belonging solely to human beings and one which they do not share with animals.

The fourth level of guidance is the level of divine revelation. This is what corrects the errors of the intellect, banishes the deceptions of the senses and maps out the way to that place where intellect alone cannot reach, removing those differences wherein the minds are in disagreement with.

> *Mankind was one single nation, and Allah sent Messengers with glad tidings and warnings; and with them He sent the Book in truth, to judge between people in matters wherein they differed; but*

the People of the Book, after the clear Signs came to them, did not differ among themselves, except through selfish contumacy. Allah by His Grace Guided the believers to the Truth, concerning that wherein they differed. For Allah guided, whom He will, to a path that is straight. [2:213]

We sent aforetime Our Messengers with Clear Signs and sent down with them the Book and the Balance (of Right and Wrong), that men may stand forth in justice... [57:25]

Belief in the Hereafter

"The wombs deliver [the new born], the earth devours [the dead]". Is this really the essence of life and of human existence or is it what the Qur'an quotes the unbelievers as saying?

"There is nothing but our life in this world! We shall die and we live! But we shall never be raised up again!" [23:37]

If this is the case, then what is the secret behind the hidden and mysterious sentiments which have overwhelmed human nature since ancient times; the overwhelming feeling that he has not been created merely for this life and for a short duration alone? What can be the mystery behind that natural intuition which says that the human being is merely a stranger or a wayfarer in this world; that he is a passing guest about to depart for his Permanent Abode?

As we know, this presentiment existed with the ancient Egyptians. It was according to this belief that they mummified their dead and built pyramids. The evidence of similar beliefs to that of the ancient Egyptians among other ancient peoples has been unearthed.

How is it possible that the stage of this life can be shaken off so easily when whoever wanted to plunder plundered, whoever wanted to steal stole, whoever wanted to murder murdered, whoever wanted to transgress transgressed and whoever wanted to tyrannise tyrannised? Not one criminal was caught and punished. Their misdeeds were rather covered up, they managed to cover-up their transgressions and they escaped the grasp of justice. Some of them even managed to subjugate innocent people by their swords and acts of tyranny.

On the other hand, what of all those people who carried out good deeds and sacrificed their lives and belongings for it, but did not receive the reward they deserved for their noble acts. Either they remain unknown soldiers or else are held in contempt by those who are simply jealous and envious of them instead of acknowledging their virtues. Or their passing away was hastened by death so that they could reap the fruits of all the good they ever did. How many a people called to truth, strictly adhered to it and defended it, but were obstructed, subjugated, persecuted, tortured or displaced by some tyrant. Such people were even made to lay their lives down at times in the cause of righteousness, whereas their tyrant adversaries enjoyed safety, good health and life of luxury and lavishness.

Is it not reasonable for the intellect that it should believe in the justice of a single God and that it should accept, and even demand, a place wherein a good person will be rewarded for their goodness and an evil person punished for their acts of cruelty? The wisdom found in every atom of existence in this universe speaks of this rationale:

We created not the heavens, the earth, and all between them, merely in (idle) sport: We created them not except for just ends: but most of them do not understand. Verily the Day of Sorting Out is the time appointed for all of them. [44:38-40]

Not without purpose did We create heaven and earth and all between! That were the thought of Unbelievers! But woe to the Unbelievers because of the Fire (of Hell)! Shall We treat those who believe and work deeds of righteousness, the same as those who do mischief on earth? Shall We treat those who guard against evil, the same as those who turn aside from the right? [38:27-28]

What! Do those who seek after evil ways think that We shall hold them equal with those who believe and do righteous deeds—that equal will be their life and their death? Ill is the Judgement that they make. Allah created the heavens and the earth for just ends, and in order that each soul may find the recompense of what it has earned, and none of them be wronged. [45:21-22]

Indeed, to Allah belongs all that is in the heavens and on earth: so that He rewards those who do evil, according to their deeds, and He rewards those who do good, with what is best. [53:31]

As far as resurrection after death is concerned, it is not at all difficult for the One who created man in the first instance:

It is He Who begins (the process of) creation; then repeats it; and for Him it is most easy. To Him belongs the loftiest similitude (we can think of) in the heavens and the earth: for He is Exalted in Might, Full of Wisdom. [30:27]

CHARACTERISTICS OF THE ISLAMIC BELIEF

Clear belief

The Islamic belief is distinguished by the merits which other faiths are not privileged enough to have.

It is a lucid and candid faith with no complications or ambiguities. It sums up to the belief that behind this wonderfully harmonious and coherent universe, there is a sole Master Who created it and put it in order. He meted out an exact measure for everything. This God or Lord does not have any partner nor is there anyone similar to Him; He does not have a spouse nor does He have any offspring:

> *...Nay, to Him belongs all that is in the heavens and on earth: everything renders worship to Him.* [2:116]

As a result, this belief is clear and acceptable. This is because the intellect always seeks correlations and unity behind diversity and profusion, and wants to attribute things to one cause.

Unlike the abstruse concepts of Trinity or Duality, the Islamic monotheistic belief does not have in it these kinds of vagueness and complications and, as a result, does not suffer from the adage so fondly used by non-Muslims, namely, "blind faith".

Natural belief

The Islamic belief is neither alien to our nature nor adverse to it. It rather conforms to it just as the correct key fits with precision into its lock. This has been unequivocally stated in the Qur'an and the Ḥadīth.

The Qur'an commands:

> *So set you your face steadily and truly to the Faith: (establish) Allah's handiwork according to the pattern on which He has made mankind: no change (let there be) in the work (wrought) by Allah: that is the standard Religion: but most among mankind understand not.* [30:30]

Furthermore, a *ḥadīth* of the Prophet (ṣ) unequivocally testifies: Every child is born in conformity with the natural disposition of Islam—and indeed it is his parents who make him a Jew, a Christian or a Zoroastrian.[3]

This indicates that Islam is man's divine nature and does not require any influence from the parents. As far as Judaism, Christianity and Zoroastrianism are concerned, these religions are imparted by parents to their children.

Firm belief

The Islamic belief is a firm and defined belief. It does not permit any addition or subtraction, nor does it accept any distortion or modification. No ruler, scientific institution or religious conference can add to it or distort it. Any addition or misrepresentation is returned back to its origin. Prophet Muḥammad (ṣ) has said:

> Anyone who innovates anything inauthentic in our doctrine, his (such) innovation is repelled back to him.[4]

The Qur'an disapprovingly states:

---

3. Unanimously agreed upon.
4. Unanimously agreed upon.

> *What! Have they partners (in godhead), who have established for them some religion without the permission of Allah?* [42:21]

Based on this fact, all innovations, myths and legends that have been interpolated into certain books, ascribed to Muslims, or that have been disseminated between ordinary Muslims are all false, discarded and inadmissible within the domain of Islam, and in no way used as sources of authority.

Substantiated belief

The Islamic belief is a "substantiated" belief. It does not determine any of its issues by mere compulsion and strict obligation, nor does it command one, like some other religions, to "believe blindly", "believe first and then realise later", "blind imitation" or that "ignorance is the mother of piety." Its Book states openly:

> *Say: "Produce your proof if you are truthful."* [2:111, 27:64]

None of the Islamic scholars can say as the Christian saint and philosopher St. Augustine has said: "I believe in it because it is inconceivable". They rather say that imitated faith is unacceptable.

Similarly, addressing the emotions and sentiments is not considered sufficient, nor does this faith rely upon them as a basis for belief. It rather presents its cases with irrefutable arguments, with manifest evidence and with lucid rationalisation, reigning the intellect and penetrating deep inside the heart. The scholars of Islam say: "The intellect is the foundation of tradition and the authentic tradition does not conflict with the common intellect."

So in case of divinity, we see the Qur'an substantiating its view on the existence of Allah based on His oneness and on his completeness, with evidence from the universe, from the human self and from history.

In case of resurrection, it corroborates the fact of His ability to create the first time, His ability to create the heavens and the earth, to revive the earth after being barren. To emphasise His wisdom, the Qur'an confirms divine justice through the rewarding of the good-doers and punishing of the evil-doers:

> *...so that He rewards those who do evil, according to their deeds, and He rewards those who do good, with what is best.* [53:31]

Balanced belief

The Islamic belief is a balanced belief which knows neither excess nor extravagance.

It is midway between those who reject everything metaphysical—for its not being reachable or comprehensible by their senses—and between those who ascribe more than one god to the universe, those who perceive incarnation of the divine spirit not only in kings and rulers, but also in some animals and plants, like cows and trees! Islamic belief rejected atheistic unfaithfulness as it rejected the ignorant concept of multiple gods and ignorant polytheism. It established for the world the oneness of God—that there is no god but Him alone:

> *Say: "To whom belong the earth and all beings therein? (Say) if you know!" They will say, "To Allah!" Say: "Yet will you not receive admonition?" Say: "Who is the Lord of the seven heavens, and the Lord of the Throne (of Glory) Supreme?" They will say, "(They*

> *belong) to Allah." Say: "Will you not then be filled with awe?" Say: "Who is it in whose hands is the governance of all things—who protects (all), but is not protected (of any)? (Say) if you know." They will say, "(It belongs) to Allah." Say: "Then how are you deluded?"* [23:84-89]

The Islamic belief is also balanced belief with regard to the attributes of Allah.

There is no exaggeration in these abstractions, which would render the attributes of God as nothing other than empty words carrying no meaning whatsoever, implying neither fear nor hope. This is unlike Greek mythology, which described God as being unlike so and so and not being like such and such, without really mentioning any positive attributes of God or the impact of such attributes their relationship to this world.

Contrary to other beliefs, the Islamic belief is free from any assimilations or anthropomorphism of God's attributes. Other beliefs, like Judaism, likened the Creator to His creation and ascribed attributes of sleep, fatigue, rest, bigotry and mercilessness to Him. They even portrayed Him as meeting one of His apostles wherein He is challenged to wrestle with and is brought down by the apostle, and the Creator is not able to liberate Himself from this helpless state until He confers a new title on the triumphant apostle!

WORSHIP

The goal of man in this existence

Why did I come to exist? What is my mission in this life? What is the purpose of my being here?

These questions are unavoidable for every human being and everyone, without exception, persists in posing these questions to themselves and pondering over their answers.

Any ignorance, however grave it may be, can be forgiven, except the ignorance of a human being about the secret behind his existence, about the purpose of his life and about the duty of his fellow human beings and his self on earth.

The worst dishonour for this creature—the human being, who has been bestowed with intellect and a will—is when he lives recklessly, eating and enjoying himself like cattle and does not reflect over his destiny nor is cognizant about his own nature and about his role in this life, until death suddenly overcomes him. He faces the biggest shame, when, without any preparation, he faces his unknown destiny and reaps the fruits of his negligence, ignorance and deviation during his worldly life whether long or short. As a result, he would at that moment wish to repent, but alas, the repentance is of no avail, and he would crave salvation, but alas, it is too late to escape.

In view of this, it is incumbent upon every prudent human being to ask himself with all earnestness: Why have I been created? What is the purpose of my creation?

Why was man created? The answer to this question, by the believer, is spontaneous. For the faithful, the answer regarding the purpose of creation lies with the Creator. Why did He create man and why did He design him in such a unique form?

Since Allah is the Designer and Creator of man, and since He governs his affairs, let us put the question directly to Him:

"O Lord, why did You create man? Did You create him just to eat and drink? Did You create him simply for fun and amusement? Did You create him to walk on the earth and merely eat what grows on it and return to there, and that is the end of the matter? Is this brief spell of life, falling between the cry at the time of birth and the final groan with the agony of death, meant for him simply to live in anguish? What then is the secret of those abilities and faculties that You have built into the human being, in the form of the intellect, the free will and the soul?"

In response to these questions Allah will reply with the same answers that have been mentioned in His timeless book, the Qur'an, saying that He created man to be His vicegerent on the earth. This fact is very clear from the story of Adam and how the angels envied him for the status granted to him by Allah:

> *Behold, your Lord said to the angels: "I will create a vicegerent on earth." They said: "Will You place therein one who will make mischief therein and shed blood?—whilst we do celebrate Your praises and glorify Your holy (name)?" He said: "I know what you know not."* [2:30]

The first thing among the prerequisites of this role is that man should fully recognise his Lord and must worship Him comprehensively. Allah says:

> *Allah is He Who created seven Firmaments and of the earth a similar number. Through the midst of them (all) descends His Command: that you may know that Allah has power over all things, and that Allah comprehends, all things in (His) Knowledge.* [65:12]

In this Qur'anic verse, recognising Allah has been described as the sole purpose of the whole of creation.

Allah, the Exalted, says:

I have only created Jinns and men, that they may serve Me. No Sustenance do I require of them, nor do I require that they should feed Me. For Allah is He Who gives (all) Sustenance—Lord of Power—Steadfast (for ever). [51:56-58]

Anyone who ponders over this universe in which we live, finds everything in it existing and living in the service of other things. We see that the water serves the soil, the soil serves the vegetation, the vegetation serves the animals, and that the animals serve man. Then who is man in the service of? This is the mystery.

The answer that is announced by nature and pronounced by various species in this universe is that man is for Allah, for knowing Him, for worshiping Him and for discharging his given duties to Him. It is not conceivable that man can be there for the service of anything else found on the earth or anywhere else in the universe, because perceptibly, all the upper realms and the lower realms of the universe are subjugated to serve him. How then can he be in the service of these things?

Hence worship by man of the forces and phenomena of nature, whether above him or below him, like the sun, the moon, the stars, the rivers, the animals, the trees etc, has been a setback to his natural disposition (*fiṭrah*) and has led to a dreadful degeneration of his status.

Thus, naturally and logically, man is created for Allah, the Exalted, not for anyone else other than Him. He has been created to worship Allah alone, not to worship any fellow human being, stone, animal, tree, the sun or the moon. Any worship to anything else other than the One God is nothing but the deceitful beautifying of wrong by Satan, the avowed enemy of man.

The first call of every divine message is "Worship Allah! You have no other god but Him". This concept of worshipping Allah alone is part of that very old covenant which He had made with man and registered with the pen of His authority in their innate nature, planting it in their disposition, right from the time when He instilled them with consciousness, planted palpitating hearts in their bosoms and placed signs all around them in the universe:

Did I not enjoin on you, O you Children of Adam, that you should not worship Satan; for that he was to you an enemy avowed?—And that you should worship Me, (for that) this was the Straight Way? [36:60-61]

It is no wonder then that the main purpose behind the deputation of the prophets, the missions of the messengers and revelations of the many holy books, has been to remind mankind of that old covenant, to remove the rust of negligence, idolatry and blind tradition gathered on their once pristine nature. It comes as no surprise that the first proclamation of every messenger has been:

"O my people! Worship Allah! You have no other god but Him..." [7:59]

Thus did Noah, Hūd, Ṣāliḥ, Abraham, Lūṭ, Shu'ayb and every other prophet sent to the rejecting nations, call his respective nation to this message. Allah says in the Glorious Qur'an:

For We assuredly sent amongst every People a messenger, (with the Command), "Serve Allah, and eschew Evil"... [16:36]

> *Not a messenger did We send before you without this inspiration sent by Us to him: that there is no god but I; therefore worship and serve Me.* [21:25]

The meaning and essence of worship

"Worship" in the Arabic language

The expressions *al-'abdiyyah*, *al-'ubūdiyyah* and *al-'ibādah*, (equivalent of worship) in the Arabic lexicon means obedience.

According to the well-known Arabic dictionary *al-Ṣaḥḥāḥ*, the root of *al-'ubūdiyyah* is submission and subservience, and *al-ta'būd* means servility. *Ṭarīq mu'abbad* (paved way) is from the same root. Similarly *al-ba'īr al-mu'abbad* means a camel which has been marked with tar on its body as a sign of which master it belongs to. *Al-'Ibādah* means obedience. *Al-ta'bbud* means devotion. As you can see the shades of the meaning change depending on their derivation. For example, in the Qur'anic verse 29 of Sūrah al-Fajr, the phrase *fadkhulī fī 'ibādī* means "join my party". This adds a connotation of loyalty to the word.

In *al-Mukhaṣṣaṣ*[5], the basis of *'ibādah* is overcoming. For example, *Ṭarīq mu'abbad* means a pathway which is well trodden. From here, the word *al-'abd* (slave) derives its meaning of subservience to one's master. All these words are similar in their meanings and connotations. Hence, it is said that so-and-so is subservient to so-and-so. Any act of submission amounts to worship. Every act of obedience to God based on submission and humility to Him is classified as worship. The concept of worship is only awarded to those of creation who have been

5. Vol. 12, p. 96.

given the greatest gifts, like that of life, comprehension, hearing and sight. The prominent dictionary *Lisān al-'Arab* also gives similar details.

Worship in the Sharī'ah

Ibn Taymiyyah views worship in a deeper and wider perspective. He has dissected its meaning to its constituent parts. Besides its linguistic meaning, which implies the highest degree of obedience and submission, he has highlighted a new aspect of utmost importance in Islam and in every other religion, a vital aspect, without which worship is not realised; this is the aspect of adoration. Without this emotional and sentimental factor, worship—for which Allah created all of creation, sent the messengers and revealed His books—ceases to exist.

Explaining this, in his book *al-'Ubūdiyyah,* Ibn Taymiyyah writes:

> Religion by its own definition implies submission and subservience. They say that so-and-so made so-and-so subservient, *i.e.*, one subjugated the other and the latter submitted. Similarly, they say that so-and-so believes in Allah and submits to Allah, *i.e.*, worships Allah, obeys Him and surrenders to His will. So devoutness to Allah is nothing but worshiping Him, obeying Him and surrendering to Him.
>
> The word *'ibādah* is the root and it also means subservience. They say *ṭarīq mu'abbad*, (a beaten path), *i.e.*, the pathway which is made and marked by frequent walking on foot. However, enjoined worship implies the meanings of subservience and adoration. It implies extreme humility to Allah and deep adoration for Him. The pinnacle of love is

enthrallment and its first stage is that of attachment. The course begins with attachment to the object of your devotion. This attachment develops into fascination and then the heart becomes enchanted by it. Then comes the stage of ardent love whereby the heart becomes captivated by the beloved. The following stage is commitment and the final stage is enthrallment. They say that so-and-so is infatuated with God *i.e.*, he is a slave of God. In other words a fascinated person is one who has become enslaved by his beloved.

He (Ibn Taymiyyah) writes further,

He who submits to a human being while there is hatred in his heart, cannot be a worshiper of him. Similarly, he who loves without submitting to the beloved cannot be an adorer of the beloved, just as some person may love his child or his friend. Hence, one of the two are enough with regards to the worship of Allah. Allah must rather be the dearest thing to the slave, above everything else. He must be Supreme to everything else; in fact Allah alone is worthy of absolute love and unreserved submission; anything one loves and which goes against the will of Allah, is a love perverted, and anything revered contrary to the law of Allah is void.

Allah says: "Say: If it be that your fathers, your sons, your brothers, your mates, or your kindred; the wealth that you have gained, the commerce in which you fear a decline, or the dwellings in which you delight—are dearer to you than Allah, or His Messenger, or the striving in His cause—then wait until Allah brings about His decision: and Allah guides not the rebellious." [9:24]

With this profound elucidation of the meaning of worship and its essence, we realise that genuine worship has the following two prerequisites:

First: Compliance with what Allah has prescribed and His messengers have called upon, whether a commandment or a prohibition, whether it be an allowance or a prohibition. This is exactly what characterises obedience and submission to Allah.

One cannot be a beloved of Allah nor His worshiper if he fails to submit to His commands or if one's arrogance holds him back from walking on His path and from obeying His prescribed laws even if one has declared that Allah is his Creator and Provider. Even the pagan Arabs used to testify to this. But the Qur'an by this sole admission alone did not qualify them as believers or the beloved of Allah. Mere verbal admission of His divinity does not amount to submission and hence does not suffice. Submission embodied in devoutness and characterised in the form of compliance and obedience is imperative. This is right owed to the Divine and with this only the essence of the claim, "You do we worship; Your aid we seek" (1:5) is realised.

The basis of submission to Allah is the conscious awareness of His Unity and of His paramount Omnipotence over everything in existence. Every existing thing is His creation and in service to Him; everything is in His hand, under His control and within His authority. In this perspective, the Qur'an states:

> *Whatever beings there are in the heavens and the earth do prostrate themselves to Allah (acknowledging subjection)—with good-will or in spite of themselves: so do their shadows in the morning and evenings. Say: "Who is the Lord and Sustainer of the heavens and*

> *the earth?" Say: "(It is) Allah." Say: "Do you then take (for worship) protectors other than Him, such as have no power either for good or for harm to themselves?" Say: "Are the blind equal with those who see? Or the depths of darkness equal with light?" Or do they assign to Allah partners who have created (anything) as He has created, so that the creation seemed to them similar? Say: "God is the Creator of all things: He is the One, the Supreme and Irresistible."* [13:15-16]

The basis of submission to Allah is being self-conscious regarding one's dependency on the One Who possesses harm and benefit; One Who controls death and life; One to Whom belongs the creation and authority; One in Whose hands lies the governance of all things; One Who when He decrees a matter, He says to it: "be", and it is. It is the self-consciousness of weakness before the Omnipotent;[6] the realisation of being ignorant in front of the One Who comprehends all things in His Knowledge; the recognition of being feeble in front of the One Who has the authority; the awareness of being destitute in front of the One who owns all the riches. In brief, it is the self-consciousness of an impermanent and destitute life of created servitude, before the Eternal and Timeless, creative divinity, which dominates everything and conducts every command independently.

The more man gains knowledge of his own self and about his God, the more these presentiments increase in clarity and strength. As a result, the more his trust in Allah increases, the

---

6. The human being is unaware about what is happening to him in his present; he is ignorant about what is going to unfold for him in the future; he does not know what he is going to acquire tomorrow; he does not know when, where and how he is going to die; he does not know what lies for him beyond the death.

more his orientation towards Him; the more his reliance on Him, the more frequently he resorts to Him; the more natural is he in serving Him. the more spontaneous is his stretching his hands out in supplication towards Him, and the more he entreats Him and knocks at His door with invocations and penitence.

On the contrary, when a human being is unconscious of his own worth and ignorant of the significance of God, these presentiments do not die, but deviate and mutate. They search for another deity to which the person may turn to, submit, and with a surety, unconsciously pursues that wrong course. This person may not deem his submission to such an unconsciously sought-after deity as a submission or obedience to a deity or to a god at all.

Second: Such attachment must emanate from a heart which loves Allah, the Exalted. There can be nothing in existence more loved than Allah. To Him belong favour and benevolence; He created from nothing and non-existence; He created for him whatever there is on the earth; He bestowed upon him His hidden and manifest blessings; He created him in best possible of moulds and fashioned him in the best of forms; He honoured him and conferred on him special favours above many of His other creatures; He provided him with delicacies; He taught him the expression; He appointed him as His vicegerent on the earth; He breathed into him of His Spirit; He commanded the angels to prostrate to him. Who then is worthier than Allah of being loved? Who can man love then instead of his Bountiful Benefactor? The foundation of love of Allah is being conscious of His benevolence and beneficence, and of His benefaction and mercy; perceiving His beauty and completeness. Whoever appreciates the benevolence and beneficence conferred upon them aught to know that Allah is their Granter and their Possessor; whoever appreciates beauty, aught to know that Allah is the source of beauty; whoever admires completeness and perfection, should know that nothing, indeed, is perfect except His completeness; whoever appreciates his own self, must know that Allah is his Creator.

Whosoever knows Allah, loves Him. The amount of one's devotion is in proportion to the knowledge one has of Him. Since he was the most knowledgeable of Allah, this is the reason why among all the people, (Muḥammad) the Messenger of Allah (ṣ) was the most intense in his love for Allah. The delight of his eyes was in prayers, because it amounted to the direct connection between his own heart and Allah. He would always beseech Allah to grant him the yearning for a meeting with Him (in the hereafter) and the pleasure of looking at His Glorious Countenance. When he was given the choice between living longer in this world and joining his Lord, he said, "I choose (to be with) the highest Companion!"

There have been some scholars of (scholastic) theology, who said that love of a human being for Allah is not conceivable in reality, that the real meaning of love for Allah (by man) is his perseverance in being obedient to Him, and that the essence of love with another person of the opposite gender is also unattainable. In his renowned book *Iḥyā' 'Ulūm al-Dīn*, al-Ghazālī has refuted meticulously such claims.[7] He has asserted that the one who deserves absolute love with all its attributes and intentions is none but Allah.

---

7. Likewise Ibn al-Qayyim, in his book *Rawḍah al-Muḥibbūn*, has rebutted such contentions and exposed their void from eighty different perspectives.

If Allah has created us with the purpose of worshiping Him *i.e.*, to obey Him in absolute submission coupled with extreme love, how then should this ardent submission manifest itself and what should be the sphere of such obedience? Answering this question will elucidate for us a vital fact: the range of the concept of worship in Islam with all its richness. This comprehensiveness has two facets:

1. It includes the whole of religion as well as the whole of life.
2. It includes all the hidden and manifest aspects of man.

Worship encompassing the whole of religion

When, in interpreting the Qur'anic verse "O Mankind! Worship your Guardian-Lord" (2:21), Ibn Taymiyyah was asked about the meaning of "worship" and its ramifications, and whether the whole religion was embraced by "worship" or not, his reply was so detailed and extensive that it took the form of a whole book penned by him, entitled *al-'Ubūdiyyah* (Worship). The book begins with the following note:

> Worship: This word is a comprehensive expression and encompasses all that is liked and approved by Allah in the form of words and deeds, whether hidden or manifest. Part of worship are acts and deeds like the five obligatory prayers; paying of mandatory charity; fasting during the month of Ramadan; performing the Pilgrimage (ḥajj); truthfulness; returning trusted possessions; filial obedience; upholding the kinship; honouring one's covenants; enjoining what is right and forbidding what is wrong; fighting the infidels and hypocrites; supporting one's neighbours, the orphans, the

poor, the wayfarers, the slaves and animals; supplication and praise of Allah, and reading and so on.

Similarly, the adoration of Allah and love of His Messenger (ṣ); fear of Allah, penitence and devotion to Him alone; patience on observing His rulings, thankfulness for His blessings, contentment with His Judgement, reliance on Him, anticipation of His mercy, fear of His punishment, and all such feats amount to worship.[8]

Thus, as explained by Ibn Taymiyyah, we realise that the horizon of worship is vast and its range is very extensive. It includes fundamental obligations: the essential rituals of *Ṣalāh* (the five obligatory prayers), *Ṣawm* (fasting during the month of Ramadan), *Zakāh* (alms) and *Hajj* (pilgrimage to Makkah).

Besides these fundamental obligations, worship also includes various forms of voluntary worship, like the recitation of the Qur'an, invoking Allah's name, seeking His forgiveness, reciting His glorification, enunciating His praise, chanting His greatness and pronouncing His excellence.

Worship also includes virtues like courtesy, the fulfilling of rights due to your fellow human beings, respecting one's parents, upholding ties of kinship, supporting the orphans and the underprivileged, helping the wayfarers, showing mercy to the weak and kindness to animals.

Worship embraces all forms of noble character and all commendable human virtues, like truthfulness, honesty, faithfulness and other attributes of a cultivated character.

It also includes what is called "divine morality" like love of Allah and His Messenger (ṣ), fear of God, repenting to Him,

---

8. *Al-'Ubūdiyyah*, 2nd edition, al-Maktab al-Islāmī, p. 38.

absolute allegiance to His religion, patience with His decrees, gratitude for His blessings, contentment with His judgement, reliance on Him, hope of His mercy, fear of His punishment and observing Him consciously, in solitude and in public.

Lastly, worship involves two fundamental obligations which constitute the vanguard of all that has been mentioned above:

1. Enjoining righteousness and forbidding evil
2. Fighting the unfaithful and hypocrites in the way of Allah.

Worship also embraces another important aspect of vital significance in the material life of people. It has been described by Ibn Taymiyyah in another place in his study as "adoption of the required means and compliance with the laws on which Allah has founded the universe". Ibn Taymiyyah says, "All means that have been prescribe by Allah for His slaves, (adopting) those means amounts to worship."[9]

Ibn Taymiyyah has gone further saying:

> The whole religion is embodied in worship, because religion implies submission and servility. (While analysing the meaning of religion) they say: I subdued him and he yielded *i.e.*, I subjugated him and he humbled himself; he embraced faith in Allah and he submits to Allah *i.e.*, he worships Allah, obeys Him and submits to Him. So the religion of Allah is worshiping Him, obeying Him and submitting to Him; worship actually means subservience as well.[10]

This is how the meaning of religion fits with the actual meaning of worship, both linguistically and with religion generally.

9. Ibid., p. 73.
10. Ibid., pp. 43-44.

Worship accommodates the whole of life

Having learnt from Ibn Taymiyyah that the essence of religion is worship, that religion came to prescribe to man the way to live life in those manifest and hidden aspects, that it came to define human behaviour and relations in accordance with the divine scheme, we discover that the worship of Allah accommodates the whole life and that it regulates all its aspects. It regulates everything from eating, drinking, private affairs to nation building, policies of governance, financial strategy, business dealings, penalties, and the principles of international relations in times of peace and war.

This is the reason why we find that the Holy Qur'an addresses the faithful servants of Allah with obligatory commands and laws dealing with different aspects of life. In one single chapter, like al-Baqarah, we find a number of obligations pronounced with the words "it is prescribed for you that...".

Let us look at the following verses:

> *O you who believe! the law of equality is prescribed to you in cases of murder..* [2:178]

> *It is prescribed, when death approaches any of you, if he leave any goods that he make a bequest to parents and next of kin, according to reasonable usage...* [2:180]

> *O you who believe! Fasting is prescribed to you as it was prescribed to those before you, that you may (learn) self-restraint.* [2:183]

> *Fighting is prescribed for you, and you dislike it. But it is possible that you dislike a thing which is good for you...* [2:216]

These commands about retribution, will, fasting and war are directed by Allah to His slaves. In other words, these are obligations incumbent upon them and they must worship Allah by fulfilling these obligations with unconditional observance.

With this elucidation one important reality, which even many Muslims are ignorant of, is made unequivocal. Upon hearing the expression *'ibādah* (worship), some people do not comprehend anything but prayers, fasting, charity, pilgrimage and related rituals like supplications and invocation. To many, it just does not occur that worship has a relationship with morality and etiquettes, with rules and regulations, or with customs and traditions.

Certainly, the worship of God is not confined to prayers, fasting and pilgrimage and related rituals like recitation of the Qur'an, glorification of Allah, supplications and invocation alone, as is thought by many Muslims when they are called to worship Allah. Many foolishly devout, religious people assume that when they perform such rituals, they accomplish the duties assigned to them and that they fulfil precisely and completely the obligations associated with their divine-given duty.

In spite of the prominence and importance of these significant and fundamental rituals in the building of Islamic personality, they amount to only a part of the system of worship of Allah and do not constitute the sum total of worship sought by Allah from His slaves.

The fact is that the domain of worship for which Allah created the human being and declared it to be the purpose of his life and his mission on the earth, is very enormous and immense. It includes all human affairs and encompasses his entire life.

Worship means total compliance with the divine order

The demand of human worship to Allah alone is that he submits all his affairs to the will of Allah and for His approval, whether it be in terms of beliefs, words or deeds. He must customise his life and behaviour according to the requirements of divine guidance and stipulations. When Allah commands man to do something or prohibits him from doing something, when He makes anything permissible for him or forbids anything, his stance should be:

> *"We hear, and we obey: (We seek) Your forgiveness, our Lord, and to You is the end of all journeys."* [2:285]

The distinction between a believer and an infidel is that the believer sets himself free from the bondage of his own self and from the slavery of created beings and opts for the bondage to his Creator alone; he moves far from the obedience of his own selfish whims and fancies to the obedience of Allah. A believer is not like a stray animal which follows its own inclinations and is guided by someone else from among creation. A believer is, rather, obligated by an agreement that he must honour, by a sacred covenant that he must conform to and by a system to which he must adhere. This kind of commitment is quite logical and stems from nature itself and the demand made by the covenant of faith (*al-mīthāq*).

The covenant of faith implies that the faithful give his life to Allah, so that His genuine and truthful Messenger can lead it on the right path and that he be guided by the impeccable divine revelation.

The covenant of faith makes it imperative that when the Lord says, "I order and I forbid", the slave must say, "I heard and I obeyed".

The covenant of faith requires that the human being set himself free from the bondage of the whims of his own self to the law of his Master.

In this context, the Glorious Qur'an reads:

> *It is not fitting for a Believer, man or woman, when a matter has been decided by Allah and His Messenger to have any option about their decision: if any one disobeys Allah and His Messenger, he is indeed on a clearly wrong Path.* [33:36]

> *The answer of the Believers, when summoned to Allah and His Messenger, in order that He may judge between them, is no other than this: they say, "We hear and we obey": it is such as these that will attain felicity.* [24:51]

Hence, he does not worship God, who says, "I worship, fast and perform Hajj, but I am at liberty to consume pork, intoxicants, and deal in usury; I am free to reject those statutes of the Sharī'ah that do not appeal to me, and to adopt thereupon norms other than the norms of Sharī'ah". Similarly he does not worship God, who performs the ceremonial rites, but does not submit himself and his family to the Islamic standards of behaviour and practices—like a male wearing pure silk, adorning himself with gold and impersonating the female; or like a woman who dresses up in a manner that manifests her attractions, does not cover her body and does not draw her veil over her bosom. In the same way, he does not worship God, who assumes that the servitude to Allah does not go beyond the walls of the mosque, and that when he enters the diverse fields of life outside the mosque, he is the slave of his own self; in other words, he considers himself free to follow his own lusts or the lusts of other created beings like him.

Beneficial social works too are worship

More than that, Islam has broadened the scope of worship and expanded its compass to accommodate a multitude of deeds that no one could ever have imagined to be recognised by religion as deeds of worship and a means of endearing oneself to Allah.

Every beneficial social work is acknowledged by Islam as being amongst the best acts of worship, as long as the intention of the doer is benevolence rather than hunting for praise and admiration or attaining wide acclaimed fame. Every sincere deed where a human being wipes the tears of a grief-stricken fellow human being, alleviates the burdens of a burdened individual, patches in bandages the wounds of the afflicted, allays the hunger of a poor person, supports one who oppressed, raises a powerless from a fall, pays off the debt of an impoverished person, lends a helping hand to a need kinsmen, guides a bewildered and confused person, teaches an unlearned person, provides shelter to a stranger, wards off a tribulation from a living being, removes a harmful thing from a passageway, provides succour to a needy person, are all essentially a feat of worship and a vehicle for achieving closeness to Allah.

Islam effectively rendered a whole host of such deeds to the status of worshipping God, to being the outcome of faith and means of achieving reward from Allah.

So acts of prayers, fasting, remembrance, invocation and supplications alone are not logged as deeds of worship that qualify for reward, certainly not! During the course of a day one can append his balance sheet of good deeds, which carries their weight and worth in the estimation of Allah, the Exalted, with many other deeds of worship and virtuous acts, however insignificant these may appear in accordance with worldly standards.

In this perspective the Messenger of Allah (ṣ) said with regards those who strive for reconciliation between adversaries:

> Shall I reveal to you something more substantial than fasting, prayers and charity? The companions (may Allah be pleased with them) said, "Yes, please tell us". He said "It is reconciliation between adversaries. Malice (on the other hand), indeed, is a sharp razor."[11]

Another narration reports further, saying, "I do not mean that it is razor which shaves off hair, it rather is blade that severs one's faith".[12]

Encouraging the visiting of the ailing and sick, and explaining its importance in the form of alleviation and consolation, the Messenger of Allah (ṣ) says:

> He who visits a sick person, an angel calls out to him from the heavens: 'Be delighted, may your steps bring delight to you, and may you be granted an abode in Paradise![13]

11. Narrated by Abū Dāwūd, Tirmidhī and Ibn Ḥayyān as authentic.
12. This addition has been narrated by Tirmidhī.
13. Narrated by Tirmidhī and categorised by Ibn Mājah as fair (with narration of Abū Hurayrah).

In fact, Islam deems these social acts as daily obligations upon every Muslim.

When we examine the Ḥadīth of the Messenger (ṣ), we find that he did not only apply this vast meaning of worship as an obligation on the believers for the benefit of their fellow human beings only, but emphasised the need for seeking it out (with passion) as if it was obligatory upon him in every sphere of life and mandatory upon every joint of his body. Abū Hurayrah narrates from the Messenger of Allah (ṣ),

> Every day the sun rises, charity becomes due on every joint of the body of a person. Administering of justice between two men is also charity. And assisting a man to ride upon his animal, or helping him load his luggage upon it, is charity; and a good word is charity; and every step that you take towards prayer is charity, and the removal of harmful things from the pathway is charity.[14]

Earning a living too is worship

The Messenger of Allah (ṣ) regarded even worldly deeds carried out by man for the sake of his own livelihood and his endeavours for himself and for his family as being part of worship and pious deeds that bring him closer to Allah, even though such actions benefits only him and his family. A farmer in his farm, a worker in his factory, a trader in his store, an employee in his office and every person in the field of his profession can turn the toil for his own livelihood into prayers and into a form of struggle for the sake of Allah if he abides by the following guidelines:

---

14. Narrated by Bukhārī and Muslim.

1. That the work done is lawful according to Islam. Those deeds that are disapproved by Islam, like work which involves usury, in pubs and night clubs and so on, are not and shall never be, treated as worship. Allah is good and accepts nothing but good.

2. That the work should be based on righteous intention: the intention of safeguarding himself, providing for his family, benefiting his nation and making the earth flourish, as ordained by Allah.

3. That the job is done with perfection and excellence. In this context, a *ḥadīth* says:

> Allah has prescribed excellence in every aspect (of human life)"[15]
>
> and
>
> Allah likes that whenever anyone of you does any job, that he does it with perfection.[16]

4. That the boundaries set by Allah are observed. A believer does not commit injustice, act treacherously, swindle and encroach on the rights of others.

5. That worldly affairs do not divert him from his religious obligations, as Allah says:

> *O you who believe! Let not your riches or your children divert you from the remembrance of Allah. If any act thus, the loss is their own.* [63:9]

---

15. Narrated by Muslim from Shaddād bin Aws (it is one of the 40 hādīths compiled by Nawawī).
16. Narrated by Bayhaqī, in *Shu'ab al-Īman*, from 'Ā'ishah. Also narrated by Abū Ya'lā and Ibn 'Asākir. Appears in *al-Fayḍ*.

> *By men whom neither traffic nor merchandise can divert from the Remembrance of Allah, nor from regular Prayer, nor from the practice of regular Charity: Their (only) fear is for the Day when hearts and eyes will be transformed (in a world wholly new).* [24:37]

Fulfilment of natural instincts as an act of worship

Indeed worship includes even the basic needs fulfilled by a Muslim in response to his human instincts. Eating, drinking and sexual interaction of husband and wife are included by Islam in the broad spectrum of worship if the "intention" is sincere. Intention is the amazing, magical substance which when added to unforbidden deeds and habits, transforms them into acts of piety and devotion.

The most unequivocal witness to this effect is the following explanation of the Messenger of Allah (ṣ) to his companions:

> "Even your having sexual intercourse is (an act of) charity". The companions asked: "Does it mean that when one of us fulfils his carnal appetite, he will be granted a reward for that?" The Messenger of Allah (ṣ) replied: "Do you understand that if one has unlawful sex, he would as a result carry a sin?" The companions said: "Of course". He then said, "Similarly, when one has lawful sex, he is deserving of a reward!"[17]

The scholars remark that this is the pinnacle of Allah's mercy upon mankind—He rewards them for fulfilling their own desires when they intend to fulfill their obligations towards

---

17. Narrated by Muslim.

their spouses and to guard their chastity. Praise be to Allah, the Most Gracious.

The implications of the comprehensiveness of worship

The comprehensiveness of the meaning and scope of worship in Islam, as described above, has positive effects on one's self and life. This is felt by the person within himself and clearly felt by others whom he comes in contact with. The most prominent and deepest of these effects are the following two aspects:

1. It taints the life and actions of a Muslim with the paint of divinity. It keeps him connected to Allah through every worldly action he performs with sincere devotion, humility and piety. This prompts him to undertake even more rewarding endeavours, to contribute to more righteous causes and to anything else which makes life easier for himself and his fellow human beings. This adds to the reserve of his virtues and pious deeds which bring him closer to Allah. This insight directs him towards excellence, diligence and perfection when performing his worldly deeds, which he does with the awareness of submission to the Glorious Cherisher and with the intention of seeking His pleasure and pleasant recompense.

2. It grants to a Muslim a sense of direction and a unity of purpose in life as a whole. In every coming day and passing night, he strives to please the only Lord and runs towards Him by all his worldly and religious endeavours. There is neither a schism, conflict nor duplicity in his personality or in his life.

He is not among those who worship God during the night and worship "society" by day. He is not among those who worship Allah within the sanctuary of the mosque and worships the "world" or "matter" in the arena of actual life. He is not among those who worship Allah on a specific day of the week and worship other things and beings for the rest of the week.

Certainly, he is not from among these! He worships only Allah and Him alone wherever he is, however he is and in whatever job and circumstance he may be. Observation of Allah does not part with him in any work, state or time:

> *To Allah belong the East and the West: Whithersoever you turn, there is the Presence of Allah. For Allah is all-Pervading, All-Knowing.* [2:115]

Thus, all his attention turns towards Allah, his heart concentrates on Allah; the integrity and harmony of his life, thought, motivation and passion do not fragment into various directions, trends and schisms.

His life is an indivisible single unit. His route therein is the worship of Allah, his purpose therein is seeking the pleasure of Allah and his guide therein is the revelation of Allah.

While dealing with subjects of jurisprudence, scholars have classified worship separately, however we find authorities like Ibn Taymiyyah stating explicitly that worship comprises the whole of religion. We also know that Ibn al-Qayyim has incorporated the whole religion in "You do we worship" [1:5]. We shall later come to his description of the fifty ranks of servitude.

Worship embraces the whole of ones personality

This is yet another facet of the comprehensiveness of worship in Islam.

As worship in Islam incorporates the whole of life, it also embraces the complete human personality.

A Muslim worships Allah with his intellect, his heart, his tongue, with the senses of hearing and vision and with all the other senses. He worships Allah by spending his wealth, dedicating his life to Him and through the act of parting with his nearest and dearest and by leaving his homeland.

A Muslim glorifies Allah with his intellect by reflecting over his own self and over the universe, contemplating the wondrous kingdom of the heavens and the earth and whatsoever is therein; by pondering over the revealed signs of Allah and on the guidance and wisdom therein; and by contemplating over the ultimate fate of nations, the events of history and the lessons and warnings contained therein.

A Muslim practises piety through divine emotions and spiritual sentiments such as love and fear of Allah; hope for His mercy and fear of His punishment, contentment with His decree, patience during trials, thankfulness for His blessings, humility towards Him, trust in Him and sincerity and devotion to Him.

A Muslim worships Allah with his tongue through invocation and glorification, recitation and supplications, and through extolment, praise and exaltation.

A Muslim venerates Allah with his body, by abstaining from and not giving into the pleasures and cravings of the carnal self—as is done in the state of fasting. He worships Allah with his body through the vitality, work and activity of the body—as is done in the canonical prayers where the whole body, including the tongue and organs, move in synergy with the heart and mind.

> *A Muslim reveres Allah by spending his wealth generously; an act which is dear to the human heart and mind—as through the act of Zakāh, charity and aid. This act has been termed by Islamic jurists as "pecuniary worship", just as the act of prayer and fasting has been termed as "bodily worship." By "body" they mean the complete human entity; not merely the physical body. Intention is the precondition for every act of worship; and the home of intention, by unanimity, is the heart. This is why the worship of an insane or a drunk person is neither valid nor accepted. The condition for being it to be accepted is: "until you can comprehend all that you say."* [4:43]

A Muslim worships Allah when he is made to part with his loved ones and his homeland for His sake, when he goes for Hajj and Umrah (pilgrimage), or as a migrant to a land where he can establish the religion of Allah, or to strive in the path of Allah, or to seek knowledge and so on. As such, he sacrifices his comforts and his wealth. This is why, consistent with the standard jurisprudential classification, we consider this type of worship as being physical and pecuniary at the same time.

Purpose of worship

Why worship Allah?

We know now that the purpose of man on this earth and this existence is to worship Allah alone. We know that worship represents utmost submission blended with ultimate love for

Allah. It encompasses the whole of religion and embraces all of life with its various aspects.

There is still one more question which remains to be answered: Why do we worship Allah? In other words, why did God make His worship and obedience incumbent upon us, while He is in no need of it? What is the purpose of making the worship obligatory on us? Does our worshipping, devoutness, calling on Him, adherence to His commandments and prohibitions, benefit Him in any way? Or does the benefit go to us, His creation? What then is that benefit? Is the purpose merely our obedience to His commands?

In fact, the worship of any of His slaves avails no benefit to Him (Praise be to Him), nor does the turning away of any arrogant person from Him harm Him in any way. The Qur'an narrates to us the statement of Solomon:

> *(Solomon) said: "This is by the Grace of my Lord!—to test me whether I am grateful or ungrateful! and if any is grateful, truly his gratitude is (a gain) for his own soul; but if any is ungrateful, truly my Lord is Free of all Needs, Supreme in Honour !"* [27:40]

Another verse of the Qur'an reads as follows:

> *O you men! It is you that have need of Allah: but Allah is the One Free of all wants, Worthy of all praise.* [35:15]

Allah reveals through a *ḥadīth qudsī*:[18]

> "O My servants, it is beyond your capability to harm Me; and it is beyond your capability to avail any benefit for Me. O My servants, if all of you—first and last, humans and jinn—were

18. Sayings of the Messenger (ṣ) that convey the meanings revealed to him by Allah.

like the one among you with the most devout heart, that would add nothing to My kingdom. O My servants, if all of you—first and last, humans and jinn—were like the one among you with the most dissolute heart, that would take nothing away from My kingdom".[19]

When God is absolutely in no need, why then has he imposed upon His servants to worship and obey Him?

I believe that after we know the answer to those perpetual questions—"From where did I come? To where shall I go? Why am here?"—it becomes easy for us to know the answer to this question too. The answer lies hidden in the nature of man himself; in the nature of his mission on the earth and in the purpose for which he was stationed in this life.

Worship is nourishment of the soul

Human beings are not just the physical exterior that we sense and sight; one which demands its portion of earthly food and drink. The essence of man rather lies in that precious substance by which he became venerated as a human being and as responsible for all creation on earth. That substance is nothing but the soul which derives its energy and purity from the intimate discourse with Allah (the Mighty and the Majestic). It is the worship of Allah which provides sustenance and nourishment to this soul and dispenses its daily requirements, never running out nor depleting.

If negligence and ignorance accumulate on this metaphysical entity and if the corrosion of denial and suspicion rust it then it is in times of great tribulations that it may stir up and extricate

19. Narrated by Muslim.

this accumulated dust; the fire of hardship and suffering may erupt and as a consequence eliminate the corrosion. It is at this instance that the human being instantaneously returns to Allah, calls out to Him and humbles himself before Him. This is the fact that has been mentioned in the Qur'an and supported by the ongoing events of human life:

> *He it is Who enables you to traverse through land and sea; so that you even board ships—they sail with them with a favourable wind, and they rejoice thereat; then comes a stormy wind and the waves come to them from all sides, and they think they are being overwhelmed: they cry unto Allah, sincerely offering (their) duty unto Him saying, "If you do deliver us from this, we shall truly show our gratitude!"* [10:22]

The human heart always feels the need for God. This is a veritable and pristine sentiment, the vacuum of which cannot be filled by anything in the existence except by a strong bond with the Lord of Existence. This exactly is the role of worship when performed aptly.

Ibn Taymiyyah states:

> By nature, the heart is destitute of Allah from two aspects: from the aspect of worship and from the aspect of recourse and reliance. The heart cannot be righteous, cannot thrive, cannot be pleasant, cannot be happy, cannot enjoy, cannot feel delighted, cannot be at peace, nor can it be contented, but by the worship of its Lord alone, with His love and by returning to Him. If the heart attains all the relished created things, it still cannot be contented nor can it be at peace, because it has its own inherent need to its Lord, who is its deity, beloved and the cherished One. With this does it (the

heart) attain delight and pleasure; enjoyment and comfort; peace and tranquillity.[20]

Worship of Allah is the road to freedom

Furthermore, absolute servitude to Allah is actually identical to freedom. It is the road to real sovereignty. It alone releases the heart from serving the creation. It alone liberates the heart and mind from submission and servitude to all sorts of gods and idols who subjugate the people and enslave them by means of the worst forms of suppression and enslavement, even though in their appearance and form they may appear to be sovereign rulers.

The reason for this is that in the human heart there is an autogenic need to attach itself with, to seek after and to strive for the gratification of a god, a deity or a lord. If this deity were not the One and Only Allah, the Almighty, the heart would be in a chaotic state of affairs by worshipping numerous deities and multiple lords, whether visible or invisible, whether rational or irrational, whether existing or nonexistent as figments of the human imagination.

There is nothing more honourable for a sensible human being than worshiping the One Who created him, then fashioned him and then appropriately modelled him.

There is nothing more effective in bringing happiness and inner tranquillity to him than directing all his worries to the One God, devoting his attention, submission and adoration to Him, so that his heart is not torn between fictitious deities and false lords. The Qur'an portrays this fact as follows:

---

20. *Al-'Ubūdiyyah*, p. 108.

Allah puts forth a Parable—a man belonging to many partners at variance with each other, and a man belonging entirely to one master: are those two equal in comparison? Praise be to Allah! but most of them have no knowledge. [39:29]

A sound person belonging to one single master is always at ease, as he knows what pleases the master; he carries out his commands cheerfully and accomplishes his wishes with gratification. In contrast, a slave owned by several masters contradicting his affairs and obligating him with conflicting orders, is in absolute misery and objectionable wretchedness!

Worship—a divine test to galvanise the personality

The worldly life that we are living now, whether long or short, is not the ultimate purpose in itself, nor is it the goal post. It is merely a transitional phase to another life, to another world; to the life of eternity and infinity. As the saying goes, "You have been created for eternity; indeed, you are transferred from one abode to another". A poet has expressed it thus:

Death is nothing but a journey; however,
from the perishable house to the Eternal Abode.

Hence, the genuinely reliable abode is the abode of the hereafter:

What is the life of this world but amusement and play? but verily the Home in the Hereafter—that is Life indeed, if they but knew. [29:64]

The human being in this impermanent house strives for that everlasting abode. He has been appointed the vicegerent in this world. He is to prepare and refine himself for the

Eternal Life. Nothing can refine, purify and prepare him as tribulation; it is the melting pot for the refinement of character and purification of the soul.

It was the will of Allah to create the human being as distinct from all other creatures. He equipped him with a duel nature, which enabled him to ascend to the heavens as well as to descend to the soil. Human beings have been provided with instincts and lusts but they have also been endowed with intellect and free will; they are the composition of matter and soul.

Humans are obliged to worship Allah

Worship, above all, is the right of Allah (the Almighty, the Creator) over His creation.

In this context Bukhārī and Muslim narrated through Mu'ādh ibn Jabal:

> I was riding a donkey with the Prophet (ṣ) when he asked me: "O Mu'ādh, are you aware of the right of Allah over man?" I said, "Only Allah and His Messenger know best." He said, "That they worship Him alone."

There is nothing strange in the fact that we owe Allah His right to be worshipped. However, it is deplorable when we worship anything else or anyone else besides Him. It is deplorable that we hand over someone else's due right to others who do not deserve it, or pretend freedom for ourselves from Allah and unjustly reject that we are His slaves.

We were nonexistent and then we came into existence, we emerged from the darkness of nonentity to the light of existence, we turned out to be the most honoured of all creation. We were created in the best form, given the best shape, taught expression and given the intellect and free will. The creatures around us were made subservient to us; the earth was made as a cradle and a bed for us, the sky as a roof and canopy; the sun provides us with light and warmth, the stars guide us and decorate our sky; in the sea, our ships sail carrying goods for our sustenance; from the sky, water rains down, as pure drink so that we may quench our thirst and with it our cattle too can drink.

Who has done and perpetuates all this? We did not create our own selves, nor did we bring into existence even an atom of our surroundings; never has any human, jinn or an angel claimed to be the creator or the designer of the universe. Who then has the vast knowledge, the utmost wisdom, the vanquishing might and the efficacious will to precisely create this wondrous universe, organise it and perfected it beautifully? Who then created the human being in the most beautiful and perfect form, subjugated to him all that is in the heavens and on earth, and generously bestowed upon him seen and unseen bounties? That supreme Power is none other than Allah, whose divinity all intuitive and sound creatures bear witness to, and of whose existence, integrity and unity all enlightened minds acknowledge.

It is no wonder then that this Gracious Creator has the right to be worshipped, to be sought for in times of need, to be implored earnestly and to be invoked in supplication, with submission, obedience and observance!

Glorify the name of your Guardian—Lord Most High, Who has created, and further, given order and proportion; Who has ordained laws. And granted guidance; And Who brings out the (green and luscious) pasture, And then does make it (but) swarthy stubble. [87:1-5]

O you people! Adore your Guardian—Lord, Who created you and those who came before you, that you may have the chance to learn righteousness; Who has made the earth your couch, and the heavens your canopy; and sent down rain from the heavens; and brought forth therewith Fruits for your sustenance; then set not up rivals unto Allah when you know (the truth). [2:21-22]

MORALITY

The significance of morals in Islam

Islamic scholars have traditionally divided Islam into four elements: Beliefs, Acts of Worship, Dealings and Morality. Since morality has been mentioned last, some people may have been deluded into thinking that morality is the least important element in Islam and has not the similar status as the other three elements. However, the reality that becomes evident to those who deliberate over Islam, through serious study and reflection on its Book and on the life of its Prophet (ṣ), is that Islam in its essence is nothing more than a message of moral refinement—with all that this element entails.

This is not merely because Islam actively encourages moral excellence and strongly warns against moral depravity, but because it demands the highest level of obedience in this regard, and speaks of extreme degrees of recompense—in reward and penalty—both in this world and in the life hereafter.

This is also not just because Islam intensively cares about morality to the extent that the Qur'an commended the Messenger (ṣ), and his paramount status with the most eloquent of expressions saying that:

And you (stand) on an exalted standard of character. [68:4]

Even the Messenger of God (ṣ), summarises, with the most succinct eloquence, the essence of his message: "I was sent to perfect the nobility of character."[21]

Morality is not a characteristic of Islam solely for this or that reason. Aside from these reasons it is because of the fact that morality circulates like blood in the whole of the Islamic system and in the Islamic teachings. It permeates its beliefs, its acts of worship, dealings, politics, economics and even its rules for peace and war.

Islamic beliefs and morals

Islamic beliefs are founded upon monotheism, the opposite of which is polytheism.

From here we discover that Islam ascribes a moral symbolic manifestation to the concept of monotheism and considers this to be justice, which is a moral virtue. On the other hand, it regards polytheism as symbolising injustice, which is a moral depravity:

False worship is indeed the highest wrong-doing. [31:13]

The Qur'an rather regards disbelief, with all its manifestations as being unjust. Allah, the Exalted, says:

---

21. Narrated by al-Ḥākim, confirmed as authentic by Dhahabī.

Those who reject Faith, they are the wrong-doers. [2:254]

When the Islamic faith becomes complete and bears its fruits, it assumes the form of moral virtues, which have been mentioned at length in various Qur'anic verses and in the prophetic traditions, for example:

> *The Believers must (eventually) win through—Those who humble themselves in their prayers; Who avoid vain talk; Who are active in deeds of charity; Who abstain from sex, Except with those joined to them in the marriage bond, or (the captives) whom their right hands possess—for (in their case) they are free from blame, But those whose desires exceed those limits are transgressors—Those who faithfully observe their trusts and their covenants. And who (strictly) guard their prayers—These will be the heirs, Who will inherit Paradise: they will dwell therein (forever).* [23:1-11]

> *For, Believers are those who, when Allah is mentioned, feel a tremor in their hearts, and when they hear His Signs rehearsed, find their faith strengthened, and put (all) their trust in their Lord; Who establish regular Prayers and spend (freely) out of the gifts We have given them for sustenance: Such in truth are the believers: they have grades of dignity with their Lord, and forgiveness, and generous sustenance.* [8:2-4]

> *Only those are Believers who have believed in Allah and His Messenger, and have never since doubted, but have striven with their belongings and their persons in the Cause of Allah: Such are the sincere ones.* [49:15]

> *And the servants of (Allah) Most Gracious are those who walk on the earth in humility, and when the ignorant address them, they*

> *say, "Peace!"; Those who spend the night in adoration of their Lord prostrate and standing; Those who say, "Our Lord! avert from us the Wrath of Hell, for its Wrath is indeed an affliction grievous,- "Evil indeed is it as an abode, and as a place to rest in"; Those who, when they spend, are not extravagant and not niggardly, but hold a just (balance) between those (extremes); Those who invoke not with Allah, any other god, nor slay such life as Allah has made sacred except for just cause, nor commit fornication—and any that does this (not only) meets punishment.* [25:63-68]

The sayings of Prophet Muḥammad (ṣ) too link moral virtues with faith and regard it as the fruits of the latter. For example:

> He who believes in Allah and in the Day of Judgement, should support the bond of kinship; He who believes in Allah and in the Day of Judgement, should refrain from hurting his neighbour; He who believes in Allah and in the Day of Judgement, should either speak good or remain silent.

Faith has more than seventy branches and the highest amongst these is the testimony of faith that "there is no god but Allah", while the lowest amongst these is the removal of a harmful object from the pathway. Shame is also a branch of faith. The Prophet (ṣ) said:

> In the act of fornication, the fornicator ceases to be a faithful believer; in the act of theft, the thief ceases to be a faithful believer; in the act of drinking alcohol, the drinker ceases to be a faithful believer.

Islamic practices of worship and morals

All major Islamic practices of worship have clear moral objectives.

Ṣalāh (the obligatory prayer), which is the foremost daily ritual in the life of a Muslim, plays a vital role in building a self motivating deterrent (of bad acts) and in cultivating God-consciousness:

> *Recite what is sent of the Book by inspiration to you, and establish regular Prayer: for Prayer restrains from shameful and unjust deeds; and remembrance of Allah is the greatest (thing in life) without doubt. And Allah knows the (deeds) that you do.* [29:45]

These prayers amount to a moral reinforcement for the believer. He resorts to these while confronting the difficulties of life:

> *O you who believe! Seek help with patient perseverance and prayer; for Allah is with those who patiently persevere.* [2:153]

Zakāh (mandatory charity), which has recurrently been mentioned alongside *Ṣalāh,* is not just a fiscal obligation collected from the rich and passed onto the poor. In the domain of morals it is rather the medium of purification, whereas in the field of finance, it acts as an important instrument of collection and all-round development.

> *Of their goods, take alms, that so you might purify and sanctify them.* [9:103]

Ṣawm (fasting) in Islam is aimed at training the self; training it to abstain from its own wicked desires and to revolt against its own habitual inclinations. In other words, it prepares the self for piety; which is the core of Islamic morality.

> *O you who believe! Fasting is prescribed to you as it was prescribed to those before you, that you may (learn) self-restraint.* [2:183]

Likewise, Hajj is meant to train the Muslim to purify the self; to train him in devotion and on rising above the vanities, extravagances, commotions and conflicts of life. That is the reason why Islam prescribes the *Iḥrām* (attire of pilgrimage) denoting entry into a life founded on simplicity, modesty, peace, seriousness and the abandoning of worldly pomp and show.

> *For Hajj are the months well known. If any one undertakes that duty therein, Let there be no obscenity, nor wickedness, nor wrangling in the Hajj.* [2:197]

When these Islamic practices of worship lose these dimensions and fail to achieve their desired goals, their significance is lost along with the essence of their purpose. Thereupon these practices turn into nothing but dead bodies having no soul. No wonder many sayings of the Prophet of Allah (ṣ) emphasise this reality in very eloquent and unequivocal terms; for example, "He whose prayers do not prevent from wicked deeds, his prayers are void. How many an awake (in supererogatory night prayers) gains from his night prayer nothing but the burning of the oil from the lamp".

About fasting, too, the Prophet (ṣ) said:

> He who does not give up spurious talk and acting upon it, Allah is in no need of his fast. How many a fasters there are who gain nothing from fasting except hunger and thirst.

Morality and the economy

Islamic morality has an impact on financial and economic affairs too, whether in production or in distribution, in delivery or in consumption.

The economy cannot grow, as some may want, without checks and balances, without being based on values or without adherence to ideals, although, there are some economists who actually advocate separation of economics and ethics.

A Muslim is not permitted to produce whatever he may desire without taking into consideration the material and moral harm this may cause to his fellow human beings, even if he was to gain heavily and profit profoundly from that production.

The cultivation of tobacco, hashish or other narcotic plants and the production of harmful substances in general may lead to lucrative gains, but Islam strictly prohibits its believers form trying to earn and gain from the loss and damage incurred by others.

The fermenting of grapes into wine may lead to high earnings and ensure high returns to vineyard owners and wine producers, but Islam denounces such profits gained by the immense wrongs caused to and the enormous harms inflicted on the minds, bodies and morals of others—manifested in the form of decadence and deterioration in the lives of individuals, families and whole groups. The Qur'an says:

> *They ask you concerning wine and gambling. Say: "In them is great sin, and some profit, for men; but the sin is greater than the profit."* [2:219]

Even in the exchange of merchandise, a Muslim must not deal in the buying and selling of wine, pork, dead meat, idols nor should he sell something to someone whom he knows will use to carrying out evil deeds, depravity or for causing damage and harm to others. For instance, one cannot sell grape juice or even grapes to someone who is known to use these for preparing wine, or sell military arms to someone who is known for murdering the innocent or uses them for acts of brutality and aggression. A *ḥadīth* of the Prophet (ṣ) puts it thus:

> When Allah forbade something, He forbade dealing in it too; so whoever withholds grapes during harvesting season to sell later it on to a Jew or a Christian or whoever ferments grapes into wine—even if it was to a fellow Muslim,—surely he is deliberately plunging himself into the fire of Hell.

A Muslim cannot hoard food provisions or the similar basic necessities of the people with the willful intention of selling it for twice or more of its original price. An authentic *ḥadīth* states: "No one other than a wrongdoer (*i.e.*, sinner) hoards."

Allah the Exalted says:

> *Pharaoh and Hāmān and (all) their hosts were men of sin.* [28:8]

A Muslim trader should not hide or cover up the defects and drawbacks of his merchandise and exaggerate its merits and advantages, as is normally done through present-day advertising, so that the deluded customers pay a price higher than what is really reasonable. This is known as swindling and the Prophet (ṣ) has said about this: "He who swindles is not from amongst us."

So too in the distribution and ownership of wealth, it is not lawful for a Muslim to possess wealth through unlawful means. He is not permitted to acquire by means of aggression nor by deceit what he otherwise does not deserve.

Since it is not permitted to possess wealth through unlawful means, it is also not legitimate to build up wealth through unlawful methods.

For this reason, Allah has prohibited usury, gambling, devouring of people's possessions through deceit, all forms of unfairness, harming others and injury of all sorts.

As far as consumption is concerned, Islam does not allow a believer to reign free, so that he spends according to his whims and fancies without being concerned about the interests of his own self, his family and his nation. It has rather regulated it through moderation and self-control. The Qur'an reads:

> *Make not your hand tied (like a niggard's) to your neck, nor stretch it forth to its utmost reach, so that you become blameworthy and destitute.* [17:29]

> *Eat and drink, but waste not by excess, for Allah loves not the wasters.* [7:31]

It has condemned extravagance and indulgence in luxuries and vain pleasures. It has prohibited all kinds of excess and pomp, like the use of gold and silver utensils, and barred their use for men as well as for women. Similarly, it has forbidden wearing of gold and silk for men.

All these guiding principles characterise and distinguish the Islamic economic model with the great peculiarity of being an "ethical economy". Many of the fair-minded scholars and honest researchers agree with this reality.

French writer Jacques Austeroi, writes in his book, *Islam and Economic Development*:

> Islam is simultaneously a system of practical life and of idealistic moral values. As these two aspects are interlinked

> and inseparable, we can say that secular economy is unacceptable to Muslims. An economy that derives its strength from the Qur'anic revelation must certainly be an ethical economy.

Such moral values are capable of redefining the concept of 'value' and of filling the intellectual void that is on the verge of emergence as a result of the mechanisation of industrialisation.

Bergis has denounced the harmful consequences of the development of the depraved industrial civilisation in the West. The economy today faces the threat arising from the domination of 'hedonism' over genuine values.

The West has begun to comprehend the harmful consequences of the economic trends leading towards an unstable world, wherein an individual finds himself suddenly terminated from his job, wherein machines have become the master, where there is an extreme culture of acquiring luxuries, and where attention is focused on absurd things. The West never bothered to slow down the fast-paced enmity of machines towards humans—although they do occupy an important place in today's civilisation.

Islam has been very conscious of the lessons learnt in Western civilisation, so replete with inconsistencies. In order to stand in the face of such glaring contradictions, while accomplishing its own economic mission, Islam introduced ethics into economy.

Thus Islam subjects the material elements of the economy in order to realise justice. This union of morality and economics has not been out of the blue in Islam since it is a faith which knows no schism between materiality and spirituality.

The rendezvous of Protestantism with the industrial revolution has been a sham and their relationship controversial, but this is something alien to the Islamic faith, as most of its statutes are divine and prohibit economic development which does not take into consideration the Divine.

The express imposition of the Western experience where the adage "Render unto Caesar what is Caesar's, render unto God what is God's" should not obscure the fact that such segregation is inconceivable in the case of Islam. Separation of religion and state, which brought in material vigour to the West, is meaningless in the Islamic context, as efficiency does not come into being from within or outside the intellectual sphere; its inspiration is rather sought from the authority of Islam and from the divine revelation inspired to the Prophet of Islam.[22]

If we examine the functional reality, we shall find the effects of this conjugation of economy and ethics very lucid and deep rooted in the history of the Muslims, especially when Islam was the foremost influencing factor in their lives and the dictator of their activity and behaviour.

Morality and politics

Just as Islam has united economics with ethics, it has also done the same regarding politics. Islamic politics is not a Machiavellian style of politics wherein the ends justify means, what ever its characteristics may be. Islamic politics is rather the politics of principles and values, which must be adhered to

22. See my book *The Role of Values and Morals in Islamic Economy*, Maktabah Wahbah—Cairo, p. 440.

and not relinquished even in the murkiest of situations or in the most perplexing times; whether it is between the relations of the Islamic state with its citizens or between the external relations with other countries and groups.

Islam vehemently rejects dirty means even if they are intended to reach noble ends: "Allah is noble and accepts nothing but noble actions."[23] Unscrupulous means are unacceptable just like their vicious ends. Inevitably, there must be clean means to achieve noble ends.

Concerning the relationship between the state and its citizens, Allah calls upon those entrusted with authority to govern the affairs of the Muslims with honesty and justice, saying:

> *Allah does command you to render back your Trusts to those to whom they are due; And when you judge between man and man, that you judge with justice: Verily how excellent is the teaching which He gives you! For Allah is He Who hears and sees all things.* [4:58]

Hence, the returning of trusts, of different material and moral types, to whom they are due and judging between all people with justice and equality, is the obligation binding on the Muslim state towards its citizens.

It is not lawful for the Muslim ruler to favour any one of his relatives or commission him with something unduly while depriving the deserving. The Messenger of Allah (ṣ) identified such overt nepotism with the signs of the hour of Doom for the Muslim nation. Once someone asked him about the timing of the Day of Judgement and he replied:

---

23. Narrated by Muslim in *Ṣaḥiḥ*.

> When trust is squandered, anticipate the hour. He was asked: "How will the squandering of trust take place." He replied: when authority will be entrusted to the undeserving, anticipate the hour.[24]

It is also illegitimate to drop a prescribed punishment against anyone deserving the punishment, because of his lineage or status or closeness to the ruler. Regarding this, a *ḥadīth* testifies:

> Verily those before you were made to perish when the highborn amongst them stole and they spared him and when a powerless stole, they imposed the penalty upon him; By Allah, if Fāṭimah—the daughter of Muḥammad—were to commit theft, I myself would chop off her hand.[25]

The internal dimensions of Islamic politics must be grounded on the foundation of justice, fairness and equality between all with regards to rights, responsibilities and penalties. It must be based on truth and frankness of people about reality, without any deception, false pretence or delusion. The Prophet (ṣ) has said that one of the three whom Allah will not look upon on the Day of Resurrection, nor exonerate them and for whom there will be an awful punishment, shall be the untruthful ruler.[26]

With regard to international relations, the Islamic state must fulfil treaties and respect its word. Allah says:

> *Fulfil the Covenant of Allah when you have entered into it, and break not your oaths after you have confirmed them; indeed you*

24. Narrated by Bukhārī.
25. Unanimously agreed upon.
26. Narrated by Muslim from Abū Hurayrah.

have made Allah your surety; for Allah knows all that you do. And be not like a woman who breaks into untwisted strands the yarn which she has spun, after it has become strong. Nor take your oaths to practise deception between yourselves, lest one party should be more numerous than another: for Allah will test you by this; and on the Day of Judgement He will certainly make clear to you (the truth of) that wherein you disagree. If Allah so willed, He could make you all one people: But He leaves straying whom He pleases, and He guides whom He pleases: but you shall certainly be called to account for all your actions. [16:91-93]

In these two Qur'anic verses, Allah emphatically enjoins upon the faithful to respect treaties and pacts by relating covenants to Himself (*i.e.*, the Covenant of Allah). He warns against breaking of oaths after the ratification of agreements, which is like the act of a foolish woman who puts in a great deal of effort into the spinning of her yarn, but once the yarn gains strength upon processing, she imprudently cuts her own produce into untwisted strands. He urges for the basing of treaties and agreements between nations upon sincerity and truthful intentions, without dishonesty and swindling intended to take undue advantage and to benefit more than the other party. That is exactly what we notice in treaties and agreements of our times.

The Prophet (ṣ) was the most perfect example when it came to respecting agreements and honouring treaties. He even respected an agreement when his companions believed that there was an unfairness towards Muslims in them, such as in the treaty of Ḥudaybiyah.

In one of the military expeditions against Quraysh, when a man wanted to join the Muslim army, the Prophet (ṣ) did not accept his request, as he had pledged to them that he would not fight them from the ranks of their enemy. The Prophet (ṣ) rather ordered him to honour his word, saying to him, "We are sufficient for them; we seek Allah's help over them".[27]

If some people think that politics knows no morals then such a notion is farthest from Islamic politics, which is essentially based on justice, faithfulness, truthfulness, integrity and the noblest of morals.

Morality and war

If such was the policy of Islam in peace, certainly its policy in war must not be detached from ethics.

War does not imply the nullification of virtue while being engaged in a dispute, abrogation of justice in dealings during conflict or abolition of one's humanity during and after battle.

War is sometimes a necessity imposed on society by the nature of man and by the nature of conflict that continues between people, as mentioned in the Qur'an:

> *Had not Allah check one set of people by means of another, there would surely have been pulled down monasteries, churches, synagogues, and mosques, in which the name of Allah is commemorated in abundant measure.* [22:40]

> *And did not Allah check one set of people by means of another, the earth would indeed be full of mischief: but Allah is full of bounty to all the worlds.* [2:251]

27. Narrated by Muslim, Aḥmad and others.

The necessity of war does not, however, mean submission to the impulses of rage, pagan fanaticism and for the satisfaction of such things as malignity, cruelty and arrogance.

If war is inevitable, let it be regulated by morality; let mean cravings not be the driving force; let it be against tyrants and transgressors, not against innocent and peace-loving people.

> *Fight in the cause of Allah those who fight you, but do not transgress limits; for Allah loves not transgressors.* [2:190]

> *And let not the hatred of some people in (once) shutting you out of the Sacred Mosque lead you to transgression (and hostility on your part). Help you one another in righteousness and piety, but help you not one another in sin and rancour: fear Allah: for Allah is strict in punishment.* [5:2]

If war is inevitable, let it be in the cause of Allah (i.e the cause of justice and equality), for that is the path to hoist the word of truth and righteousness; let it not be in the cause of tyranny, which leads to exaltation of wickedness and falsehood.

> *Those who believe fight in the cause of Allah, and those who reject Faith fight in the cause of Evil: So fight you against the friends of Satan: feeble indeed is the cunning of Satan.* [4:76]

If war is inescapable, let it be fought in order to liberate the oppressed, rather than for safeguarding the interests of powerful despots.

> *And why should you not fight in the cause of Allah and of those who, being weak, are ill-treated (and oppressed)?—Men, women, and children, whose cry is: "Our Lord! Rescue us from this town,*

> *whose people are oppressors; and raise for us from You one who will protect; and raise for us from You one who will help!"* [4:75]

Let war be regulated by the morals of mercy and nobility, even if it is to be fought against the worst of enemies who may be the most intolerable towards Muslims and ferocious in enmity towards them.

Many of the warlords and philosophers of valour do not care for anything during war except the sole retribution and destruction of their enemy, even if, in the course of military action, innocent civilians are afflicted. In contrast, Islam states as a rule that no one, other than those who are involved in fighting, be killed. Islam admonishes treachery, mutilation of the dead, cutting and uprooting of trees, destroying of buildings, killing of women (not involved in combat), children, old people, pious hermits and monks, and prohibits the killing of farmers dedicated to the tilling of the land during times of war.

In this context, we find evidence from many Qur'anic verses, commandments of the Messenger of Allah (ṣ) and testaments of the Rightly Guided Caliphs. The Qur'an reads:

> *Fight in the cause of Allah those who fight you, but do not transgress limits; for Allah loves not transgressors.* [2:190]

In a Prophetic tradition we find that the Prophet (ṣ) used to instruct his companions when proceeding to war thus:

> Fight in the name of Allah, and in His cause; fight those who reject faith in Allah; fight, but do not transgress; do not be treacherous, do not mutilate the dead, do not kill children...[28]

---

28. Narrated by Muslim in Ṣaḥiḥ.

Similarly, after the Prophet, the Rightly Guided Caliphs too used to instruct their commanders emphatically that they should not slay the old, children, women nor cut trees or destroy buildings.

They even prohibited them from confronting pious hermits and monks secluded in their hermitages, advising them to leave alone such holy men to worship as they may, since they might have dedicated themselves to gaining the sole pleasure of God.

Muslim historians report that during one of the major battles fought between Muslims and the two powerful empires of Persia and Rome during the rule of the first caliph Abū Bakr, the decapitated head of an important enemy commander was sent to him in Madīnah, the capital of the Islamic state, right from the throes of the battlefield. The Muslim commander, who had brought the severed head, thought that the Caliph would be pleased with this action of his. The Caliph, contrary to expectation, was outraged by the act, as it amounted to the mutilation of the dead and to the disgrace of human dignity. Some said to him, "But they do the same to our dead men". The Caliph replied, "Do you want to follow the ways of Persians and the Romans? Never ever should a severed human head be brought to me, ever!"

When a war comes to an end, human and moral aspects should not be forgotten in dealing with the prisoners and the victims of war. Allah describes the righteous among His slaves:

> *And they feed, for the love of Allah, the indigent, the orphan, and the captive—(Saying),"We feed you for the sake of Allah alone: no reward do we desire from you, nor thanks.* [76:8-9]

Between Islamic and Judo-Christian morals

Judaism was the religion of a certain people in a specific period in history, and as testified by Torah itself, it was not meant to be a universal message (for the whole mankind) or to be an eternal law. For this reason, Allah entrusted this divine book to the Israelite scholars instead of taking its preservation upon Himself. Vicissitudes of time took their toll on the laws of this tradition. It was subjected to distortion and modification, and in turn it began to contain many stories about prophets ascribing to them horrendous moral perversities. Its morality is characterised by worldly, material and sensual characteristics, and with hideous racist traits; it is marked by a lot of violence and cruelty with meticulous concern for ceremony and formalism.

Christianity came as a cure for the materialistic extravagance in which Judaism—for instance during the Roman empire—was steeped in. It was like a strong spiritual antidote. Often it is wise to treat extremism with similar extremism, provided it is meant for a certain period or for a temporary phase until balance is restored and harmony and moderation are achieved once again.

Such was the case with Christianity with its soaring spirituality and utopian idealism. It was not meant to be a law for all the world nor was it meant to be the message of eternity. That is why its followers—especially in the West—have been farthest from practising its teachings of asceticism, forgiveness, tolerance and loving one's enemy! Similarly, the concepts, values and traditions introduced by the Church over the ages—for instance, the concept of monasticism, especially in the West, has characterised the Christian faith with an air of austerity mixed with stagnation and the mortification of life.

As far as Islam is concerned, it embodies the final word of God to mankind, after humanity, having reached maturity, was competent enough to receive a universally eternal message. This is why Allah promised to protect His final Message, the Qur'an, the book of Islam. Over the centuries, not even one word has changed in it nor has a single character been removed from it.

> *We have, without doubt, sent down the Message; and We will assuredly guard it (from corruption).* [15:9]

Characteristics of Islamic morals

For given reasons, it was part of the divine will that the Islamic moral system be characterised by qualities which would make it distinct from that of Judaism and Christianity. These qualities have made this moral system suitable for every individual, community, race, environment, time and circumstance.

Reasonable and rational

The first of these qualities is that Islamic morality is free from the dictatorial devotional nature for which Judaism has been known, and which was understood by some scholars of ethics as being inherent and mandatory and taken as a standard when calling to morality in all religions. These people are ignorant of the fact that Islam is absolutely contrary to this notion. Islam always relies on rational wisdom and acceptable reasoning, appealing to the sound intelligence and unimpaired conscience by explaining the advantages of a certain commandment and the disadvantages of breaking a certain prohibition.

The instances of detailed Islamic justification for a certain command are as follows:

> *And establish regular Prayer: for Prayer restrains from shameful and unjust deeds...* [29:45]

> *Fasting is prescribed to you as it was prescribed to those before you, that you may (learn) self-restraint.* [2:183]

> *Nor can goodness and Evil be equal. Repel (Evil) with what is better: Then will he between whom and you was hatred become as it were your friend and intimate!* [41:34]

The instances of brief rational explanations (for commands) are as follows:

> *Hasten earnestly to the Remembrance of Allah, and leave off business (and traffic): That is best for you if you but knew!* [62:9]

> *Say: "I find not in the Message received by me by inspiration any (meat) forbidden to be eaten by one who wishes to eat it, unless it be dead meat, or blood poured forth, or the flesh of swine—for it is an abomination...* [6:145]

Universal

Morals in Islam are universal; nothing is permitted for a certain race and at the same time prohibited for another; Arabs and non-Arabs are equal therein. Even Muslims and non-Muslims are treated likewise. Usury-based dealings are forbidden with Muslims as well as with disbelievers; stealing is unlawful, whether the victim is a Muslim or not; adultery is prohibited with a

Muslim as well as with a non-Muslim. Justice must be shown to Muslims as well as with non-Muslims; aggression is illegal against Muslims and non-Muslims. Hence, the Qur'an says:

> *O you who believe! Stand out firmly for Allah, as witnesses to fair dealing, and let not the hatred of others to you make you swerve to wrong and depart from justice. Be just: that is next to piety: and fear Allah. For Allah is well-acquainted with all that you do.* [5:8]

Islamic morality is characterised by being free from the tendencies of nationalistic racialism—an attribute contrary to Jewish morality—tribal morality and primitive morals in general.

Conformity with nature

In the sphere of morality, Islam introduced what is not only congruent with human nature and its composition, but even complements it. It does not subject human nature to conflict. God would not have created the human being with a certain nature and then command him to subjugate or exterminate this very nature or neutralise or arrest it.

Thus, Islam recognises the human being exactly as he was created by Allah along with his psychological make up and natural tendencies. All that Islam has done is that it has disciplined and elevated them these natural elements of man; it has put limits on them in order to protect the interests of society as well as the interests of the individual. Hence Islamic Sharī'ah has permitted the finer things of life, and therefore made the individual ownership of property as lawful. It never considers human instincts and impulses as being innately satanic.

Islam sees cleanliness and beauty as something which should be desired for everyone. It has made this a prelude and precondition for the obligatory Prayer:

> *O Children of Adam! Wear your beautiful apparel at every time and place of prayer...* [7:31]

The Qur'an sternly rebukes those who forbid lawful pleasures:

> *Say: Who has forbidden the beautiful (gifts) of Allah, which He has produced for His servants, and the things, clean and pure, (which He has provided) for sustenance?...* [7:32]

If Christianity views the rich as having no admittance to the Kingdom of Heaven, Islam takes the opposite view and affirms, "How wonderful is lawful wealth for a righteous person."

If Christianity believes in establishing a tyrannical system of monasticism characterised by the mortification of the body and the suppression of natural inclinations, Islam, on the other hand, prohibits celibacy. Islam encourages marriage; it considers the world to be also a place of pleasure, the best of these pleasures being a righteous partner; it considers the endeavour of raising a family and the management of familial affairs as a kind of holy struggle for the sake of Allah.

Nevertheless, while being magnanimous in its approvals and sanctions in its consideration for human nature, Islam has set up such checks and balances that function only when moderation is upheld and maintained. However, these are not impenetrable, for instability and immoderation sometimes arise and turn into unpleasantness.

Realistic

Among the other characteristics of Islamic morality is that it is a system of pragmatic morals. Permissible and forbidden commands are not passed on to those who live in ivory towers or who live in a utopian fantasy. Instead, they address the humans who walk on the earth, who have motivations and desires, who have aspirations and ambitions, who have interests and needs, who have carnal desires which ground them on the earth, and who have the yearnings of a soul that soars with them to the heavens.

The Qur'an has not imposed upon man to love his enemies and to bless his executors—as does the Bible. This attitude is not endured by the human psyche unless it is a perverted one. The Qur'an, rather, ordains upon the faithful to be just to their enemies and not to let their own hostilities and hatred transgress the set boundaries of justice:

> *And let not the hatred of others to you make you swerve to wrong and depart from justice. Be just: that is next to piety.* [5:8]

This is reasonable for humans, although there still remains the struggle for reaching the apex of moral integrity, to where only the truly faithful can ascend.

The Qur'an does not say what the Bible has said:

> But whoever slaps you on your right cheek, turn the other also to him. (Matt. 5:39)

This is not feasible, as is testified by real life, for all people; and for sure, it is not possible in all circumstances. The Qur'an, rather, affirms:

> *The recompense for an injury is an injury equal thereto (in degree): but if a person forgives and makes reconciliation, his reward is due from Allah: for (Allah) loves not those who do wrong.* [42:40]

> *And if you do catch them out, catch them out no worse than they catch you out: But if you show patience, that is indeed the best (course) for those who are patient.* [16:126]

Having affirmed the principle of justice, Islam has opened the doors for those who aspire for exaltedness and perfection, and guided them to forgiveness and exoneration. The thing that Islam condemns is futile hostility.

> *Fight in the cause of Allah those who fight you, but do not transgress limits; for Allah loves not transgressors.* [2:190]

This is how Islam reconciled between the Justice of the Torah and the forgiveness of the Bible. This is the idealistic realism of Islam.

The Qur'an does not plead for what is advocated by the Bible:

> If your eye leads you (to illicit staring), you better pluck it out and throw it away; for it is better for you that a part of your body perishes than the whole body be thrown into the fire of Hell.

The Qur'an instead orders the faithful men and women to lower their gaze; just as it enjoins upon them to renounce what they might have committed or occurred without intention:

> *O you believers! Turn you all together towards Allah, that you may attain Bliss.* [24:31]

With regards to lowering one's gaze, the Prophet (ṣ) excused the first unintentional look, saying: "Do not follow the incidental look with another (intentional) glance; the first one is for you and the subsequent one is not."

The realism of Islamic morality is evident from the fact that the pious and the faithful are not assumed to be infallible, so that their own selves will never entice them to evil and vice. Certainly that is not the case. Man has been created on the basis of a dual nature: a combination of the elements of clay and the breath of the Divine Spirit. It is not condemned that when he happens to sin he reverts back with penitence. What is condemned is that he persists in sinfulness and rebellion. Adam, the father of mankind, sinned but he repented and Allah forgave him. Similarly, there is nothing wrong in that his sons and daughters follow the example of their father Adam. This is why among the pious there are those who are mentioned as:

> *Those who, having done something to be ashamed of, or wronged their own souls, earnestly bring Allah to mind, and ask for forgiveness for their sins—and who can forgive sins except Allah?—and are never obstinate in persisting knowingly in (the wrong) they have done.* [3:135]

In the same light, the Qur'an has distinguished between grave and shameless sins, and between minor misdeeds and negligible wrongdoings, from which seldom any human can escape. The latter type of offences comes in the category of tolerance and forgiveness as long as grave sins are avoided.

If you (but) eschew the most heinous of the things which you are forbidden to do, We shall expel out of you all the evil in you, and admit you to a gate of great honour. [4:31]

The realism of Islamic morality is also manifest in the fact that necessities have been taken into consideration, allowance has been made for genuine excuses and circumstances for exemption, instead of the rigidity of utopian extremists who accept no exception. That is why the Qur'an, after mentioning prohibited foods, immediately remarks:

But if one is forced by necessity, without wilful disobedience, nor transgressing due limits—then is he guiltless. For Allah is Oft-Forgiving Most Merciful. [2:173]

Positive

Among the characteristics of Islamic morality is that the Islamic morals are positive. It is inconceivable that someone adorned with Islamic morals can be blindly following the pursuit of what is modish, go along with the tide of the times or be feeble and submissive to the circumstances, and be blown like a feather thrown to the wind. On the contrary, Islamic morals promote strength and struggle to strive relentlessly with confidence and hope, and to resist incompetence, desperateness, insignificance, languor and all causes of weakness. The Qur'an demands the faithful to:

...take hold of the Book with might... [19:12]

A *ḥadīth* insists on the same:

Adhere to what is beneficial to you, seek help from Allah, don't be ineffectual, and don't say: had I done so and so, the

> outcome would have been so and so; instead, say: whatever Allah predestines and wishes, He is Omnipotent to execute that. The word "if" opens the door to Satan.

The Messenger of Allah (ṣ) instructs us to keep striving for the enhancement of life until our last breath, even if no one was going to benefit from the efforts put in. As a tribute to the one who toils in earnest he said:

> If the Hour of Resurrection was going to arise and, at that moment in time, someone has taken a seedling into his hand to plant into the soil, then he must finish the act of planting it regardless.

Islam deplores despondent resignation, as reflected in the talk of the people of Moses, when they said to him:

> *Go you and your Lord, and fight you two, while we sit here (and watch).* [5:24]

Instead Islam seeks an active, positive attitude reflected in what the companions of Muḥammad (ṣ) told him: "Go you, and your Lord, and fight you two, while we are in combat along with you."

In Islam, it does not suffice from a Muslim that he himself be good and not strive for the goodness of others. Islam does not permit anyone to be among the devoted, meritorious just for being righteous for his self alone especially if such an individual does not denounce the open corruption found in the society around him. Islam commands every Muslim—depending upon one's ability and capability—to call to good, enjoin what is right, forbid what is wrong, exhort one another to truth and to patience, compassion, show sincerity to kins through religious bonds, and to be concerned about the affairs of the Muslims as a whole.

> *You are the best of peoples, evolved for mankind, enjoining what is right, forbidding what is wrong, and believing in Allah.* [3:110]

> *By (the token of) Time (through the Ages). Verily Man is in loss. Except such as have Faith, and do righteous deeds, and (join together) in the mutual teaching of Truth, and of Patience and Constancy.* [103:1-3]

Prophet Muḥammad (ṣ) said: "Religion is sincere counselling" and "whoever is not concerned about the affairs of the Muslims, is not from amongst them".

Thus Islam repudiates passive attitudes in the face of social and political depravity and passivity in the face of moral and spiritual decadence. It requires from a Muslim to change corruption with his hand and if he is unable to do so, then he should try to change it with his words; if he is unable to do this then he should try to change it with (an intention in) his heart, which is the weakest level of faith.

The intention of wanting to change a wrong with the heart is not as negative as may be supposed by some. It represents a psychological and emotional mobilisation against depravity and decadence, which will inevitably manifest itself in the form of substantial action.

Comprehensive

Another characteristic of Islamic morality is the fact that it is a comprehensive and encompassing system. If some people believe that the morality of religious beliefs are limited to rituals of worship and holy services, then that may be true in the case of some religions, but it is not true in the case of the moral code of Islam. Islamic law has not left out from human activity, individual or collective, any of the vital spheres, whether intellectual, cultural, or spiritual, but that it has outlined the maxim for conduct in accordance with a certain principle. It has even gone beyond the relationship of an individual with his own self and with his fellow human beings to embrace his relationship with the universe with elaborate details. For all these spheres, it has laid down, in light of the divine will, beautiful rules of etiquette and a sublime doctrine. Thus, Islam not only reconciled what people had dispelled in the name of religion and philosophy, but also did much more in terms of invaluable additions to them.

Among these Islamic moral additions are those which pertain to the concept of the individual self:

1. Physical: The self's needs and necessities: the Prophet (ṣ) says, "Your body has a right over you". And in the Qur'an, Allah says:

> *Eat and drink: but waste not by excess for Allah loves not the wasters.* [7:31]

2. Intellectual: The self's talents and aspirations:

> *Say: "Behold all that is in the heavens and on the earth..."* [10:101]

> *Say: "I do admonish you on one point: that you do stand up before Allah—(It may be) in pairs, or (it may be) singly— and reflect (within yourselves)..."* [34:46]

3. Psychological: The self has emotions along with intentions and yearnings:

Truly he succeeds that purifies it. And he fails that corrupts it! [91:9-10]

As also in your own selves: Will you not then see? [51:21]

Islamic morality also includes those matters that pertain to society:

1. In etiquette and courtesies:

O you who believe! Enter not houses other than your own, until you have asked permission and saluted those in them: that is best for you, in order that you may heed (what is seemly). [24:27]

And swell not your cheek (for pride) at men, nor walk in insolence through the earth; for Allah loves not any arrogant boaster. [31:18]

2. In economics and trade:

Woe to those that deal in fraud,—Those who, when they have to receive by measure from men, exact full measure, But when they have to give by measure or weight to men, give less than due. [83:1-3]

O you who believe! Fear Allah, and give up what remains of your demand for usury, if you are indeed believers. [2:278]

The Prophet (ṣ) said: "He who swindles, is not from amongst us".

3. In politics and governance:

Allah does command you to render back your Trusts to those to whom they are due; and when you judge between man and man, that you judge with justice; verily how excellent is the teaching which He gives you! For Allah is He Who hears and sees all things. [4:58]

The Prophet (ṣ) says, "Religion is sincerity to Allah, to His Messenger, to his Book, to Muslim leaders and to the common Muslim folk".

Hence, in Islam, there is no separation between politics and morality or between economics and ethics, as advocated by some of the intellectual trends in the West.

Furthermore, Islamic morality contains those aspects pertaining to other creatures like animals.

The Prophet (ṣ) said: "(Caring) for every living being shall be rewarded" and "A women was thrown into Hell for caging a cat."

Similarly, it is related to the universe and to life in general:

> *And He has subjected to you, as from Him, all that is in the heavens and on earth: Behold, in that are Signs indeed for those who reflect.* [45:13]

> *Do they see nothing in the government of the heavens and the earth and all that Allah has created?* [7:185]

Before all this comes what is related to the Almighty Creator, glory be to Him, the fact that no other deity is worthy of being worshipped or invoked except Him.

> *You do we worship, and Your aid we seek.* [1:5]

Balanced

Islamic morality is primarily characterised by a balance. It strikes a balance between contrary positions with congruity and harmony without any exaggeration or extravagance.

This characteristic can be observed by the rights of the body and the soul. The body must not be subjected to such deprivations so that it reaches the level of torture—as is found in Indian Brahmanism, Persian Manuism, Greek Stoicism and in Christian monasticism. There is no disregard for the soul, as is largely found in Judaism and in those other materialistic ideologies, which do not recognise the existence of the soul, let alone its rights. This is the reason why the Prophet (ṣ) denounced the extremism of some of his Companions, one of whom resolved to be awake every night in prayers without ever sleeping. Another resolved to fast everyday without ever breaking his fast, and the third resolved to shun women and never marry. He said to them:

> Indeed I am the most knowledgeable about Allah amongst you and I am more God-fearing than anyone of you; yet I keep awake for prayers and sleep too, on some days I fast and on others I do not, and I marry. He, who turns away from my *sunnah*, does not belong to me.

Balance can also be found in worldly life and the Hereafter. If Judaism takes this present life as its biggest concern and if Christianity confines all its orientations to the Heavenly Kingdom—wherein lies the other world—then Islam blends the two outlooks together. It combines the two ways of living wherein this world is cultivated farm of the now bearing the harvest of the Hereafter. Allah has made man His vicegerent on earth and settled him herein, hence he aught not to ravage the earth nor disrupt it; fortunate is the one who attains good in this world and good in the Hereafter:

> *"Our Lord! Give us good in this world and good in the Hereafter, and shield us from the torment of the Fire!"* [2:201]

> *But seek, with the (wealth) which Allah has bestowed on you, the Home of the Hereafter, nor forget your portion in this world: but do you good, as Allah has been good to you, and seek not (occasions for) mischief in the land: for Allah loves not those who do mischief.* [28:77]

Balance can also be seen in rights and duties. An individual is not mollycoddled by many rights and given a free ticket to slack in the name of freedom, so that he is allowed to relax, transgress, pervert and deprave. At the same time, he is not overburdened in the name of society or in any other name, by masses of obligations and responsibilities, until he is no longer fit to bear it.

Yet another aspect is balance between reality and idealism. While recognising the reality of most people, Islam leaves the doors wide open—with encouragement and motivation—for those who are privileged with forethought, initiative and determination, to let them rise and compete in good deeds, as people vary in their capabilities:

> *But there are among them some who wrong their own souls; some who follow a middle course; and some who are, by Allah's leave, foremost in good deeds...* [35:32]

> *And those foremost (in Faith) will be foremost (in the Hereafter). These will be those Nearest to Allah:* [56:10-11]

Whoever ponders over the balanced nature of Islamic morality and the wondrous harmony therein is stunned by how divergent virtues have been harmonised, something that many consider impossible. That is the reason why it has been perplexing and difficult task for some researchers to trace and pin these morals down to some previous sort of morality or to a school of theology, whether ancient on contemporary. They wonder whether these are morals of force or of love, whether these are morals of asceticism or of life, whether these are divine or man-made, rational or religious, idealistic or realistic, individual or collective.

The truth is that Islamic morality does not belong to a particular school or doctrine. It is rather all of these comprised together, as there is a certain amount of each one of these types. It represents all the good that is contained within those while remaining free from all their pollution and overindulgences. The indubitable truth is that Islamic morality is an integrated and balanced moral system.

An appraisal

Allah wanted Islam to be the eternal universal message. It is the divine guidance sent to all people of every nation, every class and generation. Since people's talents differ, their spiritual, mental and sentimental capabilities also differ and their aspirations, expectations and degrees of concerns vary. Therefore Islamic morality has united what other religious groups and philosophical schools—idealistic and realistic—scattered concerning morals and the source of moral obligation. In fact everything that was advocated by these religions and theories was not futile nor was it wholly true. Actually, the drawback of such theorising was that it viewed morality from one angle and ignored the other; it was concerned about one aspect at the cost of another. This mishap has haunted human reasoning, which was unable to view the matter from an all-embracing perspective capable of comprehending all times and places, all races and individuals, and all circumstances and facets; this was a requirement and height of comprehension which was only possessed by God, the Omniscient and the Most Wise.

It is no wonder then that the Islamic perspective of morality is encompassing and comprehensive. This is simply because Islam is not a human theory, it is rather the revelation of the One Who is Omniscient and Who knows the true amount and detail of everything.

This is the reason why Allah has incorporated into this religion a sufficient amount of what can fully satisfy every reasonable and moderate desire, persuade every self-respecting person and accommodate every development and change. An idealist who inclines to goodness for the sake of goodness itself, finds in the Islamic morality what makes his idealism content; he who believes in measuring happiness, finds in the Islamic perspective what makes him attain happiness for himself and for those around him; he who believes in measuring individual or collective benefits, finds in Islam what satisfies his concerns of utilitarianism; he who yearns for progress to perfection, discovers in it what fulfils his ambition; he who is concerned about his sociability finds in it what goes well with his society; even he who believes in the importance of sensual pleasure, can find that too in what Allah has prepared for the faithful in Paradise, in the form of material comfort and sensual pleasures:

> *There will be there all that the souls could desire, all that their eyes could delight in...* [43:71]

Thus every ear hears its favourite tone and every soul attains the desire it so craves for.

There are three types of people for whom there is no room in the Islamic morality:

First: The one who does not believe in anything except instant sensual pleasure or in immediate personal worldly benefit, who attaches no importance to what is in store in the form of an afterlife that is better and everlasting. Such is the person about whom a poet has said:

> Whatever passed by is gone;
> whatever is expected is unknown;
> For to you belongs the hour that you are living now.

Second: An individual who rejects all values just for his selfishness and for his whims and fancies or with the pretext that moral values have been coined by one class for the sole exploitation of another class or any such drivel.

Third: A bigoted and arrogant person who is adamant on not looking at life and the living beings except from one angle and only with a narrow vision; such a person is a prisoner of a particular school of thought or a captive of a certain ideology, unable to liberate himself from his captivity and dash forth into the open horizon that is the universal message of Islam.

LEGISLATION

Among the basic constituents of Islam is its legislation. This aspect regulates the Islamic way of life with a set of practical and pragmatic legal regulations that govern the relations between people in various domains of life and elucidate to them what Allah likes from them and what He dislikes.

Legislation within and beyond the text

It is well known to the students of Islam that it has not stipulated verbatim legislation for everything. There are rather matters which have been elucidated and elaborated, matters which have been briefly expounded, and others matters which have deliberately been kept silent without pronouncing anything about.

Abū Dardā' reports that the Messenger of Allah (ṣ) said,

> Whatever Allah has made permissible is permissible; whatever He has prohibited, is forbidden; whatever He has kept silent about is a kindness, so accept the favour of Allah. Allah could not have forgotten anything. [The Prophet (ṣ) then recited the Qur'anic phrase:] "And your Lord never does forget."[29]

According to this we discover that Islam deliberately left a blank territory without obligatory legislation. Based on this *ḥadīth*, I have termed this as 'the territory of favour' (*manṭiqah al-'afw*).[30]

Another *ḥadīth* in the Forty Ḥadīth of Imam al-Nawawī, sheds light on this subject. It states that leaving this territory blank was a divine mercy upon us, a generosity towards us and simplification for us. The Messenger of Allah (ṣ) said,

---

29. The verse is from Sūrah Maryam, 64. Narrated by Bazzār and Ṭabarānī as fair and reliable (as narrated by al-Haythamī in his collection: 1/17); also narrated by Ḥākim and authenticated by Dhahabī (2/375).
30. Refer to my book *'Awāmil al-Si'ah wa al-Murūnah fī al-Sharī'ah al-Islāmiyyah* (Factors of Amplitude and Flexibility in Islamic Legislation).

> Allah has ordained obligations, therefore do not squander His obligation; He has demarcated the bounds, therefore do not transgress His bounds; He has forbidden certain things, therefore do not transgress therein; and without having forgotten, He has kept silent about certain things as a mercy for mankind, therefore do not fish for those things.[31]

Anyone who explores this blank territory finds that it relates to those spheres of life which witness swift changes, that advance rapidly and that vary considerably with different environments, periods, situations and circumstances—such as matters related to politics, military, administration and protocol.

Here, we can fill the legislative vacuum, which has been deliberately left out by the texts, through *al-qiyās* (juristic reasoning or analogy) in light of the *maṣūṣ* (prescribed in the text) with its relevant conditions, or through *al-istiḥsān* (application of discretion) when *al-qiyās* does not suffice, or through *al-istiṣlāḥ* (that which is best for society) with appropriate provisions, or through *al-istiṣḥāb* (accommodation), or by honouring *al-'urf* (custom/convention of particular people), or in light of *sad al-dharā'i'* (impeding potential ploys by an enemy), or in light of *ri'āyah al-maqāṣid* (considering the purpose of the Sharī'ah), and so on.

Sometimes, in some fields, Islam lays down a complete method in such a manner that it defines the foundations, establishes the principles and lays out a general framework, but leaves the details for the process of *al-ijtihād* (diligent interpretation) by competent legal experts who select what is

31. Narrated by Dārquṭnī, Ṭabarānī and Bayhaqī; rated as fair by al-Nawawī and Ibn Sama'ānī (in *Amālī*); contested by Ibn Rajab in *al-'Ulūm wa al-Ḥikam*.

appropriate for the people by considering what is beneficial for them in their given place, time and situation.

The standard for this is the principle of *Shūrā* (consultation), which has been stipulated in the Qur'an and the Sunnah through verses such as:

> *...who (conduct) their affairs by mutual Consultation...* [42:38]

> *...and consult them in affairs (of moment)...* [3:159]

That the Messenger of God (ṣ) consulted his Companions on various occasions is an established fact, yet he did not elaborate to us specific details like: who are to be consulted? How should they be selected? Who shall select them? For how long are they to remain in that position? On what subjects should they be consulted? Is the opinion of the majority obligatory or not?

The Sharī'ah has not given us details in this regard to any specific options that may suit a certain period but may not be appropriate to some other period, and may be suitable for one place but inappropriate to another. It did not desire to freeze us in a certain state of affairs, but rather left space and freedom for us to exert our own diligent interpretations and to acquire and adapt from other sources if the need arise.

When do the texts adjudicate in legislation?

In some areas the Islamic Sharī'ah is decisively definitive. This is the case where constancy is primary and variation seldom occurs; for example, in family affairs and inheritance or in what is termed these days as personal statutes.

In these areas the Qur'an elaborates in detail, so that people do not stray from the right path or remain puzzled and lose their sense of direction in this regard. Allah, the Exalted, elucidates this fact—within the context of inheritance—in the last verse of Sūrāh al-Nisā' in the Holy Qur'an, saying:

> *Thus does Allah make clear to you (His law), lest you err. And Allah has knowledge of all things.* [4:176]

God loathes that His slaves wander away from His mercy and perish. Islamic stipulations are of two types. Firstly, the type which has been clearly defined by the texts through categorical support and meaning. Although less, it is of the utmost significance, because it unites the Ummah on oneness of purpose and embodies its unity in practice and conduct besides the unity of belief and conscience.

The second type is the one which has been defined through presumptive substantiation or connotation or through both. The majority of the stipulations of the Sharī'ah fall into this category. Here there is scope for diversity of views, inclinations and interpretations.

Objectives of legislation in Islam

Legislation in Islam has sublime objectives and noble purposes, and the Prudent Lawgiver intends the actualisation of these in the lives of people.

This indicates that the rules of Sharī'ah are well-founded, comprehensible, and linked to the interests and welfare of humans and other created beings. This has been unanimously agreed upon by all Muslims with exception of a small group of Ẓāhirites and those who followed their suit.

Supporting this are innumerable verses of the Holy Qur'an and sayings of the Messenger (ṣ), which explain and justify commands, prohibitions and edicts, and even practices of worship. Prayers, for example, restrain from evil deeds:

> *Prayer restrains from shameful and unjust deeds.* [29:45]

Zakāh is taken from the rich to spiritually cleanse them:

> *...that so you might purify and sanctify them.* [9:103]

Fasting during the month of Ramadan is prescribed for piety:

> *...that you may learn self-restraint.* [2:183]

Similarly Hajj was proclaimed with the purpose:

> *...that they may witness the benefits (provided) for them, and celebrate the name of Allah, through the Days appointed.* [22:28]

These and numerous other instances substantiate the fact that Sharī'ah, in its code, is based on wisdom and it has its objectives, which must be explored and honoured. Some of these objectives are explained in the following paragraphs:

Dealings and transactions between people must be based on justice, which is revered by the heavens and all on earth. There is no prejudice against the poor in favour of the rich; there is no nepotism in favour of the strong against the weak; there is no preference to a local over a foreigner or to a white over a black, except in terms of piety. Justice is the objective of all the heavenly religions, as declared by Allah, the Exalted:

> *We sent aforetime Our Messengers with Clear Signs and sent down with them the Book and the Balance (of Right and Wrong), that men may stand forth in justice...* [57:25]

Brotherhood prevail between people, trust and understanding remain intact, and roots of hostility and discord vanish. This has been done by defining rights and responsibilities, by explaining the basis and stipulations of dealings and transactions, and by averting injustice, deception and vulgarity. Thus, every deserving individual gets his fair share. Hearts and minds are satisfied; sanctity, life, honour and wealth are preserved; dealings and transactions are kept together on a solid basis.

The safeguarding of the interests of the people on three levels: the basic necessities without which humans cannot survive; the intellectual needs without which humans would remain in perplexity and destitution; welfare by which human kind accomplishes itself, recreates and strides on the best of courses and circumstances.

After taking care of their dealings and transactions and fulfilling their material and human necessities, people may dedicate themselves to their mission on earth. That mission is worshiping Allah, developing His planet, shouldering the responsibilities of being His vicegerents, calling the people to His message—the message which He designed to be a mercy to the whole of creation, that aims at truth, benevolence and the noblest of morals, pursues the path of faith, noble deeds and mutual advocacy of truth and patience. Thus are human beings, as individuals and as a society, saved from loss in this world and in the Hereafter. This is what has been eloquently summarised in the Sūrah al-ʿAṣr of the Holy Qur'an:

> *By (the token of) Time (through the Ages), verily Man is in loss, except such as have Faith, and do righteous deeds, and (join*

together) in the mutual teaching of Truth, and of Patience and Constancy. [103:1-3]

Significance of ḥudūd (penalty) in the Sharīʿah

Here, I would like to clarify two important issues:

Firstly, the legislative or legal aspect of Islam is not the whole or the bulk of Islam, as is imagined by some or as they are made to envision. Islam is a system of belief that is harmonious with nature. It is a worship that nourishes the soul, a morality that purifies the self, an etiquette that beautifies life, an endeavour that benefits people and stays firmly rooted.

It is a call of guidance to Allah for the whole world, to struggle in the path of truth and benevolence. It is mutual advocacy of patience, mercy and compassion. At the same time, it is a legal system that disciplines the course of life, systematises the relations of human beings with their Cherisher, organises their relation with their families, societies and countries, as well as regulating the relation of their countries to them and the relation with other countries whether friendly or hostile.

In fact, Islam stands primarily for guidance and the development of the individual and society, before being a law or cannon.

Secondly, penalties, requital and sanctions are a limited part of the vast Islamic law. As is known, from amongst about six thousand verses of the Qur'an the number of verses related to penalties and requitals does not exceed ten.

Punishment is meant only for the most terrible of people. Certainly these evil people are not the majority nor do they form the criterion of judgement. They, rather, are deviant exceptions from the mainstream of mankind.

Islam, essentially, did not come to cure the incorrigible, perverted individuals, rather it came to guide the sound-minded bulk of humanity and to protect them from deviating.

Punishment, from the Islamic viewpoint, is not the major factor in tackling crime. The major factor, rather, is to prevent crime by averting the causes leading to it. Prevention has always been better than a cure.

Significance of the penalty for zinā (illicit sex)

If we look at adultery, we find that the Qur'an has prescribed the punishment for this crime in only one verse, at the beginning of Sūrah al-Nūr, wherein Allah says:

> *The woman and the man guilty of adultery or fornication—flog each of them with a hundred stripes: Let not compassion move you in their case, in a matter prescribed by Allah, if you believe in Allah and the Last Day.* [24:2]

But the same Sūrah contains tens of other verses that are directed at preventing the widespread publication of such penalties. It is sufficient to quote the following:

> *Those who love (to see) scandal broadcast among the Believers, will have a grievous Penalty in this life and in the Hereafter: Allah knows, and you know not.* [24:19]

In the context of regulating social visiting and spelling out the relevant decencies, and specifying the sanctity and sacredness of homes, Allah says:

> *O you who believe! enter not houses other than your own, until you have asked permission and saluted those in them: that is best for you, in order that you may heed (what is seemly).* [24:27]

Etiquettes of seeking permission by servants and children who have not attained puberty, fall in the same context:

> *O you who believe! let those whom your right hands possess, and the (children) among you who have not come of age ask your permission (before they come to your presence), on three occasions: before morning prayer; while you take off your clothes for the noonday heat; and after the late-night prayer: these are your three times of undress.* [24:58]

Even more important is teaching the Muslim men and women the virtues and morals of chastity and modesty by lowering their gaze and guarding their private parts:

> *Say to the believing men that they should lower their gaze and guard their modesty: that will make for greater purity for them: And Allah is well acquainted with all that they do. And say to the believing women that they should lower their gaze and guard their modesty; that they should not display their beauty and ornaments except what (must ordinarily) appear thereof; that they should draw their veils over their bosoms...* [24:30-31]

Here a new element emerged towards prevention from illicit sex and sex-related crimes, *i.e.*, forbidding women from emerging with seductive appearances which can allure men and provoke their instincts and fantasies. The Qur'anic verse reads as follows:

> *...and that they should not strike their feet in order to draw attention to their hidden Ornaments...* [24:31]

The verse concludes saying:

> *And O you Believers! Turn you all together towards Allah, that you may attain Bliss.* [24:31]

Still more important than all this is the collective directive to the society as a whole—in their capacity of being socially responsible—to marrying off the single men and women:

> *Marry those among you who are single, or the virtuous ones among yourselves, male or female: if they are in poverty, God will give them means out of His grace: for God encompasses all, and he knows all things.* [24:32]

The responsibility of society—and the government in the first place—here, besides obstructing ways leading to illicit affairs, is to pave the way for legitimate relationships, by removing the material and social hurdles faced by those who want to marry, such as exorbitant dowries, extravagant gifts, wasteful feasts and lavish furnishing. It should not leave any stone unturned in this direction.

Inflicting the penalty of *ḥudūd* alone is not sufficient to solve the problem of illicit sex. The fact is that the penalty in this case cannot be inflicted with required legitimacy except upon confession made four times in front of the board of adjudicators (as specified by many schools of jurisprudence) or upon witness of four trustworthy persons who would have directly witnessed the act taking place; this is difficult to come across in real life. Indeed, the real intention here is to deter people from overtly committing the crime in public. As far as anyone having been smitten by this sin without having been seen by anyone else, he would not be subjected to the penalty in this world; his matter will be dealt with in the divine court of the Hereafter.

It is in the light of all this that we demand the Islamic Sharī'ah and its penalties be founded and implemented. We believe that laws and punishments alone neither protect societies nor build nations; nations are built and societies are protected by genuine faith, ideal morality, prudent counselling and constant guidance, supported by equitable legislation and a coherent legal system that does not discriminate between the ruling and those ruled.

Significance of the penalty for theft

If we look at the crime of stealing, we find that the Qur'an speaks about its punishment in just two verses of Sūrah al-Mā'idah:

> *As to the thief, male or female, cut off his or her hands: a punishment by way of example, from Allah, for their crime: and Allah is Exalted in Power, Full of Wisdom. But if the thief repents after his crime, and amends his conduct, Allah turns to him in forgiveness; for Allah is Oft-Forgiving, Most Merciful.* [5:38-39]

The verse prescribing the amputation of the hand of a thief was revealed towards the final stages of revelation to the Messenger (ṣ), *i.e.*, after the foundations of the Islamic society, established by him in Madīnah, were consolidated. That was the society based on justice, solidarity and brotherhood; its members were like one single family, like a solid structure, its affluent lent a helping hand to its poor, its rich gave generously to its needy, its members stood shoulder to shoulder through thick and thin. In that society, one who slept after a full meal while his neighbour remained hungry was not deemed to be pious; similarly one who amassed wealth while depriving his brother in faith was not considered a believer. A wealthy person was considered a trustee of what belongs to Allah, wherein there was a recognised right for the needy and the destitute. *Zakāh* was a religious obligation of great socio-economic importance. It was collected from the wealth accumulated from society and *given back* to the needy. It is the third of the five pillars of Islam; if one refused to pay it voluntarily, it was taken from him forcibly. He who refused to pay *zakāh*, war was declared against him until he did, even though it might have been as meagre as a rope or a headband of a camel, as was done by the first caliph Abū Bakr who declared war to retrieve the rights of the poor from the miserly clutches of the rich.

Zakāh is the first of the rights in wealth, not the last; he who has it, should invest it to make it yield for the less fortunate.

Prior to the verses prescribing penalty for theft, hundreds of verses were revealed enjoining payment of *Zakāh*, encouraging the feeding of the poor, calling to spending in the cause of Allah, urging the establishment of justice and equality between all people, forbidding injustice in all its forms, and warning about the awful destiny of the tyrants of this world and in the Hereafter.

Hence it is unimaginable that in the shade of the correct implementation of Islam, the hand of a thief will be chopped off in a society in which unemployment is rampant, the hungry are not fed, the naked are not clothed, the sick are not treated and the illiterate are not educated, while at the same time a small number of people play with millions of dollars, squandering them on anything except to help the poor and the destitute!

Characteristics of legislation in Islam

Comprehensiveness

Among the characteristics of legislation in Islam is the fact that it is comprehensive.

It does not enact laws for the individual while disregarding the family, or for the family while ignoring the society, or for the society in isolation from other societies of the Islamic nation, or for the Islamic nation while turning a blind eye to other non-Muslim nations of the world.

Islamic legislation includes legislation for the individual in his worship and devotion to his God. This is what is elaborated under the section "Worship" in the books of Islamic jurisprudence, and is not found in the conventional laws.

Islamic legislation deals with private and public behaviour of the individual. This aspect covers what is called *al-ḥalāl wa al-ḥarām* (the lawful and the prohibited).

Islamic legislation covers all that is related to family affairs, including marriage, divorce, maintenance, weaning, inheritance, and personal and financial guardianship. This is known today as personal statute.

Islamic legislation for society includes both its social and commercial relations as well as exchange of funds and utilities—whether compensated or otherwise—like selling and leasing, loans, lending, mortgage, remittance, security bonds and guarantees. This comes under the scope of social commercial laws in the current parlance.

Islamic legislation includes matters related to crime and the relevant punishments prescribed in the Sharī'ah, like *Ḥudūd* (penalties) and *Qiṣāṣ* (retribution), and those left to the acumen of the relevant specialist, as in the case of punishment. This is known nowadays as Criminal Law or the Penal Code.

Islamic legislation deals with obligations of the government towards its subjects and with the responsibilities of the subjects towards the rulers. It regulates the relation between the two sides. This has been dealt with in the books of jurisprudence on subjects like the Sharī'ah-based polity, tribute and assets, and on rules of governance. This is what has been embraced in modern times by constitutional, administrative and financial legislation.

Islamic legislation also handles regulation of international relations in times of peace and war between Muslims and others. This has been the subject of the books of Islamic jurisprudence related to accounts of *jihād*, which cover matters that are governed by International Law in modern times.

Hence there is no aspect of human life which Islamic legislation has not striven to cover by enjoining or by prohibiting.

It is perhaps sufficient to hint that the longest verse revealed in the Qur'an is the one to regulate the civic affairs, *i.e.*, mutual loans and record of credit.

The comprehensiveness of Islamic legislative system is also obvious from one more fact: it penetrates into various problems, their causes and effects and looks at them from a comprehensive and encompassing perspective based on knowledge of the human nature, on the reality of its intentions, ambitions and yearnings, on knowledge of human life and its varying needs and inconsistencies. It correlates legislation with religious and moral values in such a way that legislations serve values and morals instead of being a pickax for their demolition.

Whoever comprehended this fact well was able to understand the attitude of Islamic Sharī'ah and its brilliance regarding various issues, like divorce, polygamy, inheritance, usury, penalties, and retribution. Studies have proven the precedence of Islam in these areas and its superiority over all other legislative models, past or present.

The shortcoming, which is inseparable from the limited nature of human beings, is that they tend to see things and matters from a single perspective while ignoring other perspectives. Certainly they are helpless and cannot be blamed for this shortcoming, as an ambient and all encompassing view that can grasp a matter from all its aspects, know all its requirements and requisites, and comprehend all its possibilities and prospects, is the sole domain of none but the Lord of all humans and the Designer of the universe.

> *Should He not know,—He that created? and He is the One that understands the finest mysteries (and) is well-acquainted (with them).* [67:14]

Pragmatism

Among the characteristics of legislation in Islam is pragmatism. It has never ignored the reality when legislating and while prohibiting what it prohibited. It did not disregard reality while setting up its regulations and laws for the individual, the family, society, state and humanity.

Some aspects of pragmatism of Islamic legislation:

Permissions and prohibitions

The Islamic Sharīʻah did not prohibit the human being anything that may be a necessity in real life; similarly, it did not permit anything that may be harmful.

Hence the Qur'an disapproved of the forbidding of adornment and delights and declared their permissibility for all humans with condition of moderation in their use:

> *O Children of Adam! wear your beautiful apparel at every time and place of prayer: eat and drink: But waste not by excess, for Allah loves not the wasters. Say: Who has forbidden the beautiful (gifts) of Allah, which He has produced for His servants, and the things, clean and pure, (which He has provided) for sustenance? Say: They are, in the life of this world, for those who believe, (and) purely for them on the Day of Judgement. Thus do We explain the signs in detail for those who understand.* [7:31-32]

The Sharīʻah has taken into consideration the natural inclination of humans towards entertainment and recreation and thus permitted genuine types of amusement, like racing and horseback riding, provided they are not associated with gambling or anything illegitimate, or does not dissuade one from the remembrance of Allah and submission to Him, especially on festive occasions like weddings and specific festivals. When two slave girls sung in the house of ʻĀ'ishah, Abū Bakr rebuked the girls, but the Messenger of Allah (ṣ) said:

"Let them be, O Abū Bakr! These are the days of 'Īd."[32] That is when he also said: "Let the Jews know that in our religion there is tolerance and that I have been sent with great generosity!"[33] He also allowed the Abyssinians (folk martial art performers) to perform with their spears and permitted his wife 'Ā'ishah to watch them perform until she was satisfied.

The Sharī'ah has taken into account the nature of women and their desire to adorn themselves and make themselves look beautiful. That is why it approved for them some of the things that have been forbidden for men, like wearing jewellery and silk.

The pragmatism of the Sharī'ah is corroborated by the fact that it has considered and appreciated the compelling pressures that a human being encounters somewhere in his life. That is why it has permitted taking of prohibited items proportionate to the necessity. Hence, based on the Qur'anic pronouncements in the context of prohibited foods, like in the following verse, scholars of the Sharī'ah have resolved that there is exception during an emergency:

> *He has only forbidden you dead meat, and blood, and the flesh of swine, and that on which any other name has been invoked besides that of Allah. But if one is forced by necessity, without wilful disobedience, nor transgressing due limits—then is he guiltless. For God is Oft-Forgiving Most Merciful.* [2:173]

The pragmatism of Sharī'ah is evident by its awareness of human weakness in the face of many of the prohibited things. That is why it has blocked the ways leading thereto. It has

32. Narrated by Bukhārī and Muslim.
33. Narrated by Aḥmad in his *Musnad*.

prohibited things whether in big or small amount—as in the case of liquor, because a small amount leads to plenty. Likewise, in order to obstruct means leading to the illegitimate, and keeping in view the reality of human beings when exposed to the forbidden, it has classified as *ḥarām* those things leading to the *ḥarām*. That is the reason for the prohibition of secluded privacy with the opposite sex, in order to close all doors of evil lust. Similarly, it is prohibited is look lustfully at the opposite sex. The eye is the envoy of the heart and a lustful look communicates seduction. This is something a poet has elaborated on:

> All episodes originate from a look,
> As most fires ignite from simple sparks.

A famous contemporary Arab poet Aḥmad Shawqī puts it thus:

> A look, a smile, a greeting,
> A word, then a date and an audience!

Marriage and family

What substantiates the Islamic Sharī'ah being pragmatic is the fact that it considers the intensity of the sexual drive of humans and does not disregard it, nor does it look at it with scorn or consider it filthy, as was done by some religious cults and creeds. At the same time it did not approve for humans to be driven by urges and instincts alone, as was advocated by some philosophies. By legitimising the institution of marriage, the Islamic Sharī'ah allowed fulfilment of the sexual urge in a manner that ensures continuity of the human race, upholding of human dignity and the ascension of humans above the rank of animals. The Qur'an has hinted to this—after mentioning the women who cannot be married and those who can be married upon meeting relevant conditions—saying:

> *Allah does wish to make clear to you and to show you the ordinances of those before you; and (He does wish to) turn to you (in Mercy): And Allah is All-knowing, All-wise. Allah does wish to Turn to you, but the wish of those who follow their lusts is that you should turn away (from Him)—far, far away. Allah does wish to lighten your (difficulties): For man was created Weak (in flesh).* [4:26-28]

The weakness referred to here is the weakness in the face of sexual impulses.

Prohibition of polygeny as prescribed in the Sharī'ah, was based on this pragmatic approach to life and to the humans.

Penalties, requital and castigation

Another aspect of the pragmatism of the Sharī'ah is that it vigorously strives to cleanse the society from the root causes of crimes and to guide individuals on the basis of integrity. At the same time, although very persistent about it, it does not rely on the moral deterrent alone. Although a religious and social necessity, right upbringing alone does not suffice. Among the people, there are those who are not deterred by anything other than stern punishment and to whom polite advice nor right guidance bear fruit. That is why along with guidance from the Qur'an the law's whip is an imperative. In this context 'Uthmān is reported to have said: "Allah restrains with the authority of His power that what is not deterred by the Qur'an!"

Hence the Sharī'ah has prescribed sanctions, penalties, requital and reprimand. It does not endorse the position of the fanciful, who advocate abolition of the death penalty on the pretext of mercy to the pitiable murderer, without bothering to look at the ordeal of the victim and his family, the devastation afflicted upon them, and the safety of society in general; or those who plead to suspend the penalty for theft, on the plea of kindness to someone who was not kind to himself nor to others for desecrating private sanctity, who threatened the peace of society, who cared for his own selfish objectives and who shed the blood of the innocent. In the context of requital, Allah says:

> *In the Law of Equality there is (saving of) Life to you, O you men of understanding; that you may restrain yourselves.* [2:179]

Regarding theft, He says:

> *As to the thief, male or female, cut off his or her hands: a punishment by way of example, from Allah, for their crime: and Allah is Exalted in power.* [5:38]

Simplicity and leniency

Among the features of the Islamic legislative system is the simplicity and lenience shown towards its subjects. In fact this spirit of runs throughout the whole body of the Sharī'ah. This is based on the consideration of the weakness of the human being, his burdens and pressures of life. The Author of this religion is the Most Compassionate, the Most Merciful; He does not like to see agony and anguish come upon His slaves; He desired welfare, felicity, wellbeing and bliss for them in this world and in the Hereafter.

Islam has not come for a people, region or period, but for the whole of mankind, spanning all age groups, and throughout the globe in all epochs. No doubt that an open system characterised by such comprehensiveness must lean towards simplification and relief so that it can accommodate all peoples with all their diversities of locations, times and circumstances.

In fact, this is the reality discerned by everyone who happens to have an encounter with Islam.

The Qur'an is an easy book to refer to for guidance; the Islamic system of belief is simple to comprehend and the Sharī'ah is easy to implement and execute. There is no trust or obligation which burdens the subjects. How can it be on the contrary when the Qur'an proclaims this fact explicitly in more than one place. It says:

> *On no soul does Allah place a burden greater than it can bear.* [2:286]

> *No soul shall have a burden laid on it greater than it can bear.* [2:233]

> *Allah puts no burden on any person beyond what He has given him.* [65:7]

It implores the faithful to supplicate by saying:

> *Our Lord! Lay not on us a burden greater than we have strength to bear.* [2:286]

An authentic saying of the Messenger (ṣ) suggests that supplicating with this invocation is granted by Allah.

The Qur'an denies the existence of any difficulty or intricacy in its Sharī'ah. While refuting having any coercion or hardship, it affirms its being characterised by relief and ease. While granting concession for fasting in the month of Ramadan to those on journey or sick, Allah says:

> *Allah intends every facility for you; He does not want to put to difficulties.* [2:185]

Similarly the tradition of the Messenger of Allah (ṣ) confirms the Qur'anic orientation of easiness towards humanity. For example, the Messenger (ṣ) has said:

> I have been sent with magnanimity of truth.[34]

> You have been (decorated with this faith) as envoys of ease, not as emissaries of hardship.[35]

> Facilitate (for the people) and don't complicate; be harbingers of good tidings and don't spread grief.[36]

The unique characteristics of the Messenger of Allah (ṣ), with which he had been depicted in the previously revealed heavenly books, was his being the simplifier and the reliever from burdens and shackles that had overburdened the followers of previous religions. Allah the Exalted says:

> *...whom they find mentioned in their own (Scriptures),—in the law and the Gospel;—for he commands them what is just and forbids them what is evil; he allows them as lawful what is good (and pure) and prohibits them from what is bad (and impure); He releases them from their heavy burdens and from the yokes that are upon them.* [7:157]

---

34. Narrated by Aḥmad from 'Ā'ishah.
35. Narrated Bukhārī, Tirmidhī and al-Nasā'ī from Abū Hurayrah.
36. Unanimously agreed upon (Narrated from Anas).

Among the supplications the Qur'an has taught the faithful is:

Our Lord! Lay not on us a burden like that which You did lay on those before us. [2:286]

Islam has provided ease wherever the need may arise. For example, the accommodation of performing *tayammum*[37]—in place of ablution—owing to health or climatic conditions.

...nor kill (or destroy) yourselves: for verily Allah has been to you Most Merciful! [4:29]

...and make not your own hands contribute to (your) destruction... [2:195]

Similarly, there is accommodation, for whosoever cannot perform prayers in the standing posture, to pray sitting; or to pray by gesticulation while reclining or lying down.

Likewise, there is accommodation for pregnant women and suckling mothers to skip fasting if they fear for themselves or for their babies; as there is permission for those who are sick or on journey to defer fasting as recompense for the missed days. In the same way, those who are travelling can shorten and combine their prayers.

The Messenger of Allah (ṣ) has said: "Allah likes his relaxations to be availed of as he dislikes committing of any disobedience to Him".[38]

The Messenger of Allah (ṣ) denounced the person who afflicts austerity on himself by fasting while travelling, in spite

37. To rub with clean sand or earth.
38. Narrated by Aḥmad.

of feeling the severity of hardship and need to eat and drink. He said: "It is no piety to fast while travelling".[39]

As a consequence of this approach is the marvellous principle of *al-mashaqqah tajlib al-taysīr (i.e.*, hardship naturally begets relief) essentially became one of the unanimously established fundamentals of Islamic jurisprudence, with all the Islamic schools of jurisprudence. This root principle has numerous exuberant branches in various sections of the Islamic jurisprudence. The great scholar Ibn Nujaym al-Ḥanafī has described the derivatives of this principle and emphasised their significance in his book *al-Ashbāh wa al-Naẓā'ir.*

There are many things that have been considered by the Sharī'ah on the grounds of accommodation; for example, sickness, travel, coercion, mistakes and forgetfulness, and calamity. Provisions for all these have been well detailed in the books of Sharī'ah.

A gradual approach

Among the instances of respite Islam gives to mankind is that its approach with them with regard to legislation, whether of a permissible or forbidden nature, is implementation through a gradual process.

For example, when *Ṣalāh* (the obligatory prayer) and *Zakāh* (alms) were enjoined on believers, it was done gradually in stages till their culmination in the final format.

Prayers were enjoined in the least of measures of two *rak'ahs* (units of prayer). Finally the measure was affirmed to this very number (of two) for travellers and raised to the measures of

---

39. Narrated by Bukhārī.

four *rak'ahs* in normal conditions (for noon, afternoon and night prayers).

Ṣawm (fasting) was enjoined as an act of worship with two options of either fasting or paying ransom for not being able to fast. In case of the latter, one is to feed a poor person for each day of fast missed. This has been narrated by Bukhārī from Salamah ibn Akwa', as interpretation of the following Qur'anic verse :

> *For those who can do it (with hardship), is a ransom, the feeding of one that is indigent. But he that will give more, of his own free will—it is better for him. And it is better for you that you fast, if you only knew.* [2:184]

Later on, fasting was made obligatory upon every person without any excuse.

> *So every one of you who is present (at his home) during that month should spend it in fasting...* [2:185]

Zakāh was enjoined in the pre-migration period of Makkah as an open obligation with no criterion or yardstick, proportions or term. It was rather left to the discretion and conscience of the Muslims and then to the requirements of the community and the individuals, until, in the post-migration period of Madīnah, it was made obligatory with fixed rates and proportions.

Prohibitions too were not effected all at once. Allah the Exalted was aware of their powerful effect over people and of their powerful permeation through their lives and through society as a whole.

It would not have been wise to dissuade and wean away addicts from those vices by way of direct commands to them.

Acumen demanded that the people be prepared psychologically and mentally for their acceptance; it required that the situation be handled by gradual proscription, so that when the final unequivocal commandment came, they would promptly submit and implement what was being prescribed and say: "We heard and we submit wholeheartedly".

Perhaps the most evident example in this regard is the gradual prohibition of liquor, well known in the history of Islamic legislation. When the final categorical verses of its prohibition were revealed—in Sūrah al-Mā'idah—and concluded with the inquisitive statement: "...will you not then abstain?" (5:91), the faithful replied unambiguously, "Our Lord, the matter is over forever!"

Evidently Islam's consideration of the gradualist approach was the reason for leaving the deep-rooted institution of slavery intact. Slavery was prevalent throughout the world at the time of the advent of Islam. Its hasty abolition would have rocked the social and economic fabric of life. Wisdom demanded tightening its sources and filling them up whenever an opportunity presented itself. At the same time it maximised its strain on it and thus ensured its gradual eradication from society altogether.

This divine principle (of the gradual application of laws) ought to be followed in governing the people's affairs and when implementing the Islamic system; it aught to be pursued for actualisation of an integrated and wide-ranging Islamic renascence.

If we want to establish a true Islamic society, we should not be under the illusion that it can be actualised by the stroke of a pen or by the ordaining of a royal edict or by an adjudication of a revolutionary command or even by a parliamentary resolution.

This is going to be realised only by following the same gradual approach, the approach of intellectual adaptation, psychological preparation, moral grounding and social underpinning.

This is precisely the same methodology pursued by the Messenger of Allah (ṣ) for the transformation of the pagan life of Arabia to the Islamic way of life. He stayed in Makkah for thirteen years. His mission then remained limited only to guide a generation of the believers, who could shoulder the responsibility of calling to Allah and could put up with the duty of *jihād* to guard the mission and propagate it throughout the peninsula.

This is why the Makkan period did not feature legislation and codification of laws. It was rather the phase of nurturing the torch bearers of the faith.

During that phase and before moving on to the enactment of laws and the elaboration thereof, the Qur'an itself focused its attention, before anything else, on the rectification and consolidation of the creed, and on transmitting its rays on the inner self and to the conduct of the Muslims, so that it manifested in the form of the finest morals and righteous deeds.

Chapter 3

The Characteristics of Islam

RABBĀNIYYAH (GODLINESS)

One of the foremost characteristics of Islam is called *al-rabbāniyyah* (Godliness).

The Arabic word *rabbāniyyah* denotes the attribute of being 'related to God'. A person may be attributed with this characteristic by virtue of being intimate with Allah, learned about His religion and His book, as if he were a milestone in his own right on the way to Allah. The Qur'ān defines such people in the following terms:

> *Be you worshippers of Him Who is truly the Cherisher of all: For you have taught the Book and you have studied it earnestly.* [3:79]

Godliness in the above verse has two aspects:

1. Godliness of the Purpose of Life.
2. Godliness of the divine source and methodology.

Godliness of purpose

By godliness of purpose, we mean to say that a Muslim establishes a devout relationship with Allah and strives to attain His pleasure. This should be the highest aspiration of the faithful:

> *O you man! Verily you are ever toiling on towards your Lord-painfully toiling,—but you shall meet Him.* [84:6]

> *That to your Lord is the final Goal;* [53:42]

Indeed Islam deals with other humanitarian and social objectives as well, but upon reflection we find that these goals are in fact subordinate to the highest goal of attaining the pleasure of Allah and qualifying for His gracious reward; this is the paramount aim of Islam.

Certainly, Islam has other legislations which cover various social dealings and transactions, but these are meant to regulate life and point a greater goal—Allah. Islam desires that human beings settle down and free themselves from the endless struggle for possessions, so that they may devout themselves to Allah, to His worship and to the pursuit of attaining His sole pleasure.

In Islam there exists the concept of *jihād* and the struggling against one's enemies but the ultimate purpose of such a thing is to:

> *Fight them until there is no more tumult or oppression, and there prevail justice and faith in God altogether and everywhere...* [8:39]

Islam encourages man to travel the world and to partake of the good therein, but the ultimate aim is to thank Allah for His blessings and bounties, and to repay His debt through gratitude:

> *Eat of the Sustenance (provided) by your Lord, and be grateful to Him: a territory fair and happy, and a Lord Oft-Forgiving!* [34:15]

Every legal instruction or guidance in Islam intends to prepare man on how to be the devout and faithful slave of Allah alone. This is why *tawḥīd* (belief in the Unity of Allah) is regarded as the essence of the Islamic belief.

The benefits of Godliness for the self and life

What is unequivocal is that *rabbāniyyah* has many profound benefits for the self and life. Besides the many rewards in the Hereafter, man also reaps the important fruits of this world too. Some of the profound benefits of *rabbāniyyah* are the following:

Awareness of the purpose of human existence

Knowing the purpose of one's existence, being conscious of the direction of one's journey and being able to define one's mission in life, make a person feel that his existence has value and meaning, that his life has an essence and is to be enjoyed. As a result, he feels neither lost nor abandoned to the vagaries of life unlike those who have chosen to disbelieve and as a consequence are in disarray.

After acknowledging Allah and His unity, such as person is guided by a divine light. He is aware of his affairs and is fully focused on his purpose in life.

Self discovery

Another fruit born by *rabbāniyyah* is that a person begins to discover his own innate, natural disposition (*fiṭrah*). This is the nature on which Allah created him. It is a nature which demands faith in Allah alone, a faith which cannot be substituted by anything else:

> *So set you your face steadily and truly to the Faith: (establish) God's handiwork according to the pattern on which He has made mankind: no change (let there be) in the work (wrought) by God.* [30:30]

Self discovery is not an easy task. It is a profound and insightful discovery whereby man begins to live in peace and harmony with his own self as well as with the whole of existence; a godly existence which glorifies and praises Allah in turn:

> *There is not a thing but celebrates His praise.* [17:44]

In fact there is a spiritual void in human nature which cannot be filled by knowledge, culture or philosophy alone. This void can only be filled by having faith in Allah, the Exalted. This is because human nature will continue to feel spiritually famished unless it believes in Allah and follows the guidance He has prescribed for the well-being of mankind.

Protection from a divided self

Rabbāniyyah ensures that the self is not divided. It seeks to do away with the internal schisms that can afflict one's personality and pull it towards conflicting goals. Islam has abridged all the objectives of man into the single goal of attaining the pleasure of Allah, the Exalted.

Nothing else relieves a man of the burden of existence than the discovery of a purpose in his life accompanied by guidance. Only then can he know where to begin his struggle with life.

Far too often man is made despondent by the contradiction of his aims and the conflict of his interests. He vacillates indecisively from one decision to another and, as a result, pleases some people whilst enraging others. In the end, he is always left bewildered. A poet once remarked in this regard:

> Who among the people can please all?
> When the passions of the people are poles apart.

The belief in unity (*tawḥīd*) convinces a Muslim that there is no deity to be feared other than Allah. It teaches him that he is answerable to none other than God. Such a belief protects him from taking false deities as gods and also drives away the idols of materialism and desire from his heart until he becomes content with Allah alone as his Lord. He submits his soul to Allah and places his trust in Him. He turns to Him in repentance, seeks His blessings, derives strength from His Omnipotence, longs for His affection, appeals to Him in times of affliction and seeks constant refuge in Him.

> *Whoever holds firmly to God will be shown a way that is straight.* [3:101]

Freeing oneself from selfishness and lust

In time, *rabbāniyyah* becomes deeply rooted in one's self and it liberates one from the bondage of selfishness and lust, from vain sensual pleasures and holds one back from submitting to such things.

This is because faith in Allah and in the Day of Judgement place a person who is blessed with the virtue of *rabbāniyyah* in a state where he is able to achieve a balance between his desires and the requirements of his religion. In such a state, he is able strike a balance between his own wishes and the wishes of his Lord. He is in a state of constant awareness in which today's pleasures and delights are regulated by the trials and reckoning of the Hereafter.

Such an acute awareness of one's responsibilities is enough to liberate him from the yoke of his futile desires. He is elevated above the rank of selfishness and animalistic cravings to the rank of a liberated self which conducts itself with integrity. It is no longer dictated by desire and lust alone.

Godliness of the divine source and methodology

So far we have mentioned the foremost characteristic of *rabbāniyyah* as being aware of one's purpose in life. Let us now examine the second characteristic: the godliness of the divine source and methodology in Islam. These are the methods which have clearly been outlined by Islam and it is by them we accomplish the divine objectives of the faith since their origin lie in the revelation from Allah sent to His final Messenger, Muḥammad (ṣ).

We believe this method is not the creation of any individual, family, class, party or people. It stems directly from the divine will of Allah, serving as a source of guidance and light for us all. It is the glad tidings, the source of healing and mercy mentioned in the Qur'an:

> *O Mankind! Verily there has come to you a convincing proof from your Lord: For We have sent unto you a light (that is) manifest.* [4:174]

> *O Mankind! There has come to you a direction from your Lord and a healing for the (diseases) in your hearts,—and for those who believe, a guidance and a mercy.* [10:57]

The Prophet's place in the divine scheme

Allah is the author of this path (of Islam). This is why in Arabic Islam is also known as *minhāj Allāh* ('the way of Allah') and in the Qur'an we also see that it is referred to as *ṣirāṭ Allāh* ('the path of Allah'). Such close associations with Allah tell us two important things, namely that as well as being the Compiler of the path, Allah is also the purpose of the path itself.

The Messenger's role was to invite people to this path. He was given the responsibility of teaching people about this divine path and was sent to strengthen their faith by replacing doubt with conviction by clarifying the message. Allah addresses His Messenger saying:

> *And thus have We, by Our Command, sent inspiration to you: you knewest not (before) what was Revelation, and what was Faith; but We have made the (Qur'an) a Light, wherewith We guide such of Our servants as We will; and verily you do guide (men) to the Straight Way. The Way of God, to Whom belongs whatever is in the heavens and whatever is on earth. Behold (how) all affairs tend towards God!* [26:52-53]

That which distinguishes Islam from other religions

Islam is the only religion in the world whose divine sources have not been distorted or marred by the fallibilities of man. All religions in our own time fall under one of the three following categories:

1. Secular ideologies based on the intellectual or philosophical reasoning of a single ideologue or a group of thinkers. These include such ideologies as Communism, Capitalism and Existentialism.

2. Those religions which are solely the product of human thought having no established recourse to the divine. For example, Chinese, Japanese or Indian Buddhism, which have no divinely inspired revelations.

3. Distorted religions. These are religions which we recognise as having divine origins, but which in time have been distorted through false interpolations and malicious omissions. As a result, the original revelations were contaminated and so too was lost the faith people had originally had in them as being the immaculate word of God. Judaism and Christianity serve as prime examples of this. Apart from the established and self apparent distortions of the Old and New Testaments, there have also been obvious interpolations by people. All of this has greatly tainted the original word of God.

Islam is a unique faith whose sources have remained free from any kind of human distortion. This is because Allah has taken it upon Himself to protect His revelation (the Qur'an). He confirmed this with His Messenger (ṣ) and with his nation when He said:

> *We have, without doubt, sent down the Message; and We will assuredly guard it (from corruption).* [15:9]

The pristine path of Islam

Islam remains the unchanged divine path. Its various branches of beliefs, rituals, etiquettes, morals and laws are all rooted in divine soil. This is implied in the broadest sense, affecting all the facets of our life.

A divine credo

The Islamic credo is divine. It is derived from the Qur'an, a source which we believe to be guarded from any type of falsehood. Its foundations are further augmented by the authentic prophetic traditions which serve to further elucidate the Qur'an as well as the Islamic credo in general.

One should note that the Islamic credo has not been compiled by a few select members nor has it been decreed by any kind of papal-like authority. None of the Companions of Prophet Muḥammad (ṣ) or any great Imam has been given authority to alter anything in the Islamic credo by way of additions or reductions, as was done by Saint Paul in the case of Christianity. History tells us that Saint Paul distorted the original Christian credo to such an extent that some contemporary western theologians refer to present-day Christianity as 'Pauline Christianity' as opposed to being that of the original Christianity of Jesus Christ.

The divine rituals of worship in Islam

The Islamic rituals of worship are all divinely inspired rituals of worship. It is through revelation that we know the manner in which our worship should be performed as well as the conditions surrounding them.

New forms of worship are rejected outright by Islam no matter who introduces it. In Islam, such an act would be heresy and akin to liking oneself to Allah, the Exalted, Who is the only authority regarding such matters.

Islamic worship is defined by two key principles and these principles are taken to be absolute and unchangeable:

1. No one except Allah is worthy of worship and nothing should be set up as a co-equal with Him. This is the essence of *rabbāniyyah*.

2. Allah is *only* to be worshipped by the established practices prescribed by Him. These practices have been elucidated by the many messengers He has sent to mankind. The last of these messengers being Muḥammad (ṣ), whose Sharī'ah replaced all the previously established practices of other messengers sent by Allah and destined to remain so until the end of time.

Anything in the way of worship invented outside these two principles are to be rejected and considered as bad innovations despite the good intentions which may accompany them. In Islam, sincere intentions alone do not grant the endorsement of an act; intentions must also conform to the Sunnah of the Prophet.

There are two conditions laid down in Islam before any action can be accepted. Firstly, the action must be carried out for the sake of Allah alone. Secondly, any action should be corroborated by the Sunnah (the traditions) of Prophet Muḥammad (ṣ).

Divine morality

Islamic morality also has its roots in divinity with its fundamental aspects clearly defined. This is an important fact to bear in mind since it tells us that there exists then an Islamic personality based on these unequivocal moral precepts. The Islamic character is an integrated, coherent and exemplary one. It is a religion which is aware of its ethical purpose unlike other beliefs which wrestle with the moral relativism created by their own value systems.

The principles of Islamic ethics have been clearly mapped out in the Qur'an. This is both at the individual and collective level, where piety and good deeds are encouraged and all types of pernicious immoral behaviour is to be avoided. The ethics mentioned in the Qur'an include the following: kindness to parents (especially when they attain old age), benevolence to kith and kin, patronage of orphans, honouring one's neighbours, fellow-travelers, wayfarers and servants, caring for the poor and destitute, liberating the enslaved, fulfilling one's oath, being honest when it comes to earning one's livelihood, lowering the gaze and guarding modesty, exhorting oneself and others to truth, patience and compassion, calling to righteousness, enjoining the right and forbidding evil, returning borrowed goods to their owners, judging with impartiality, fulfilling the covenants one has made, renouncing abominable deeds, avoiding anything which will lead to *shirk* as well as black magic, murder, adultery, drunkenness, usury, devouring the wealth of orphans, slandering faithful women (regarding their chastity) and a warning not to flee from collective responsibility in times of war.

Divine legislation

The divine Islamic law was designed with all aspects of human life in mind and deals with everything from the individual, family, society to international relations. These God-given laws exist so that humanity may organise itself on equitable and solid foundations, free from human infallibilities.

This is the uniqueness of Islamic law over all other man-made legislative systems found in the past and in the present. Islamic laws are legislated in accordance with divine revelation which is too exalted to permit any form of injustice:

And the words of your Lord have been perfected in Truth and Justice, and His words are constant, He is the All-Hearing, the All-Knowing. [6:115]

In Islam the sole Law-giver is God. This is by the virtue of His Sovereignty, Divinity and Authority over all His creation. He is the One Who ordains and prescribes, Who permits and prohibits, and entrusts and obligates. He is the Lord of mankind, Supreme Ruler of mankind, the God of mankind, the Creator and Governor. To Him belong all praise in this life and the next; His is the command, and unto Him we will all return.

No one other than Him has the right to legislate except those cases which He has allowed or left open for humanity to decide. It is the latter which forms the basis of jurisprudence (*fiqh*). No human being has been given the absolute right of legislation and governance. Even the Messenger (ṣ) was not a law-giver since he was, by virtue of being God's messenger, simply applying the commandments of Allah here on earth:

Whosoever obeys the Messenger, obeys God. [4:80]

The Qur'an refers to those who have invested legislative authority in the hands of other humans such as a clergy as being 'polytheists' because such people change the divine words of Allah and misinterpret His laws. In doing so they commit forgery in the name of Allah and in due course they legitimise what Allah has forbidden and forbid what Allah has made permissible. This is an act of great transgression.

AL-INSĀNIYYAH (HUMANITY)

After *rabbāniyyah* (godliness) comes the characteristic of *al-insāniyyah* (humanity). Islam is unique in its stress on humanity, which is reflected greatly in its beliefs, rituals and laws. It is in essence the religion of humanity.

Between godliness and humanity

Many people may find a contradiction between the quality of "godliness" and the quality of "humanity", but this is often based on the flawed assumption that the establishment of one of these qualities automatically negates the other, in other words: If *rabbāniyyah* is established, there remains no room for *al-insāniyyah* and vice versa.

We have already mentioned that by godliness we mean that a person infuses the quality of godliness into the purpose behind his life and through the virtue of *rabbāniyyah*, establishes a good relationship with Allah. Seeking His pleasure is the purpose of man's existence and the objective of Islam. We have also said that it is an awareness of the divine nature of the sources and methodology which underpins Islam. Does this mean then that there is no place for human beings in such a divinely orientated scheme?

Man is not co-equal with God

Many people make the mistake of seeing man as being somehow co-equal with Allah. They forget that Allah is far beyond and above such comparison to man!

Allah is the Master and sole Creator of the universe:

> *Say: "Shall I seek for (my) Cherisher other than God, when He is the Cherisher of all things (that exist)?"* [6:164]

Man is just one creation among the many creations of Allah, the Exalted. It is illogical to draw comparisons between the Creator and His creation and to compare the finite with the Infinite:

> *Say: He is God, the One and Only; God, the Eternal, Absolute; He begets not, nor is He begotten; And there is none like unto Him.* [112:1-4]

Man is a creation of Allah, but he has been endowed with a special status not afforded to others and has been granted an important role in the totality of existence. The granter of this honourable status is the Creator Himself.

Let us look at man based on this truth and perception.

Although a created being, man enjoys this unique status of being the most honoured of all the creation of Allah.

Harmony between *Rabbāniyyah* and *Insāniyyah*

When we comprehend the above, we begin to realise that Islam takes into consideration the spiritual and material objectives of life. Taken together we see that man indeed has a place in the divine scheme of Islam vis-à-vis the quality of godliness and that there exists no schism between the qualities of godliness and humanity; in fact, we could describe the two as complementing each other.

This compatibility cannot be stressed enough since honouring humanity is itself a source of godliness and one of the cornerstones of the Islamic narrative. Allah ennobled man by breathing into him of His spirit. He then made him His vicegerent on earth and subjugated to him all therein as well as bestowing upon him His innumerable apparent and hidden graces.

If the source of Islam is divine, then man is the one who is most capable of comprehending this source since he himself is derived from the same Divine Origin and is able to apply such knowledge to everyday lived reality.

From all this we gather that it is spirituality which is the essence of every Muslim's life. We must be keenly aware then that the purpose of such spirituality exists to make man feel a sense of happiness in this life and to help him attain everlasting felicity in the Hereafter with his Lord.

Godliness is the message to every Muslim and its objectives are to achieve a healthy society and to elevate mankind while at the same time preventing them from going astray.

The spiritual ideals of faith, monotheism, piety, hope and fear represent human values because in Islam they are part of the spiritual make-up in which God created man when He breathed into him of His spirit causing him to come to life. As is mentioned in the Qur'an:

> *When I have fashioned him (in due proportion) and breathed into him of My spirit* ... [15:29]

The Islamic position stresses that a man cannot truly be 'spiritual' without being human and that he cannot be totally human without being spiritual.

Godliness calls for sincere intentions and actions for the sake of Allah alone. It demands seeking the pleasure of Allah and His reward as the ultimate objective behind every word and deed. However, it must be noted that the rationale which underpins all this is the idea of liberating man, making him feel happy, protected and elevating him to higher station of nobility. These have always been the fundamental objectives which have informed Islam since its inception.

The Qur'an: the Book of humanity

When we reflect over the Qur'an and its verses we can see that its main theme is man. Indeed, the Qur'an could be described as being a discourse between mankind and God.

The word *al-'insān* (mankind) occurs sixty three times in the Qur'an. In addition to this, man has been mentioned by other generic synonymous terms such as *Banī Ādam* (Children of Adam), which occurs six times and *al-nās* (people) which occurs two hundred and forty times.Perhaps the best illustration that the Qur'an is the book of humanity is in the first divine revelation sent to Muḥammad, the Messenger of Allah (ṣ), in the form of the first five verses of Sūrah al-'Alaq (The Clot), which makes mention of man twice. On closer reading we see that the entire chapter is dedicated to human affairs:

> *Proclaim! (or read!) in the name of your Lord and Cherisher, Who created—created man, out of a (mere) clot of congealed blood: Proclaim! And your Lord is Most Bountiful,—He Who taught (the use of) the pen,—Taught man that which he knew not.* [96:1-5]

Muḥammad (ṣ): Man and Messenger

When we observe the human being in whose personality Allah personified Islam, whom He made a living example of the teachings of Islam and whose character was that of the Qur'an, we can say that he was "the human messenger". The Prophet (ṣ) was not divine in nature nor was he an angel: he was a man of flesh and blood just like the rest of us. On various occasions the Qur'an is especially keen to emphasise this human dimension of the Messenger (ṣ):

> *Say: "I am but a man like yourselves, (but) the inspiration has come to me, that your God is one God...* [18:110]

The human dimension of Islam

Anyone who studies Islam, its Book and the traditions of its Messenger (ṣ), will find explicitly that it has stressed the human dimensions in its teachings. It has made many concessions for man when issuing its decrees and directives.

When it comes to Islamic jurisprudence the bulk of it, a third or more, deals with the issue of worship while the rest deals with personal relations, commercial transactions and penal codes.

Moreover, upon reflection we discover that one of the major pillars of Islam, *Zakāh* (mandatory charity), is only there for the sole benefit of mankind. *Zakāh* is taken from the rich and distributed to the poor. For the former it is a means of spiritual purification, and for the latter it is something which tries to deliver them from the shackles of abject poverty.

There are also other practices of worship rich with human dimensions. *Ṣalāh* (the five-time obligatory prayers), is a form comfort and support for mankind designed to release him from the difficulties of life:

> *O you who believe! seek help with patient perseverance and prayer; for God is with those who patiently persevere.* [2:153]

Ṣawm (fasting) cultivates the virtue of patience in the face of hardship. It gives us the opportunity to empathise with those less fortunate than ourselves and encourages compassion towards them. This is why the Messenger (ṣ) referred to Ramadan as "the month of patience" and the "month of sympathy".[1]

Hajj is a divinely arranged human conference calling on all the faithful servants of Allah to gather:

> *That they may witness the benefits (provided) for them, and celebrate the name of God, through the Days appointed...* [22:28]

"Witnessing the benefits" in the above verse means to see the communal objectives of hajj.

Furthermore, we also find in the traditions of the Prophet (ṣ) sayings which tell us that every good deed performed by a believer for the welfare and happiness of humanity is considered by Allah to be an act of worship.

Benefits of the human dimensions of Islam

Brotherhood, equality and freedom

Islam's concept of the universal brotherhood of man is based on its humanistic foundations. This is an essential basis from which ideas of equality and freedom can be further developed and advocated. Islam holds these three principles in high regard and puts forth a practical framework for their application. These principles are strongly integrated into its beliefs, rituals

---

1. As narrated by Salmān.

and ethics. In doing so they do not remain mere ideals or futile aspirations held by a few.

It is enough for us in this context to discuss the principle of equality since it is intrinsic to brotherhood and an immediate outcome of it.

The principle of human equality

The principle of human equality is advocated by Islam. It stems from the honour Islam has bestowed on every human being regardless of their race or creed. Islam is against any form of racial discrimination or prejudice. As Allah reminds us in the Qur'an:

> *O mankind! We created you from a single (pair) of a male and a female, and made you into nations and tribes, that you may know each other (not that you may despise (each other). Verily the most honoured of you in the sight of God is (he who is) the most righteous of you. And God has full knowledge and is well acquainted (with all things).* [49:13]

It is a fact of life that people belong to different ethnic backgrounds. There are those of us who are Aryan, Semite, Arab, Persian and so on. People also vary in their social and economic standing coming from either an aristocratic class or a lower class.

Furthermore, people differ in regards to their professions in life. Some are rulers whilst others subjects, some are accomplished professionals and others ordinary workers, some are professors and others are simply caretakers at the same university.

The point is that all these variations in human life need not diminish the value of any human being. These differences in rank and wealth exist, but the honour of a human being is not in proportion to his standing in life.

In Islam every human being is valued regardless of their race and socio-economic rank. According to our Prophet (ṣ), all human beings are equal like the teeth of a comb. Based on this reality, Islam regards aggression against any human being as an act of transgression against the whole of mankind just as it deems the saving of a single life akin to the saving of the whole of humanity. This is clearly stated in the Qur'an:

> *If any one slew a person—unless it be for murder or for spreading mischief in the land—it would be as if he slew the whole people: and if any one saved a life, it would be as if he saved the life of the whole people.* [5:32]

How Islamic rituals emphasise equality

Equality is not merely a theory in Islam. It is a practical reality demonstrated through a host of Islamic teachings and practices. The obligatory pillars of Islam such as *ṣalāh*, *zakāh*, fasting and hajj are all manifestations of this reality. These are central pillars which constitute the Islamic way of life.

Equality before Islamic law

All people are treated equally before the law of Islam. Whatever is *ḥalāl* is permitted to everyone and whatever is *ḥarām* is prohibited for everyone.[2] Religious obligations fall equally upon everyone and penalties are meted out with partiality.

2. For details, refer to my *al-Ḥalāl wa al-Ḥarām fī al-Islām* (The Lawful and The Prohibited in Islam).

When one of the Arab tribes, upon their acceptance of the Islamic faith, pleaded for a temporary exemption from the obligatory prayers, the Messenger of Allah (ṣ) rejected their plea saying, "There is no virtue in religion without prayers".

On another occasion, some of the companions tried their best through Usāmah ibn Zayd, to intercede on behalf of a noble Quraysh woman from the Banī Makhzūm clan who was to have her hands chopped off for committing theft. When Usāmah ibn Zayd approached the Prophet on this occasion the compassionate Prophet (ṣ) turned red with anger and then uttered this historical statement:

> Verily, those before you perished (for not applying equality), so that when a noble stole, they let him go, and when someone poor committed theft, they imposed the penalty on him. I swear by Allah that even if Fāṭimah, the daughter of Muḥammad, had stolen, Muḥammad would have chopped off her hand!

During the reign of the Rightly Guided Caliphs, there were many examples of equality for all before the Islamic law. It is sufficient to refer to the episode of Jablah ibn Ayham, a Ghassānide prince. Once when a simple bedouin complained to the Commander of the Faithful, 'Umar ibn al-Khaṭṭāb, that Jablah had slapped him in the face for no reason, 'Umar immediately called for Jablah to be summoned before him. 'Umar then gave the bedouin the opportunity to take revenge by slapping Jablah saying that this was the only way to maintain equality before the law or the bedouin could forgive him if he wished to do so. It was too much for the Ghassānide prince who turned to 'Umar and asked, "How can he take revenge on me, I belong to royalty and he is a commoner?"

'Umar then replied, "Islam has made you all equal."

The poor prince was taken aback by such an idea. He then fled Madīnah and apostated from Islam. His pride could not take a faith which taught such equality before the law.

Neither 'Umar nor the other noble Companions felt any loss by the desertion of such man of noble descent from Islam. For them it was a matter of principle: the loss of an individual was not comparable to the loss of a principle such as equality.

THE HOLISTIC NATURE OF ISLAM

Islam's holistic nature is another aspect which distinguishes it from all the other religions and man made ideologies of the world. It encompasses the whole of man's life and existence.

The late Ḥasan al-Bannā[3] eloquently elucidated the holistic dimensions of Islam, saying:

> It is an eternal message for all time and its nature is such that it appeals to all the diverse nations of the world. Moreover, it is the only faith which balances the affairs of this life and the life hereafter in perfect measure.

A timeless message

Islam is an eternal message which is applicable to all times. It is not a temporal message meant for a specific period like the messages of those prophets who came before Muḥammad (ṣ) and were succeeded by other prophets.

---

3. Ḥasan al-Bannā (1906—1949), Egyptian reformer who founded the Muslim Brotherhood in 1928.

As for Muḥammad (ṣ), he was seal of the prophets, the last among them, and his eternal message was destined by Allah to remain until the Day of Judgement, guiding people to the straight path. Therefore, there shall be no revelation after Islam, no divinely revealed book after the Qur'an and no other prophet after Muḥammad (ṣ).

Prior to Muḥammad (ṣ) none of the prophets ever declared that their message was the final divine message and that they were the last prophet to be sent by Allah. On the contrary, the Torah heralded the one who would come after Moses. The New Testament too announced that after Jesus Christ a Messenger would appear whose name would be "Paraclete" (meaning advocate or comforter). He would be sent to elaborate the truth and that his words would not be his own but in fact would be divinely inspired revelation. Islam is the message of the past and of the future. Its essence, ethics and articles of faith are similar to the message of every prophet of the past sent by God. All the prophets preached the monotheistic message of Islam and warned people against all kinds of vice. The Qur'an emphasises this point on many occasions:

> *Not a messenger did We send before you without this inspiration sent by Us to him: that there is no god but I; therefore worship and serve Me.* [21:25]

> *For We assuredly sent amongst every people a messenger, (with the Command), "Serve God, and eschew Evil"* [16:36]

A message for the whole world

The message of Islam is not limited to a particular time. It is likewise not limited to any one place, nation, people or social class. It is an encompassing message addressed to all nations, races, peoples and classes. It is not a message meant for a so-called 'chosen people' who claim that God has favoured them above the rest of humanity and therefore they should submit to them! Nor is it a message which can be used by imperialists to justify their colonisation of weaker nations and subsequently rob them of their wealth. Similarly it is not a message concentrated into the hands of an elite class who uses it to exploit the week section of society.

Islam is a message which belongs to everyone regardless of their social or economic standing. No one group has a monopoly over the interpretation and understanding of Islam. It is a guidance and a mercy for all from the Lord of mankind. This inclusive attitude is shown by the early Makkan verses of the Qur'an:

> *We sent you not, but as a Mercy for all creatures.* [21:107]
>
> *"O men! I am sent unto you all, as the Messenger of God…"* [7:158]

A holistic message

Islam approaches man holistically, treating him like one indivisible entity, never trying to divorce any part of his character from the other. This means that it does not attempt to single out and direct itself solely at the intellect, soul or emotions, but appeals to them all in unison.

A message for every phase of one's life

The holism of Islam signifies that it guides man throughout every phase of his life from the moment he is born to the moment he reaches old age. The message can be likened to a light which directs him, in every stage of life, towards that which pleases Allah.

This is why we find sacred rituals and directives ready to be applied as soon as a newborn enters the world: we whisper the *adhān* softly into his ears, bless him with a good name, offer sacrifice on his behalf as a token of our gratitude to Allah, and so on.

Such holism is demonstrated by great scholars like Ibn al-Qayyim who even penned a voluminous book entitled *Tuḥfah al-Mawdūd fī Aḥkām al-Mawlūd* (Gift for the Darling on Provisions for the Newborn) which deals exclusively with the rituals surrounding the birth of a baby.

Moreover, as well as addressing issues related to the birth of a baby, Islam also deals with the subject of death and the rituals that should be carried out when it occurs.

A message for all aspects of one's life

Islamic holism covers every field of human activity and has something to say regarding every aspect of existence. Decisions regarding human affairs are made with a full understanding of the circumstances surrounding a certain issue. So depending on this, corrections, modifications and eventually decisions are made regarding a particular problem. The result could either be that a precautionary measure is implemented or a severe punishment.

What is important to note is that Islam never leaves man without a set of guidelines in life. It sets down a framework which can be applied to his spiritual and material life, his personal and public life, his intellectual, political, economic as well as the ethical dimensions of his life.

Islam, as 'Abbās Maḥmūd al-'Aqqād remarked, is the ideal belief for man on an individual and collective basis, on a spiritual and material basis whether he wishes to aim for this world or the hereafter. It is the ideal during times of war and of peace. It allows him to fulfil his own commitments as well as his duties to others.

A person is not a Muslim if he seeks the hereafter by abandoning this world or vice versa. Nor is he a Muslim if he cares only for his soul and neglects his body. He cannot be selective regarding the application of Islam. A good Muslim strives to take the holistic approach as outlined by Islam and achieves a balance in his private and public life.

THE HOLISTIC NATURE OF ISLAMIC TEACHINGS

So far we have witnessed the holism of Islam and how it permeates through all phases and aspects of one's personal and private life. Such holism is also present in the creed of Islam itself.

Holism of the Islamic belief

The holism of the Islamic belief is metaphysically encompassing. It deals with those perennial questions of our existence such as the Divine, the nature of the universe and man, prophethood and fate. All of these questions need decisive answers which will relieve man of the doubt, emptiness and conflicting philosophies of modern times.

Many philosophies deal with one aspect of life whilst ignoring another. For example, a philosopher may deal with the nature of the divine but fail to deal with issues of prophethood or the life hereafter. However, the holism of Islam simultaneously deals with all aspects of belief in one whole and with a great clarity rarely found in other ways of thinking.

Islam does not divide man's nature between two conflicting gods, one being for good and the other for evil as was done by the Zoroastrian religion. The Bible too confuses people by assigning divine attributes to Satan making it seem as if the universe is divided between Satan and God; the worldly kingdom belonging to Satan and the heavenly one to God. In fact, the Satan of Christianity is very similar to Ahriman, the god of darkness, found in Zoroastrianism.[4]

The Islamic faith is not based on feelings and intuition alone like the belief of some 'mystics' and certain branches of Christianity, which vehemently refuse to acknowledge the intellect's role in formulating a belief and call for absolute submission of the self or, as they put it, for 'blind faith'.

However, Islam also does not depend on the intellect alone like secular philosophies, which claim that reason is the only way of knowing god and that the intellect is the only faculty which can solve the mysteries of existence.

Islam tells us that intellect and intuition should work together in trying to comprehend existence, in other words, the heart and the mind should equally be employed. It considers them as complementary tools in attaining human knowledge, which when employed in synergy, yield the desired fruits of life.

---

4. Al-'Aqqād, *Ḥaqā'iq al-Islām* (Facts of Islam), p. 103.

In the end, what Islam asks is that it be accepted in its entirety without fragmentation. It asks the adherents to cast away any doubts and suspicions they may have. If someone believes in a part of Islam and rejects another part of it, he is not considered a Muslim. For the Muslim is defined as a person who has surrendered his entire being to Allah and who follows what He has revealed without any reservations.

Holistic worship in Islam

As with everything else discussed so far the Islamic concept of worship, like its stated belief, is also holistic by nature.

Islamic worship does not utilise the tongue, body, mind or senses in isolation. Instead it strives to use all these faculties simultaneously in a single act of worship. So whilst the tongue recites the praises of Allah, the body is busy with the sacred postures of prayer, fasting and physical exertion for the sake of Allah (*jihād*). Internally, worship consists of using the heart to fear, have hope in and ultimately love Allah all at once. Finally, the intellect plays a part in worship by reflecting on the creation and nature of Allah. Thus all of man's faculties are involved in the single act of prayer.

Worship in Islam does not exclusively consist of the known acts of the five daily prayers, charity, fasting and hajj, but encompasses every beneficial act which helps people and makes life better. In this way *jihād* for the cause of Allah with the intention of defending truth, justice and the protecting rights of people is worship *par excellence*. Again, it must be emphasised that in Islam any useful action, no matter how big or small, done with the intention of helping society is considered an act of worship.

Moralistic holism in Islam

In dealing with morals too Islam takes a holistic approach. Islamic morals are much more than 'religious moral codes' which are restricted to rituals and a list of 'dos' and 'donts'. It is a moral code which encompasses all spheres of human life.

Morals in Islam touch every aspect of an individual's life, be it spiritual or material. Whether on an individual or collective basis, Islamic morality has constructed a framework for right conduct. Whereas people throughout history have failed by bifurcating morality in the name of religion, philosophy, or some social convention, Islamic morality, on the other hand, has successfully embraced all fields of life with relative ease.

Fully submitting oneself to Islam

Islam's ability to deal with life and human affairs in such a holistic manner makes it stand apart from all other religions. Therefore, it is only right that it should ask for a similar commitment from its followers. Muslims are asked not to adopt one part of its teachings whilst consciously neglecting another.

The Qur'an criticises the Children of Israel for dividing the rules of their religion according to their desires:

> *Then is it only a part of the Book that you believe in, and do you reject the rest? but what is the reward for those among you who behave like this but disgrace in this life?- and on the Day of Judgement they shall be consigned to the most grievous penalty. For God is not unmindful of what you do. These are the people who buy the life of this world at the price of the Hereafter: their penalty shall not be lightened nor shall they be helped.* [2:85-86]

Islam is not a faith which permits such crass selectivity when it comes to its teachings. Such an attitude leads people to claim that sins are not harmful if one has strong faith or that good deeds are of no use if one has no faith. Islam teaches that good deeds complement one's faith acting like a fortress which protects it from corruption. Both the Qur'an and the Ḥadīth, have elaborated on this point:

> *For believers are those who, when God is mentioned, feel a tremor in their hearts, and when they hear His signs rehearsed, find their faith strengthened, and put (all) their trust in their Lord; Who establish regular prayers and spend (freely) out of the gifts We have given them for sustenance: Such in truth are the believers: they have grades of dignity with their Lord, and forgiveness, and generous sustenance:* [8:2-4]

Some people wrongly devote their entire attention to acts of worship alone and neglect morality. They fail to realise that moral virtue is in fact one of the branches of faith. The Messenger (ṣ) said: "Faith has over seventy branches and modesty is one of the branches of faith".[5] In another *ḥadīth* dealing with morality the Prophet (ṣ) informs us about the characteristics of a hypocrite: "The signs of a hypocrite are three even if he prays, fasts and professes to be a Muslim: when he speaks he tells a lie; when he makes a promise, he breaks it; when he is trusted with something, he betrays the trust." The Qur'an also emphasises the importance of prayers:

> *Recite what is sent of the Book by inspiration to you, and establish regular Prayer: for Prayer restrains from shameful and unjust*

5. Narrated by Bukhārī.

deeds; and remembrance of God is the greatest (thing in life) without doubt. And God knows the (deeds) that you do. [29:45]

On the other hand, Islam does not allow one to focus on morals and disregard worship completely. This is because man has been innately created to know and worship Allah:

I have only created Jinns and men that they may serve Me. [51:56]

Allah has to be worshiped by the practices and obligations He has prescribed and revealed to His Messenger (ṣ). It is these which form the fundamentals of Islam.

The very first virtue that a Muslim must inculcate in his life is gratitude to Allah by thanking Him for His blessings. This is expressed by fulfilling the duties laid down by Allah such as the daily prayers, *zakāh*, fasting and hajj. However, if one refuses to show gratitude to Allah then He stands in no need of him:

But if any deny faith, God stands not in need of any of His creatures. [3:97]

A similar commitment is required to another aspect of Islam: the Sharī'ah, which organises life according to the decrees of the Qur'an with the aim of establishing justice in the world. Therefore, it is not legitimate for someone to deliberately disregard the divinely ordained Sharī'ah and adopt man-made laws in place of them. That is why Allah warns His Messenger, and every ruler after him, against the disregarding of even a part of the law in order to appease a certain group of people:

And this (He commands): Judge you between them by what Allah has revealed, and follow not their vain desires, but beware of them lest they beguile you from any of that (teaching) which Allah has

> *sent down to you. And if they turn away, be assured that for some of their crime it is Allah's purpose to punish them. And truly most men are rebellious. Do they then seek after a judgement of (the days of) ignorance? But who, for a people whose faith is assured, can give better judgement than Allah.* [5:49-50]

MODERATION IN ISLAM

Moderation is another important feature in Islam. Moderation means to maintain equilibrium in life often between two opposing ends without letting one end overcome the other. The balancing of such opposites as human nature, spirituality and materialism as well as achieving a balance between this life and the hereafter, revelation and reason, the past and the future, individuality and collectivity and between realism and idealism.

Moderation entails that every aspect of one's life should be cared for without excess or shortfall. The Qur'an addresses this theme of moderation:

> *And the Firmament has He raised high, and He has set up the Balance (of Justice), in order that you may not transgress (due) balance. So establish weight with justice and fall not short in the balance.* [55:7-9]

Man's inability to establish a balanced system

Man is unable to achieve this delicate balance because of his myopic vision and lack of encompassing knowledge. This often leads him to follow his own desires as well making him susceptible to familial, ethnic or political influences when making a decision. Furthermore, history has demonstrated the acute deficiencies of man-made systems which are replete with imbalances.

The only One capable of achieving such balance is Allah Himself who with His infinite knowledge and mercy created man and the universe. Such balance is seen in His creation as well as in His divine decrees on which we are told to model our own system of life on.

Some manifestations of moderation in Islam

Islam encourages moderation in all of its teachings and practices. Let us examine some of these in more detail.

Moderation in worship

Islam achieves a unique balance between the extremes of other religions. It neither sides with religions such as Buddhism which have given no thought to divinity, concentrating on the ethical dimensions of human life alone, nor is it on the side of Christian asceticism which advocates a life lived apart from the rest of humanity for a life of unproductive seclusion. A Qur'anic verse highlights this point when dealing with the Friday congregation prayer:

> *O you who believe! When the call is proclaimed to prayer on Friday (the Day of Assembly), hasten earnestly to the remembrance of God, and leave off business (and traffic): That is best for you if you but knew! And when the Prayer is finished, then may you disperse through the land, and seek of the Bounty of God: and celebrate the Praises of God often (and without stint): that you may prosper.* [62:9-10]

Such is the life of a Muslim which is carefully balanced between the responsibilities of the world and his religion. Even on a sacred day like Friday a Muslim occupies himself with his worldly livelihood, buying and selling his goods, but when the call to Friday prayer is made, he must hasten to it and leave his business transactions aside for a while. Then, after the prayer is over, he returns to earn his livelihood, never neglecting the remembrance of Allah since success ultimately comes from Him.

Moderation in morality

Islam achieves a balance in its moral framework by not holding exaggerated ideals that require man to be almost angelic in nature. At the same time it refuses to side with those realists who claim that man is only an animal and can be nothing more than this. The first group of people are fanatically idealistic in their conception of man thinking him to be perfect whilst the latter undermine his nature.

The human being, from the Islamic perspective, is a complex creature who lies between the two extremes of his bestial and angelic qualities. Islam informs him of the reality of both these qualities and believes that man has an inclination for both the good and the evil. However, the choice lies with man who is a free agent. His goal in life is to resist the temptations of his baser self and to purify it:

> *By the Soul, and the proportion and order given to it; And its enlightenment as to its wrong and its right—Truly he succeeds that purifies it, And he fails that corrupts it!* [91:7-10]

Moderation in legislation

Islam consists of laws and practices which strive for moderation on a collective and individual basis.

In the Islamic worldview the individual and society are arranged into a wonderful balance, a balance which takes into consideration the interests of the individual and society giving a host of responsibilities to each.

In the past, as in the present, philosophers have struggled to solve the problem of the individual and his relationship with the rest of society, it has remained an enigma: what comes first—the individual or society? Is it the individual since he is at the centre of society or is it the society since it in turn shapes the individual's culture and outlook on life? The question remains insoluble with philosophers, legislators, politicians, economists, sociologists and others still coming to no unanimous conclusion.

For instance, Aristotle believed in the individuality of man. He advocated a system based on individualism. His mentor, Plato, however, was an adherent of collectivism, as is evident from his book *The Republic*. Greek philosophy, the most prominent among ancient human philosophies, could not solve this problem. Every time a particular philosopher thought they had found the answer to this dilemma, his successor would soon brush that theory aside.

In Persia, two irreconcilable schools of thought emerged. The first advocated a life of asceticism so that man could hasten the destruction of this 'evil' world full of wickedness and sorrow. This was the teaching of Mani and it led to an extreme kind of individualism.

The second school of thought to emerge in Persia was Zoroastrianism. This was a faith which called for a radical form of collectivism which led to individual wealth and women becoming the common possessions of all. Eventually this led to tribal conflict over these very same possessions and created anarchy in Persia.

All of the revealed religions in the past originally came to promote a balanced life full of peace and mutual co-operation, but sooner or later the followers of these religions changed the divine revelation.[6] Thus once the divine source was lost these religious eventually lost any credibility.

The tribe of Israel, as mentioned in the Qur'an, displayed a haughty kind of individuality which they were condemned for:

> *That they took usury, though they were forbidden; and that they devoured men's substance wrongfully...* [4:161]

Christianity also follows suit with its concept of individual salvation taking precedence over everything else, leaving the affairs of society in the hands of 'Caesar' alone. This is what was understood by Jesus' saying: "Give unto Caesar what belongs to Caesar; and give unto God, what belongs to God".

Our own world today is no different. We are witnessing a conflict between individual interests and the interests of society as a whole. The ideology of capitalism idolises individuality and places the individual wrongly at the centre of the universe. It bestows on the individual an unhealthy amount of rights in the form of wealth, free speech and entertainment at the expense

---

6. See Qur'an: "We sent aforetime our messengers with Clear Signs and sent down with them the Book and the Balance (of Right and Wrong), that men may stand forth in justice." [57:25]

of others. In the name of 'personal liberty', the individual is free to accumulate wealth through unfair monopolisation, swindling and usury. He is allowed to spend his wealth as he pleases on alcohol and debauchery and is free to ignore those who are less fortunate than himself in society such as the sick and needy. No one can claim authority over him because he is simply 'free'.

At the other extreme end, socialist ideologies such as radical Marxism devalue the rights of the individual whilst at the same time increasing his responsibilities toward society. For them individuals are nothing but small units in the machine of society. It believes that society is the state and views the state as the ruling party. As a result, this totalitarian 'state' turns out to be nothing but a dictator.

In such a society the individual is deprived of his right to ownership apart from a few meager personal possessions such as furniture. He is not in position to question the policies implemented by his country. If he criticises or questions the decisions made by the state, he is faced with imprisonment, exile or even death.

This has been the disastrous outcome of man-made ideologies and corrupted religions in the past. Islam, on the other hand, has formulated a unique stance regarding the individual and what his relationship with society should be.

Working from the premise that Allah is the One who created man, Islam follows this up by concluding that He would never reveal a law which would disagree with human nature. In Islam, we believe that Allah created man with a double nature: an individual and a collective nature. It recognises that individuality is an innate trait of human nature and man demonstrates this by his independence. However, man also has a natural disposition for wanting to be part of a group which gives him a sense of belonging. In this regard we see how in our society solitary confinement is a punishment for man because it violates his collective nature.

An ideal system would be one that balances the individual and society and this is what Islam has achieved. From the Islamic perspective, the individual is not allowed to abuse the shared values held by a given society and similarly society is not allowed to exploit the individual. Society should strive to safeguard the rights of the individual, fulfil his basic needs and preserve his dignity at all times.

Islam and the rights of the individual

1. Islam affirmed the sanctity of human life. The Qur'an says:

> *We ordained for the Children of Israel that if any one slew a person—unless it be for murder or for spreading mischief in the land—it would be as if he slew the whole people: and if any one saved a life, it would be as if he saved the life of the whole people.* [5:32]

If someone intentionally takes the life of another human being, the Sharīʿah has made retribution obligatory unless the relatives of the murdered individual forgive the murderer. It has also made payment of blood money and penance incumbent on the one who takes the life of a human being by mistake.

2. Islam endowed every human being with honour and dignity. It is not permitted in Islam for a person to humiliate or offend another by word or gesture.

> *O you who believe! Let not some men among you laugh at others: It may be that the (latter) are better than the (former): Nor let some women laugh at others: It may be that the (latter are better than the (former): Nor defame nor be sarcastic to each other, nor call each other by (offensive) nicknames: Ill-seeming is a name connoting wickedness, (to be used of one) after he has believed: And those who do not desist are (indeed) doing wrong. O you who believe! Avoid suspicion as much (as possible): for suspicion in some cases is a sin: And spy not on each other behind their backs. Would any of you like to eat the flesh of his dead brother? Nay, you would abhor it ...But fear God: For God is Oft-Returning, Most Merciful.* [49:11-12]

3. Wealth and property are sanctified in Islam, assuring that every individual has the right of ownership. A person's wealth cannot be taken without his permission. The state or any other individual has no right to confiscate a person's possessions illegitimately. The Messenger of Allah (ṣ) even proclaimed this important principle in his Farewell Pilgrimage:

> O People, just as the sanctity of this very day, of this very month and of this very land, there is also the sanctity of life, of wealth and of honour between you.[7]

4. The home is also a sanctified space in Islam. This has to do with the principle of everyone's right to privacy. No one is allowed to spy on another person in their home or enter another's home without permission. Allah says:

> *And spy not on each other...* [49:12]

---

7. Narrated by Muslim.

> *O you who believe! Enter not houses other than your own, until you have asked permission and saluted those in them: that is best for you, in order that you may heed (what is seemly).* [24:27]

5. Freedom of belief is a principle which Islam protects. No one is allowed to force somebody against their will to convert to a specific belief. The Qur'an says:

> *Let there be no compulsion in religion: Truth stands out clear from Error.* [2:256]

> *Will you then compel mankind, against their will, to believe!* [10:99]

6. Islam grants to the individual freedom of expression and thought. It encourages active contemplation and thought, recognising the mistakes that can be made by judgements. This is the reason why Islam still rewards a jurist for his efforts even if he fails to arrive the correct ruling. According to a *ḥadīth*:

> If a diligent jurist errs, he shall get one reward, but if he makes a correct ruling, he shall have two rewards.[8]

7. Freedom to criticise is also endorsed by Islam. If one sees something wrong or unjust, one is required to raise an objection to it. This is one of the central teachings of Islam which 'enjoins the good and forbids the bad'.

8. Individual responsibility is a subject stressed throughout the Qur'an. The following verses require not further explanation in this regard:

---

8. Unanimously agreed upon.

Every soul will be (held) in pledge for its deeds. [74:38]

On no soul doth Allah Place a burden greater than it can bear. It gets every good that it earns, and it suffers every ill that it earns. (Pray:) "Our Lord! Condemn us not if we forget or fall into error; our Lord! Lay not on us a burden Like that which Thou didst lay on those before us; Our Lord! Lay not on us a burden greater than we have strength to bear. Blot out our sins, and grant us forgiveness. Have mercy on us. Thou art our Protector; Help us against those who stand against faith. [2:286]

No bearer of burdens can bear the burden of another: nor would We visit with Our Wrath until We had sent an apostle (to give warning). [17:15]

Islam and the rights of society

As well as granting individual rights and liberties, Islam has equally entrusted him with obligations towards society. Individual rights and liberties do not come in isolation, rather they must corroborate with the welfare of society. One is not permitted to harm others or inflict any kind of self-harm. Furthermore, when individual rights begin to harm the rights of the whole of society, the latter is given precedence.

While Islam safeguards the life of every member of society it also asks the individual to be prepared to defend his society at all costs. Defending the society is a noble act in Islam and one should derive a sense of pride and contentment in doing so. Islam in this regard upholds the right for one to retaliate in cases of murder, aggression by another nation and the punishment of death for the apostate.

The right to accumulate wealth in Islam is by all means permissible but is regulated by some preconditions. The foremost is that all the money one earns should be acquired through lawful means and once acquired, should be spent reasonably. One's wealth should be offered to the community in times of need despite what some say about wealth being an absolute possession. Absolute wealth in Islam does not exist since everything is regulated by the laws of Allah which has the best interests of society at the centre of its message. Therefore, at times it is permissible by law to utilise an individual's wealth for the collective good, but this is on the condition that the individual should be compensated in full once the situation becomes better. The Islamic position is that all wealth and possessions ultimately belong to Allah and the individual is but a trustee. In other words, man has been placed in a position to look after wealth and ensure fair distribution of wealth and possessions. If he attempts to abuse this privileged position then the community must try to restrain him. In addition to this, the community has a stake in the individual's wealth in the form of the *zakāh* (alms). But there are can also be other rights of wealth as mentioned in a *ḥadīth*: "In wealth there are rights other than that of *zakāh*." This can be imposed by the ruler in times of need.

All liberties and rights are regulated by the ethical framework of society. Freedom of expression does not mean that it is permissible to slander Islam, Muslims, spread atheism, reject morality or promote promiscuity. Freedom used to destabilise the social order is something which is neither accepted by law or reason.

The Islamic concept of individual responsibility is closely related to the individual's responsibility towards his community.

This concept is embodied in an authentic *ḥadīth*: "Each one of you is a shepherd and each one of you is accountable for his herd"[9]. This is applicable to all levels of society, for example, a ruler responsible for his subjects, a husband responsible for his family, a wife for her household, and a servant for the possessions of his employer. In a wider context, every Muslim then is a guardian of Islam. He carries out this responsibility by enjoining the good and forbidding the evil and fulfils his responsibility towards society. As a Muslim he is aware that he must uphold the values of society and that whenever he is able to prevent a wrong, he must do so with his hand. If he cannot, then with his tongue and if he is unable to do even this then he must abhor it in his heart. This is considered to be the weakest level of faith.

To give advice is a core principle of Islam. Advice should be given to the layman as well as the rulers. One who is not concerned about the affairs of the Muslims is not one of the Ummah. A Muslim cannot live a reclusive life in which the only person who matters is himself. This leads him to ignore corruption taking place in society which will spread like a wild fire to consume him as well. The Qur'an highlights this:

> *And fear tumult or oppression, which affects not in particular (only) those of you who do wrong: and know that God is strict in punishment.* [8:25]

A *ḥadīth* also states clearly,

> When people see a tyrant and do not attempt to restrain him in his tyranny, they are all likely to be punished by Allah.

9. Unanimously agreed upon by Ibn 'Umar.

It is imperative upon the Muslim community to bear responsibility for what is known as *furūḍ al-kifāyah* (legal obligations that must be discharged by the Muslim community as a whole). The community must strive to ensure that every branch of knowledge, industry, craft and institution is duly taken care of. This leads to an organised and healthy society and leads to the good in this life as well as the hereafter. When a sufficient number of people shoulder these responsibilities, their action absolves everyone from sin. If these collective commitments are not fulfilled, the whole community bears a collective sin for not fulfilling their duty.

The Muslim community is responsible for the implementation of Sharī'ah. The Qur'an clearly addresses the whole of the community by its repetition of "O you who believe!". This form of address employed by the Qur'an is also a call for solidarity and joint responsibility in implementing all that Allah has ordained in the Sharī'ah:

> *As to the thief, male or female, cut off his or her hands: a punishment by way of example, from Allah, for their crime: and Allah is Exalted in power.* [5:38]

> *The woman and the man guilty of adultery or fornication, flog each of them with a hundred stripes; Let not compassion move you in their case, in a matter prescribed by God, if you believe in God and the Last Day; and let a party of the believers witness their punishment.* [24:2]

Although the implementation of penalties is handled by the government and the high courts, the Qur'an addresses the Muslim community as a whole. This is because every

Muslim bears the responsibility of ensuring that the Sharīʻah is implemented in society. Should they fail to do so then they deserve punishment from Allah.

Even in worship, which is a bond between the slave and his Lord, Islam emphasises this communal spirit. It calls for congregational prayers and reminds us that they are far superior to prayers performed individually. The reward is twenty-seven times more, and the larger the size of the congregation, the greater the reward from Allah. The Messenger of Allah (ṣ) even expressed his anger in wanting to burn down the houses of those who stayed at home and failed to attend the congregational prayers in his time. He did not exempt even a blind man who heard the *adhān* to skip the congregational prayers and pray at home. He even went to the extent of saying about a person standing alone for prayers behind a full row: "The prayers of a lone person behind a row is null".[10] All of this demonstrates Islam's aversion towards a life of solitude. Even when a Muslim offers his prayers alone, he is with the community in spirit. When he whispers to Allah, he does so in the first person plural (we). He supplicates to Allah on behalf of the entire Ummah.

> *You do we worship, and Your aid we seek. Show us the straight way.* [1:5-6]

Special prayers such as the Friday congregational prayer, the Eid prayers and hajj are rituals that must be performed collectively thus maintaining the communal spirit of Islam.

Regarding collective etiquette Islam urges the observation of a number of set protocols. These aim at encouraging the

---

10. Narrated by Abū Dāwūd.

Muslim away from individualism towards a more involved and shared communal life. These etiquettes include such things as the Islamic greeting, shaking someone's hand upon meeting them, invoking the mercy of Allah for a person who has just sneezed, visiting one another, exchanging gifts, visiting the sick, consoling those who are grieving, promoting the bonds of kinship, kindness to one's neighbours, honouring the guest, good companionship while travelling, kindness towards orphans and the poor, and many other social obligations which create a harmonious community atmosphere.

Islamic morality consists of mutual love, brotherhood, altruism and cooperation in good deeds. It calls for compassion, tolerance, generosity, sacrifice, discipline and obedience towards one's elders. In relation to this it warns us against unhealthy character traits as envy, hatred, malice, disunity, conflict and all those vices that stem from selfishness and desire.

It is through such legislations and educational models that Islam strives to achieve a healthy and balanced society. It tries to take the best from individualism and collectivism and this is the meaning of moderation in Islam.

STABILITY AND CONTINGENCY IN ISLAM

The distinct moderate nature Islam is most evident in the stability and contingent nature of its laws and regulations. Laws are adhered to strictly when stability is required, and, on the other hand, a degree of contingency is adopted when change is most needed. This versatility is rarely found in other systems of thought.

Secularists have often accused religion in the past for being rigid in adhering to religious laws to the extent that it has on occasion stifled the progress of man especially in the fields of science and political freedom.

Secular laws are generally characterised by their relativism and therefore are forever changing. Even constitutions, which are considered to be the mother of all laws, are often abolished by the stroke of a pen of a tyrannical ruler or a possibly corrupt parliament. This is so common that people are never sure of the stability of an article of law and whether it is defunct or still worthy of being respected.

Islam takes a different approach whereby divine revelation is taken to be constant and contingent, making it applicable to all times and varied situations. This is a miraculous feature of Islam and again relates to its innate holism.

We may define the constant and contingent nature of Islamic law as being constant in its methodology and principles relating to morality and ethics and contingent in dealing with worldly and scientific matters.

Examples of constancy and contingency in Islam

Examples of constancy and contingency in Islam are found in the historical legal texts of Islam. Constancy is a feature of the original sources of Islamic jurisprudence, the Qur'an and Ḥadīth. The Qur'an is similar to a constitution and the Ḥadīth assists one in interpreting the Qur'an and putting it into practice. They are both equally divine and infallible sources which no Muslim can dispense with. The Qur'an states:

Say: "Obey God, and obey the Messenger" [24:54]

> *The answer of the believers, when summoned to God and His Messenger, in order that He may judge between them, is no other than this: they say, "We hear and we obey": it is such as these that will attain felicity.* [24:51]

In the branch of Islamic jurisprudence known as *ijtihād* (diligent interpretation), contingency is a key feature. This is of course a concept which Islamic scholars have differed over as to the extent of its use and method which has varied according to liberals, conservatives, fundamentalists, and dialecticians. *Ijtihād* is a rich conceptual tool comprising of such things as *ijmā'* (consensus), *qiyās* (juristic reasoning by analogy), *istiḥsān* (application of discretion in a legal decision), *maṣāliḥ al-mursalah* (that which is in the public's interest), sayings of the Companions of the Messenger (ṣ), and the laws of the earlier prophets and more.

The rules of the Islamic Sharī'ah[11] fall into two major categories: those of a fixed and constant nature; and those given to flexibility and contingency.

An example of a fixed attitude would be shown by the five basic tenets of the Islamic creed: faith in Allah, His angels, His revealed books, His Messengers and in the Day of Resurrection. These have been mentioned many times in the Qur'an, for example:

> *It is not righteousness that you turn your faces towards east or west; but it is righteousness to believe in God and the Last Day, and the Angels, and the Book, and the Messengers.* [2:177]

---

11. By "Sharī'ah" we mean what is more universal than just the "legal aspect" of the message of Islam. It is what Muḥammad (ṣ) was sent with in the form of beliefs, acts of worship, dealings, morality, etc. This is how Sharī'ah has been defined by Thānawī in his book *Kashshāf Iṣṭilāḥāt al-'Ulūm wa al-Funūn.*

Any who denies God, His angels, His Books, His Messenger, and the Day of Judgement, has gone far, far astray. [4:136]

A constant stance is also adopted with regards to the five pillars of Islam: declaration of faith, establishing obligatory prayers, fasting during the month of Ramadan, paying the *zakāh* and pilgrimage to Makkah. These are the pillars of Islam as taught to us by the Messenger of Allah (ṣ).

The definitive prohibitions mentioned in the Qur'an and Ḥadīth relating to things such as black magic, murder, adultery, usury, abusing the wealth of orphans, slandering chaste women, desertion in the battlefield, extortion, theft, backbiting, defamation and so on are also examples of prohibitions which are not up for compromise.

This is similar to the virtues such as honesty, chastity, patience, fidelity, modesty and other noble characteristics that have been described in the Qur'an and Ḥadīth as belonging to the branches of faith. The Islamic laws on matrimony, divorce, inheritance, penalties and retribution are areas where no compromise can be made.

In his book *Ighāthah al-Lahfān*, Ibn al-Qayyim has divided Islamic regulations into two categories:

i. Regulations which are deemed to be absolute and which do not change with the time, place or according to the diligent interpretations made by scholars. Examples of such regulations are displayed in specified penalties for crimes and the like.

ii. Regulations which adapt to the needs of the time, place and circumstance of a community. An example of this would be to what degree a given law should be implemented. The courts in such a situation will adopt a course which they feel is in the best interests of the community. Ibn al-Qayyim quotes several examples of this from the life of the Messenger (ṣ) and from the traditions of the Rightly Guided Caliphs after him. He goes on to say:

> This is a vast field, wherein many have confused the firm and imperative regulations with mandatory or otherwise redundant reinforcements that are auxiliary to interests.[12]

The constant and contingent nature of Qur'anic guidance

Anyone who examines the Qur'an will find ample evidence of its balanced constant and contingent nature.

A constant trait of the Qur'an is displayed when it describes the community of the faithful believers and their rights:

> *...who (conduct) their affairs by mutual Consultation...* [26:38]

> *...and consult them in affairs (of moment)...* [3:159]

No ruler is allowed to eliminate the institution of *Shūrā* from the social and political life of Islam. Furthermore, no ruler can force his people to do something which they are unhappy with.

There is no definite format for *Shūrā* that should be strictly abided by. This is because Islam with its wisdom is aware that the social and political milieu of a given culture will differ from one another and so leaves the format to them. The faithful should be able to implement the principle of *Shūrā* in the manner that suits their given conditions and

---

12. *Ighāthah al-Lahfān*, vol. 1; pp. 346 and 349.

circumstances. They should ensure that it is in harmony with the changing times of their society without adhering rigidly to any stagnated format.

Constancy is further displayed in the Qur'an in universal principled statements as:

> *And when you judge between man and man, that you judge with justice.* [4:58]

> *And this (He commands): Judge you between them by what Allah has revealed, and follow not their vain desires, but beware of them lest they beguile you from any of that (teaching) which Allah has sent down to you.* [5:49]

No compromise being allowed here, it is clear that one should adhere to justice and all that Allah has revealed without following vain desires. Where no compromise is given in an aspect of law then this is taken to be absolute.

The format of the judiciary system is very flexible in Islam and has also been left open to the community to decide. No single judge, collective, criminal or civil court has been made mandatory in Islam. This decision must be made by those who have been elected to power by the people. The legislator's ultimate duty is to establish justice, eliminate oppression and corruption and execute that which is best for his nation.

The Supreme Lawgiver, Allah, made it His concern to mark out the principal ethical objectives for man, but left the myriad of means in which these principles may be fulfilled to man, allowing him to take into consideration the social, cultural and political make up of a particular community and then make decisions based on that knowledge.

Constancy and contingency in prophetic guidance

When we deliberate over the authentic traditions of the Messenger of Allah (ṣ), we find it laden with various examples of constancy and contingency all expressed in a fine balance.

Constancy is shown in his refusal to give up proclaiming what was revealed to him and his refusal to concede anything related to the fundamentals of the religion such as its doctrine and moral precepts. This was in spite of the persistent attempts of his opponents who tried to dissuade him from these essentials, by cajoling, intimidation and other means. His stance regarding such matters was always a categorical rejection. It was in fact the Qur'an which guided him through these various situations so that when the polytheists offered him a compromise whereby he would accept some of their rituals and they would accept some of the Islamic practices of worship, taking their deities for worship a certain time and they in turn would his, his response was unequivocally stated in the Qur'anic revelation which vehemently ruled out any kind of compromise:

> *Say : O you that reject Faith! I worship not that which you worship, Nor will you worship that which I worship. And I will not worship that which you have been wont to worship, Nor will you worship that which I worship. To you be your Way, and to me mine.* [109:1-6]

When he read to them the lucid verses denouncing their polytheism and stubbornness, reproaching them for their perversity and infidelity, they replied:

> *"Bring us a reading other than this, or change this."* [10:15]

Again his reply to this was categorical:

> *Say: "It is not for me, of my own accord, to change it: I follow naught but what is revealed unto me: if I were to disobey my Lord, I should myself fear the penalty of a Great Day (to come)." Say: "If God had so willed, I should not have rehearsed it to you, nor would He have made it known to you. A whole life-time before this have I tarried amongst you: will you not then understand?"* [10:15-16]

All this demonstrates the fact that he was guided by the divine revelation which told him that there could be no compromise in matters of belief and faith.

In contrast to this, we find immense contingency in dealing with politics, military tactics and confronting the enemies, depending on the situation. He had an unparalleled skill and ability to grasp and comprehend all circumstances, solving problems without any kind of narrow-mindedness.

In the battle of *Aḥzāb,* for example, he accepted the advice from Salmān al-Fārisī who proposed the digging of a trench around Madīnah to protect it from the enemy. Similarly, on another occasion, he consulted some chieftains of Madīnah asking them about the possibility of granting a portion of the yield of Madīnah's dates to some supporters of the invading Quraysh in order to tactfully disunite them from their allies allowing them to bide their time.

In the battle filed when Na'īm bin Mas'ūd al-Ashja'ī, who had only just converted to Islam, wanted to join the ranks of the Muslim fighters, he suggested to Na'īm the act of pretending to betray the Muslims so that he could contribute in a more productive way by stirring up discord between the Quraysh tribe and their allies from among the tribe of Ghatafān and the Jews of Banū Qurayẓah.

However, it was on the occasion of Ḥudaybiyah that the Prophet's flexibility in matters was shown most. On this occasion he remarked: "I swear by Allah that if Quraysh today put forward to me a plan uniting the bond of kinship, I would grant it to them".

The Prophet was willing to compromise when an objection was raised by the Quraysh while preparing a draft for the agreement of a ceasefire. He agreed to replace the Islamic opening "In the name of Allah, the Gracious, the Merciful" with a common Arabic expression "By your name, O Lord." Similarly he submitted to the objections raised by the enemy when his name was accompanied by the appellation of "The Messenger of Allah". They called for it to be erased but his scribe, 'Alī, was reluctant to do so after having penned it. The Prophet's (ṣ) resilience was evident from his acceptance of the conditions, which were so evidently against the favour of the Muslims. The long-term outcome proved to be nothing but a blessing in disguise.

The secret behind such contingent and constant measures depend on the requirements of a given situation. In matters related to beliefs and morality a firm stance was adopted. In matters related to politics, a more relaxed approach was adopted.

When the delegation of the Banū Thaqīf offered to enter Islam on the condition that they were allowed to keep their deity called al-Lāt for three more years, the Messenger of Allah (ṣ) rejected their offer outright. They persisted in bargaining with him until they scaled down their demand for one year and then for one month only. But he firmly rejected their request and sent Abū Sufyān ibn Ḥarb and Mughīrah ibn Shu'bah to destroy it.

Beside their requests to keep their idol, they had also asked for exemption from the obligatory prayers and from the command to destroy their idols with their own hands. The Messenger of Allah (ṣ) replied:

> So far as smashing the idols yourself is concerned, we grant you an exemption from that, but without regular prayers religion has no worth.[13]

The Messenger of Allah (ṣ) made no compromise on matters of belief, as we saw in the case of the idol of Banū Thaqīf. However, in lesser matters, he was willing to compromise and show compassion like exempting Banū Thaqīf from the command of destroying the idols with their own hands which was neither a matter of principle nor faith.

Islamic jurisprudence between constancy and evolution

Having explained the position of the Qur'an and the Prophetic traditions regarding constancy and flexibility in matters of law thus far, we should now look at Islamic jurisprudence and how it with its various schools of thought and their respective approaches, adopts the same principle of firmness with regards to doctrine and the fundamentals of faith and, on the other hand, flexibility and pragmatism regarding more minor issues of law.

Islamic jurisprudence does not grant a Muslim absolute liberty to organise his life to the detriment of his beliefs, values and doctrine. Similarly, it does not restrict his freedom with unchangeable rigid regulations, so as to make him remain in their captivity forever.

---

13. *Sīrah Ibn Hishām* (Third edition), vol. 4, pp. 184-185.

The Muslim jurist is restricted by precise and immutable texts from the Qur'an and the Sunnah, which are authentic in their origin and meaning. These are sources which the Wise Lawgiver, Allah, desired to be unanimous and above differences so as to enable the faithful to build their society on. These texts form the basis of the intellectual and moral unity of Muslim society. They are like fixed mountains in the earth which prevent it from shaking. These texts are few, but in spite of this, the Muslim jurist is given a degree of intellectual freedom with concepts as diligent interpretation (*ijtihād*) and the application of prudent discretion (*istiḥsān*) at his disposal.

Area of legislative void

The first spectrum for freedom can be termed as an "area of legislative void". This is any area which has been purposely left void by the texts for diligent interpretation (*ijtihād*) by those who are at the head of legal affairs. This is achieved by complying with the objectives of the Sharī'ah and ensuring that the best option is taken. God has not dictated a long list of restrictions, a list of do's or don'ts. This is the area that some of the jurists have called *al-'afw* (favour). The term is derived from some of the traditions of the Messenger of Allah (ṣ):

> Whatever Allah has legitimised in His book (the Qur'an), it is legitimate; whatever He has forbidden, it is illegitimate; that which He has preferred to keep silent about, it is His favour upon you. So accept His compassion, as He does not forget anything. He (s) then recited: "...and your Lord never does forget".[14]

14. Narrated by Bazzār and authenticated by Ḥākim; the Qur'anic verse is from 19:64.

Another *ḥadīth* relates:

> Allah has set certain boundaries; do not desecrate them. He has prescribed certain obligations, do not squander them. He has forbidden certain things, do not violate them. He did this out of His mercy for you, not out of forgetfulness. He has preferred silence over certain things; do not hunt for them.[15]

There are boundaries set by the Sharī'ah which must not be transgressed. For example divorce can only be repealed twice; the *'iddah* (period prescribed for a divorced woman or a widow before she can marry again) is fixed to three monthly courses or till the delivery (in case of the pregnant) of a baby; specified portions of inheritance by the deceased must be based on the outlined Qur'anic injunctions; defining the minimum amount of wealth liable in payment of *zakāh*; the fixing of a penalty to hundred lashes or eighty lashes or the cutting of a hand.

A similar approach is taken with the fundamental acts of worship (*ṣalāh*, *zakāh*, *ṣawm* and hajj) which constitute the pillars of Islam. Also so with regard to *jihād*, enjoining what is right, forbidding what is wrong, filial devotion to parents, joining the bonds of kinship, kindness to neighbours, fulfilling one's oath and the implementation of justice in a government are all fundamental points of Islamic law which will allow for no exemptions. Likewise, there are explicit prohibitions such as polytheism, magic, murder, usury, stealing the wealth of orphans, slandering chaste women, adultery, drinking of alcohol, burglary and perjury.

---

15. Narrated by Dārquṭnī; agreeable according to Nawawī; contested by some, as mentioned by Ibn Rajab al-Ḥanbalī in his book *Jāmi' al-'Ulūm wa al-Ḥikam*.

Other than these boundaries, religious obligations and prohibitions, there are those matters which require diligent interpretation (*ijtihād*). This is a mercy for the Islamic nation and allows Muslims the freedom in life without the feeling they are committing sin.

As far as filling the "legislative vacuum" is concerned, there are several approaches and methods that can be applied. Islamic jurists differ about their merits and scope:

1. *Qiyās* (juristic reasoning) with its restrictions and requirements, although some Mu'tazilites, Ẓāhirites and Imāmites disagree about its application.

2. *Istiḥsān* (juristic preference), which has been adopted by Ḥanafī and Malikī Schools. Some of them even went to the extent to say: "*Istiḥsān* is one tenth of knowledge".

3. *Istiṣlāḥ* (that which is deemed most advantageous) or treating as *maṣāliḥ al-mursalah* (that which is in the best interest of the public).

All of these methods are adopted when there is no particular confirmatory text on a matter.

Upon scrutinising the books of jurisprudence we find that although all the four Sunni schools of thought have adopted this instrument for substantiation, it has been more widely employed by the Malikī school of thought.

Another point to be considered is *al-'urf* (custom of a given society) which is duly recognised in Islam. According to the fundamentals of Islamic legal system, *al-'urf* is significant. The rule is that custom is impenetrable and any virtuous practice of a society is akin to a verifiable text in its own right.

Texts and their interpretations

The second spectrum for freedom lies within the allegorical texts. These are the texts which God wished to reveal and deliberately leaves open to different interpretations. Such openness would allow people from all points of view to unite on their differences as opposed to being disunited by them.

In these varying interpretations scope is allowed for weighing the different opinions and adopting the one which, as well as meeting the requirements of the Sharī'ah, also takes into consideration the time and circumstances of a certain society.

Similarly, in the Islamic system there are places of unanimity, where no two Muslim scholars have ever differed. These are the firmly established foundations of the Islamic system. This includes legal issues as the ownership of land by an individual, the legitimacy of its exploitation and the legality of its being transmitted by inheritance. None of the Muslim jurists have deviated from the agreed consensus regarding such a matter.

However, on the matter of cultivating the land, we find several schools and differing opinions, wherein every one of them depends on differing legal evidences. There are those who forbid temporary share-cropping contracts and approve leasing for farming on the grounds of what has been reported in the earlier sources in this regard and on the basis of commonly agreed principles of leasing and tenancy. On the other hand, there are those who approve temporary share-cropping, on the basis of what is authentically reported about the Messenger of Allah (ṣ) having dealt this way with the people of Khaybar, as well as for the reasons of profit and loss of harvests. The same people forbid leasing for farming on the grounds of the destruction of seeds, expenses and labour, without any return profit for tenant whilst guaranteeing profit to the owner. In temporary share-cropping, there is the sharing of profit equally, regardless of gain or loss.

Yet there are those who endorse both views—temporary sharecropping as well as leasing for farming, provided there is no invalid condition attached to the share-cropping agreement. Their argument is that there is no substantiation towards categorical prohibition of either of the two.

Regarding leasing for farming, some scholars rule that the land owner must reduce the rent in case of natural disasters or plant diseases proportionate to the damage. They base their edict on the *ḥadīth*, wherein the Messenger of Allah (ṣ) directed to provide relief when natural disasters strike.

Despite this there are those who approve neither temporary sharecropping nor leasing for farming and impose on the land owner one of the two following options: either to cultivate his land himself with his own equipment or to lend the land to someone who can cultivate it without any charges. They base their edict on the unanimously agreed *ḥadīth* that states: "Whoever has a piece of land should cultivate it himself or lend it to his brother."

The flexibility and array of options open to a Muslim jurist are simply immense. As a result of such diverse opinions and juristic elasticity, Muslim society is at ease.

Each one of these opinions bases itself on an established juristic authority. Each opinion is valid as the other as long as it is based on a substantiated authority. We may adopt whatever we find most preferable, pertinent and most likely to achieve the best result in the interests of society, taking into perspective the circumstances of our society and time, without fear of rejection by even a single jurist, as the unanimously agreed rule is that: no condemnation of a diligent interpreter in matters of diligent interpretation.

This is the magnanimous Sharīʿah of Islam. Had it been the will of Allah, He would have definitively composed all its rules and regulations in black and white and there would not have remained any scope for any diligent interpretations (*ijtihād*), diversity of interpretations, divergence of schools of thoughts and the evolution of opinions that accompanied them. Instead of flexibility in *fatwā* (scholarly religious opinion) shifting with the change of time, place and circumstance, there would have been fixed, rigid laws.

Change of *fatwā* with change of circumstances

In view of the above, inquiring Muslim jurists throughout the ages never saw anything wrong in rulings which called for the adjustment of a *fatwā* with changing times, places, cultures and circumstances.

It is appropriate to quote Ibn al-Qayyim regarding the changing of *fatwās* in his book *Iʿlām al-Muwaqqiʿīn*:

> This subject is of great avail. As a result of the prevalent ignorance about it, horrendous damage has been afflicted to the Sharīʿah. Consequently, unwarranted embarrassment,

> hardship and burden have been imposed. It is needless to state that the marvelous Sharī'ah, which ranks lofty in catering to the interests (of people), would never have led to such adversity. Surely, the edifice and foundation of the Sharī'ah stand on good governance and on the realisation of the interests of the people—in this world and in the hereafter. The Sharī'ah embodies justice, mercy and advantage; any matter shifting from justice to unfairness, from mercy to malice, from advantage to disadvantage and from wisdom to futility is no way related to Sharī'ah, even if it might have been introduced through the interpretation (of the texts).[16]

Imam al-Qarāfī al-Mālikī also wrote in his book *al-Aḥkām* explaining that rigid insistence on the continuation of rules based on convention and custom even after their foundations have undergone acute changes, is a violation of consensus and ignorance about the spirit of the religion. In his book, *al-Furūq*, he deals with this subject with the same zeal.

In the thirteenth century of Hijrah, a great scholar amongst the later Ḥanafite scholars, named Ibn 'Ābidīn, wrote his famous treatise *Nashr al-'Arf fī Binā' ba'dh al-Aḥkām 'Alā al-'Urf* and extracted the various different rulings and opinions of the scholars belonging to same school of jurisprudence in various times (supporting flexibility pliability).

In this valuable treatise he has emphasised that many rules vary with the variation of time, because the local conventions change, a necessity arises or because the people of the time fall into depravity. Had the rules remained as they were, it would have caused hardship and adversity to the people, hence

---

16. Ibn al-Qayyim: *I'lām al-Muwaqqi'īn*, vol. 3.

it would have gone against the spirit of the Sharī'ah, which is founded on moderation, facilitation, and deflecting harm.

Hence we find that many of the great scholars belonging to the same school having disagreed with what the founder of the school had held. This is because the founder held this view based on the various factors existing in his own time. Had the founder been alive, he too would have adjusted the rulings without having violated the principles of the school.[17]

Examples of the variation of scholarly opinions and edicts with the changing environments, times and circumstances have been seen in the past.

When 'Umar ibn 'Abd al-'Azīz was the governor of Madīnah, he used to give his verdict in favour of the plaintiff upon producing one witness and the swearing of an oath. In other words, he used to treat the swearing of the oath as a substitute for the second witness. But when he took over as the caliph and resided in the capital Damascus, he necessitated the producing of two male witnesses (or one man and two women). When asked about this change, he said, "We found the people of Syria unlike the people of Madīnah".[18]

What 'Umar did in Syria did not contradict the prophetic tradition by passing judgement based on one witness and the taking of an oath. The prophetic judgement was his source of authority and legitimacy, but it was not a binding obligation. Thus it is permissible to judge with one witness and a single oath in some cases depending on the situation as 'Umar did.

---

17. Ibn 'Ābidīn: Majmū'ah Rasā'il: Vol: 2 Page: 125.
18. Please refer to *Uṣūl al-Tashrī'* by Ali Hasbullah; Page: 84 -85. Also see Ibn al-Qayyim: *I'lām al-Muwaqqi'īn*, Chapter "Ikhtilāf al-Fatāwā", Vol: 3, Page: 27 onwards.

The *ḥadīth* about judging on the basis of one witness and an oath is authentic, it is not wise to reject the *ḥadīth* outright and absolutely disallow its practice.

Chapter 4
The Objectives of Islam

THE MAKING OF A VIRTUOUS HUMAN BEING

The foremost aim of Islam is to form a virtuous human being who is worthy of being the vicegerent of Allah on earth. He is the One who ennobled man to the highest of stations, created him in the most excellent of forms and subjected to him all that is in the heavens and in the earth. Man has been bestowed with all the divine favours and honours and has been fitted with all the characteristics which elevate him from the mere status of animals and beasts. For Islam, such a virtuous human being is the foundation of a virtuous family and therefore the preamble to forming a virtuous society and nation.

A person of faith and belief

The person who belongs to the Islamic religion is above all a person of pure faith and belief; one who in their thoughts is clear about their own being and about the world around them.

They are not like an unwanted weed plant which grows without having been sown. They are aware that the universe around them has not emerged of its own accord without a Creator or Designer. They rather believe that they have a Lord, Who created them, then fashioned them in due proportion and shaped them exactly. One Who taught them the art of speech, Who endowed them with an intellect and an independent will, Who sent His messengers to them, Who revealed His books (of guidance) for their benefit, Who established clear evidence for their benefit and defined for them the purpose and correct path to take in life.

Just as they are aware of a great Creator behind this marvellous world, Who created all things and devised them in due proportion, Who gave everything its nature, then guided it aright, and shall one day wipe it all out and replace it with another creation—the world of eternity, wherein every soul shall be given its due in full and shall be recompensed for all their actions (good or bad), without any injustice:

> *Not without purpose did We create heaven and earth and all between! That were the thought of Unbelievers! But woe to the Unbelievers because of the Fire (of Hell)! Shall We treat those who believe and work deeds of righteousness, the same as those who do mischief on earth? Shall We treat those who guard against evil, the same as those who turn aside from the right?* [38:27-28]

> *Not your desires, nor those of the People of the Book (can prevail): whoever works evil, will be requited accordingly. Nor will he find, besides Allah, any protector or helper. If any do deeds of righteousness,—be they male or female—and have faith, they will enter Heaven, and not the least injustice will be done to them.* [4:123-124]

This is how the Muslim (one who submits to God) lives with pure faith in Allah, in His various messages and in all His revealed Books and Messengers—the last of whom was Muḥammad (ṣ). He is cognizant of the fact that he shall one day come face to face with Allah and be held to account for his deeds and that he shall be fairly rewarded on "the day when neither wealth nor sons will avail anyone, excepting him who will come to Allah with a sound heart":

> *On that Day shall no intercession avail except for those for whom permission has been granted by (Allah) Most Gracious and whose word is acceptable to Him. He knows what (appears to His creatures as) before or after or behind them: but they shall not compass it with their knowledge. (All) faces shall be humbled before (Him)—the Living, the Self-Subsisting, Eternal: hopeless indeed will be the man that carries iniquity (on his back). But he who works deeds of righteousness, and has faith, will have no fear of harm nor of any curtailment (of what is his due).* [20:109-112]

This kind of faith is the first factor that distinguishes the Muslim from others. He is equipped with firm faith, the essence of which is embodied in the belief of the unity of Allah (*tawḥīd*), which means that there is no creator, but Allah and that there is no deity, but the One and only Allah; this means believing in unity of His Lordship and in the unity of His divinity. Neither of these two can suffice alone nor substitute for one another. The Arab polytheists too, as the Qur'an relates, used to testify that Allah alone was the Creator of the heavens and the earth:

> *If indeed you ask them who has created the heavens and the earth and subjected the sun and the moon (to his Law), they will certainly reply, "Allah"...* [29:61]

Yet, despite their acknowledging the unity of His lordship, they worshipped other gods besides Allah—without any authority or evidence whatsoever, except false claims such as:

> *"These are our intercessors with Allah."* [10:18]

> *"We only serve them in order that they may bring us nearer to Allah."* [39:3]

Islam came as a movement of liberation. It came to liberate the man from every form of worship other than the sole worship of Allah. It came to free man from the worship of nature and inanimate objects, whether on the earth or in the skies; freeing him from the worshipping of animals, from the worship of the Devil and other human beings, whether they be kings or priests. It even came to free man from the worship of his own self and of his desires. None other than Him is worthy of worship and nothing else should be set up as deity along with Him. This was the purpose for which the Messenger of Allah (ṣ) sent his many envoys and emissaries to various kings and rulers calling them to Islam. The letters dispatched with those envoys concluded with the Qur'anic verse:

> *"O People of the Book! Come to common terms as between us and you: That we worship none but Allah; that we associate no partners with Him; that we erect not, from among ourselves, Lords and patrons other than Allah."* [3:64]

The person of prayer and devotion

The person of Islam is also a person of prayer and devotion. He knows that the universe around him has been created for him, but he himself has been created to serve Allah alone. This knowledge unravels to him the purpose of his life and the secret of his existence.

The worship of Allah—who has no partners—is his paramount goal. He has been created for this purpose and for this very purpose, everything existing in the heavens and on the earth, has been subjugated to him. Allah, the Omnipotent, says:

> *I have only created Jinns and men, that they may serve Me. No sustenance do I require of them, nor do I require that they should feed Me. For Allah is He Who gives (all) sustenance—Lord of Power—Steadfast (for ever).* [51:56-58]

All of creation serves each other in some way or another; a certain species serves some other species; the nutrient soil of the earth serves the plants, in turn, the plants serve the animals and animals serve mankind. Who then does man serve?

Man was created solely to serve his Designer, *i.e.*, for the sole worship of Him alone, without ascribing anything or anyone from among His creation, be it on the earth or in the heavens, as His partners.

With this mission, Allah sent His messengers throughout the ages and epochs:

> *For We assuredly sent amongst every people a messenger, (with the Command), "Serve God, and eschew Evil".* [16:36]

> *Not a messenger did We send before you without this inspiration sent by Us to him: that there is no god but I; therefore worship and serve Me.* [21:25]

The Muslim who complies with this divine mission is loved by Allah for being obedient to His commandments, for abstaining from His prohibitions and for making His fear and piety his prime objective:

> *Allah does accept of the sacrifice of those who are righteous.* [5:27]

Devotion to God, before anything else, is manifested through the establishment of the major practices of worship that Islam has made obligatory and are understood to be its fundamental pillars. These are the regular obligatory prayers, fasting, mandatory charity and pilgrimage to Makkah, and are complimented by acts of remembrance, glorification, veneration and exaltation of Allah, supplication to Him and through the recitation of His Book, the Glorious Qur'an.

The Muslim remembers his Lord all the time and at every moment; he remembers Him while eating and drinking, when going to sleep and when waking up, in the mornings and in the evenings, when entering and leaving a place or gathering, when setting out on journey and when returning from it, when wearing his clothes, and getting into his vehicle; he does not forget the remembrance of Allah, the Exalted, even in the most distracting circumstances, even when he has sexual relations with his spouse:

> *Men who celebrate the praises of Allah, standing, sitting, and lying down on their sides...* [3:191]

Followers of some religions worship their gods once a week. The Muslim, however, is obligated to observe his appointments with his Lord five times a day. Moreover, he is ever in touch with Him through voluntary supererogatory prayers (*nawāfil*), constant remembrance (*dhikr*), supplications and by seeking His forgiveness.

O you who believe! Celebrate the praises of Allah, and do this often; and glorify Him morning and evening. [33:41-42]

In brief, the Muslim can take pride in the fact that his whole life is an uninterrupted system of worship, that is, if he adheres to the way of life set out by Allah and aims to gain His sole pleasure.

A human being of virtuous character

A Muslim, besides being a person of faith, belief, devotion and worship, is also a person of good character and virtue. He embodies purity with all its overt manifestations, and exemplifies the virtues of justice, mercy and altruism. He has taken the Messenger of Allah (ṣ) as his moral compass since he was sent by Allah to perfect the nobility of character and to embody the perfection of morality. From this greatest guide of all times, he obtains the light of faith and guidance, and so he endeavours to follow this right path. From him, he acquires his model character so as to be close to him on the Day of Judgement. Thus, having rectified himself by the continuous inculcation of virtuous characteristics, by struggling and constantly taking himself to account, he triumphs over his temptations and desires and transforms himself from a "soul which is given to evil [actions]" to that of a "self-reproaching spirit". This continuous struggle entitles him to the ultimate success for having willed his piety to triumph over the lewdness of his soul.

By the Soul, and the proportion and order given to it; and its enlightenment as to its wrong and its right—truly he succeeds that purifies it, and he fails that corrupts it! [91:7-10]

Islam has taught us that good character and virtue are the requisites of belief and fundamentals of faith, just as they are the innate fruit born of faithful worship. If worship does not bear the fruits of nobleness and righteousness, it demonstrates nothing but the falsity of one's worship.

The Qur'an emphasises that nobleness and virtue are inseparable parts of belief, as in the following verses:

> *The believers must (eventually) win through—Those who humble themselves in their prayers, Who avoid vain talk, Who are active in deeds of charity, Who abstain from sex. Except with those joined to them in the marriage bond, or (the captives) whom their right hands possess—for (in their case) they are free from blame, but those whose desires exceed those limits are transgressors* [23:1-7]

The benevolent Messenger (ṣ) enlightens us regarding the existence of faith in the form of morals, noble deeds and virtues. For example, in some of his magnificent traditions he says:

> He who believes in Allah and in the Day of Judgement should maintain the bonds of kinship; he who believes in Allah and in the Day of Judgement should not harm his neighbour; he who believes in Allah and in the Day of Judgement should utter good or otherwise remain silent.

> Faith comprises of seventy branches and more; the highest of these branches is (declaration of faith) that 'there is no god, but the One and only Allah' and the lowest of these branches is removing of a harmful object from the road; and modesty is one of the branches of faith.

Taking a leaf from the above prophetic saying, Imam al-Bayhaqī compiled his voluminous book *al-Jāmi' li Shu'ab al-Īmān*

(The Anthology of the Branches of Faith). The book embraces most of the virtues and noble deeds on which Islam is built and demonstrates them as being the branches of faith (based on the above prophetic saying).

The obligatory ritual practices of worship must lead to the purification of the soul, so that it can bear the fruits of virtue and purge all vices, just as the glorious Qur'an encourages. About the regular prayers (*ṣalāh)*, it says:

> *...for Prayer restrains from shameful and unjust deeds...* [29:45]

Regarding mandatory charity (*zakāh*), it says:

> *Of their goods, take alms, that so you might purify and sanctify them.* [9:103]

Regarding fasting (*sāwm)*, it says:

> *Fasting is prescribed to you as it was prescribed to those before you, that you may (learn) self-restraint.* [2:183]

A *ḥadīth*, narrated by al-Bukhārī, complements this:

> Whoever does not give up uttering lies and acting on them, Allah is in no need of him giving up his food and drink (for fasting). Many a faster does not gain anything from his fasting except hunger, and many a person standing (in prayer) by night, does not gain anything from his standing (in prayer) except loss of sleep.

A Muslim's character is not divided. It is unlike the character of a Jew, who prohibits usury in dealings with another Jew but at the same time permits it with non-Jews. It is also not the character of an imperialist, who deals in his own country with ideal morals and virtues, but he steals, oppresses, tyrannise and behaves arrogantly in foreign lands.

The Muslim treats equally with justice those who he loves and those he hates; he treats equally with justice those closest to him as well as those who are his bitterest enemy:

> *Stand out firmly for justice, as witnesses to God, even as against yourselves, or your parents, or your kin…* [4:135]

> *And let not the hatred of others to you make you swerve to wrong and depart from justice. Be just: that is next to piety: and fear Allah.* [5:8]

A person of Sharīʻah and discipline

Beside complying with morality and virtue, a Muslim also complies with the divine injunctions. He strictly adheres to the coherent Sharīʻah that has been made incumbent upon him by his Lord. The Sharīʻah has made permissible for him all that is legitimate and clearly outlined for him all that is forbidden; it has outlined his responsibilities, elucidated for him his rights and made clear to him his needs. It has not neglected him and left him to be the victim of contradicting philosophies and man-made systems of belief, which would leave him in disarray. It outlines for him the right path to strive for and puts him under obligation to follow its course. It is considerate of his extenuating circumstances, and for this it allows concessions and relieves him of unbearable tasks. It appreciates the emerging needs of time, and in this regard it permits what might otherwise be impermissible, to the extent to which it is required, everything from the amount to a specific period, without extremes. In this very context, for example, Allah says about the prohibited foods:

> *But if one is forced by necessity, without wilful disobedience, nor transgressing due limits—then is he guiltless. For Allah is Oft-Forgiving Most Merciful.* [2:173]

Throughout his life, a Muslim is bound by what Allah has permitted to him; he is not given a free rein to do whatever he wishes. Rather, he is disciplined and remains ever-vigilant concerning 'all the good which should be done'.

If we take the example of food, a Muslim does not eat carcass, blood, pork and any animal which has not been slaughtered in the Islamic manner. It is also not lawful for him to eat what has not been slaughtered, or that which has been slaughtered on fixed stones (such as altars, graves, memorial sites) or that which has been slaughtered in the name of other than Allah.

Similarly, it is not lawful for him to eat food which has been unlawfully taken from its real owner, which has been stolen and was wrongfully procured, since it would be unlawful for him to eat someone else's food without that person's permission.

In fact, condemnation in this regard is very strong. Every person who has been nourished by unlawful food is himself fit for the fire of Hell.

Likewise, it is not permitted for a Muslim to take any food or substance which harms him. Since he is not the owner of his own self, harming the self is an unlawful act, because it amounts to a type of slow suicide. Allah says:

> *Nor kill (or destroy) yourselves: for verily Allah has been to you Most Merciful!* [4:29]

The Messenger of Allah says: No damaging and self-harming is lawful (do not damage your own selves and do not harm others.)

It is for this reason that the use of tobacco and its products, especially after its harmful properties have been scientifically, medically and effectively proven, is without a doubt forbidden. Narcotic substances, which fall into the category of poisons, are even worse. In fact, in Islam, the label 'prohibited' is applied to everything noxious and harmful:

> *For he commands them what is just and forbids them what is evil.* [7:157]

In the same way, to protect his intellect, body and character, the Muslim does not drink alcoholic beverages. He treats alcohol as being the mother of all impurities, an abomination of Satan's handiwork and a major sinful transgression. This has been underlined in the authentic *ḥadīth* that reads:

> An adulterer ceases to be a believer whilst in the act of adultery; a thief ceases to be a believer whilst he is in the act of stealing, a drunkard ceases to be a believer whilst in the act of drinking (an intoxicant).

Moreover, even after having ascertained that his food and drink are lawful, a Muslim also refrains from eating or drinking from utensils made out of gold or silver. Whoever eats or drinks in utensils of gold or silver, swallows nothing but the hellfire into his belly. This too has been emphasised in an authentic *ḥadīth*.

When the Muslim does partake of food or drink which is lawful, he does so without falling into excess. Allah says:

> *O Children of Adam! Wear your beautiful apparel at every time and place of prayer: eat and drink: But waste not by excess, for Allah loves not the wasters.* [7:31]

In his domestic, social, economic and political relations, the Muslim is duty-bound by the divine law: he marries and divorces by it, inherits and bequeaths, rules and seeks judgement, reconciles and fights all in the light of the divine mandate and interdictions of Sharī'ah, according to its requisites and preferences. Whatever Allah has made lawful is lawful; whatever He has forbidden, is unlawful; and that which He has remained silent about is a favour from Him.

A person endowed with mission and struggle

Above all, the Muslim is a person with a mission and struggle. This is to say that he does not stop at reformation of himself alone. He also strives to reform others and call them to the guidance of Allah.

This is why Sūrah al-'Aṣr of the Qur'an calls for mutual counselling towards the truth and of patience as well as of faith and righteous deeds, for the deliverance of the human being from loss and failure in this world and in the hereafter.

> *By (the token of) Time (through the ages), verily man is in loss, except such as have faith, and do righteous deeds, and (join together) in the mutual teaching of truth, and of patience and constancy.* [103:1-3]

Mutual counselling here means counselling others towards truth and calling them to it as well as accepting the same advice from others. Every Muslim is an advisor and is open to advice at the same time.

A Muslim, by nature, is a message bearer, as he believes that his message is for the whole world, for all times and encompasses the whole of life. Consequently, he strives to spread its light and to extend its mercy throughout the world:

> *We sent you not, but as a mercy for all creatures.* [21:107]

Given that the Qur'an tells us that Muḥammad (ṣ) was sent as "mercy for all creatures", and he too said, "I am the gift of mercy", his nation stands delegated with the same mission on his behalf. Consequently, everyone who follows him is a caller according to his own capacity. When addressing Muḥammad (ṣ), Allah says:

> *Say you: "This is my way: I do invite unto Allah—on evidence clear as the seeing with one's eyes—I and whoever follows me …* [12:108]

Hence it is clear that whoever follows him is a caller by conviction, or must at least strive to be so.

This is exactly what Rib'ī bin 'Āmir, the envoy of the Messenger of Allah (ṣ), said to Rustum, the commander of the Persians:

> Surely, Allah has dispatched us to liberate the people from the servitude of the people to the worship of Allah alone, from the constrictions of this world to the freedom found therein, and from the oppression of other religions to the justice of Islam.

A Muslim starts his calling with his immediate personal surroundings *i.e.*, his household, children and family. Allah says:

> *O you who believe! Save yourselves and your families from a Fire whose fuel is men and stones.* [66:6]

> *Enjoin prayer on your people, and be constant therein. We ask you not to provide sustenance: We provide it for you. But the (fruit of) the Hereafter is for righteousness.* [20:132]

Subsequently, he reaches out to the society that surrounds him, calls to rectitude, warns against evil, leads people to righteousness and prohibits them from wickedness. He is not supposed to sit back as a silent spectator indifferent to the scenes of abomination or to the suspension of morality; there is no choice for him but to step forward so as to:

> Replace the evil with his hand; if he can't afford to do so he should change it with his tongue; if he can't afford to do so, then he should try to change it with (a wish in) his heart; this is the weakest (level) of faith.[1]

From the saying "change with the heart", no one should understand that it denotes a negative attitude. It, rather, reflects surge of indignation from within in the face of prevalent wickedness supported and patronised by tyrannical forces. This surge of passion must manifest itself one day into positive action which will play an important role in transforming society.

It is important that wickedness must not gain legitimacy, since it brings down the curse of Allah on societies and warrants His wrath and indignation:

> *Curses were pronounced on those among the Children of Israel who rejected Faith, by the tongue of David and of Jesus the son of Mary: because they disobeyed and persisted in excesses. Nor did they (usually) forbid one another the iniquities which they committed: evil indeed were the deeds which they did.* [5:78-79]

---

1. Related by Muslim.

Even if those who indulge in wickedness or patronise it are from the ruling class or the elites of society, it is imperative upon the Muslim that he should not lose heart in facing them and giving them advice and forbidding them [from committing injustices] based on wisdom and prudent exhortation. In this respect he must draw upon the power of truth on his side and derive his strength from the conviction that his sustenance is in the hands of the Almighty, which no one can diminish, and that the moment of his demise is destined by Allah, which can neither be delayed nor advanced.

This is the "internal *jihād*" which was regarded by the glorious Prophet (ṣ) as being the apex of all forms of *jihād*. When asked about the best type of *jihād*, he said, "A word of truth in the face of a tyrant ruler." In the *ḥadīth* narrated by Ibn Mas'ūd, he said: "Never was a prophet sent by Allah, prior to me, but he had his (loyal) disciples."

A Muslim does not limit the boundary of "internal *jihād*" to propagation and advice, but performs his *jihād* and strives with his tongue, his being and his possessions, so that the word of Allah can reach the whole of mankind. The Messenger of Allah (ṣ) said, "Strive against the polytheists with your hands, tongues and possessions."[2]

The Qur'an views the act of propagating the Call as part of a greater *jihād*. Allah commands His Prophet:

> *Therefore listen not to the Unbelievers, but strive against them with the utmost strenuousness, with the (Qur'an).* [25:52]

---

2. Narrated by Aḥmad, Abū Dāwūd, Nasā'ī, Ibn Ḥayyān and Ḥākim through Anas; *Saḥīḥ al-Jāmi' al-Kabīr*: 309.

This verse was revealed during the Makkan period, before active combat was permitted.

If man-made religions as well as the distorted revealed religions strive to propagate their Call [to their religion] across the globe, it is even more appropriate that the eternal and final religion (of Islam) should have people who shoulder the responsibility of spreading its message throughout the planet so that the promise of Allah is actualised:

> *...that he may proclaim it over all religion...* [61:9]

> *Soon will We show them Our Signs in the (furthest) regions (of the earth), and in their own souls, until it becomes manifest to them that this is the Truth.* [41:53]

The person of intellect and knowledge

If the Muslim is a person of faith and belief, he is at the same time a human being of intellect and knowledge, as there is no contradiction in Islam between faith and intellect or between religion and knowledge.

Unlike other religions, the Islamic faith does not demand from the Muslim to believe blindly. It calls on him to be well acquainted with his God, to base his belief on conviction instead of assumption and to rely on evidence instead of blind tradition.

The Qur'an calls upon the people of different creeds and faiths to do the same:

> *Say, "Bring forth your argument, if you are telling the truth!"* [27:64]

> *Say: "Have you any (certain) knowledge? If so, produce it before us. You follow nothing but conjecture: you do nothing but lie."* [6:148]

It invalidates the assumptions of the polytheists, saying:

> *They follow nothing but conjecture; and conjecture avails nothing against Truth.* [53:28]

Just as the Qur'an disapproves of believing by mere assumption where conviction is required, it similarly condemns the following of one's desires and being led by emotions where absolute objectivity is required. It portrays the idol worshipers as:

> *They follow nothing but conjecture and what their own souls desire!—Even though there has already come to them Guidance from their Lord!* [53:23]

Islam vehemently assails following others blindly, an action whereby the human being abrogates his own intellect and thinks by others' heads instead of using his own. They could be venerated fathers, forefathers, chieftains and notables holding influential positions and power; their exaltation can reach to the extent of their deification on the earth, at least among the common folks and ignorant masses.

In condemnation of blindly following the tradition of one's parents and ancestors, there are many Qur'anic verses of the Makkan period such as:

> *Just in the same way, whenever We sent a Warner before you to any people, the wealthy ones among them said: "We found our fathers following a certain religion, and we will certainly follow in their footsteps." He said: "What! Even if I brought you better guidance than that which you found your fathers following?"* [43:23-24]

In the Madīnite portions too, we find verses like:

> *When it is said to them: "Come to what Allah has revealed; come to the Messenger". They say: "Enough for us are the ways we found our fathers following." What! Even though their fathers were void of knowledge and guidance?* [5:104]

Likewise, when criticising the blind following of the elders and the powerful, we find the Makkan portions of the Qur'an depicting some of the scenes of the hereafter and of the attitude of those condemned to Hell towards each other—be it the followers or the masters, the subordinates or the superiors:

> *Every time a new people enters, it curses its sister-people (that went before), until they follow each other, all into the Fire. Says the last about the first: "Our Lord! It is these that misled us: so give them a double penalty in the Fire." He will say: "Doubled for all", but this you do not understand. Then the first will say to the last: "See then! No advantage have you over us; so taste you of the penalty for all that you did !"* [7:38-39]

This mutual blaming and cursing repeats itself often in the Makkan portions of the Qur'an.

Among Madīnite portions of the Qur'an we read:

> *Then would those who are followed clear themselves of those who follow (them); They would see the penalty, and all relations between them would be cut off. And those who followed would say: "If only We had one more chance, we would clear ourselves of them, as they have cleared themselves of us." Thus will Allah show them (the fruits of) their deeds as (nothing but) regrets. Nor will there be a way for them out of the Fire.* [2:166-167]

Blindly imitating the masses and being carried away by the public, especially if they are misguided, is strongly denounced. The *ḥadīth* warns against this kind of submissiveness saying:

> None of you should be a sycophant and say: 'I am with the people; if they act rightly, I too shall do good, and if they do bad, I too shall do bad'; be prudent, so that if people act rightly, do right, but if they behave wrongly, do not be unfair.[3]

On the other hand, the Qur'an motivates us with its eloquent style to reflect, reason and ponder over the divine signs in the visible universe as well as in the revealed signs—both readable and audible. In other words, it encourages contemplation over the silent divine book, *i.e.*, the universe, and over the articulated divine book, the Qur'an.

Let us read the following verses:

> *Say: "Behold all that is in the heavens and on earth;"* [10:101]

> *Do they see nothing in the government of the heavens and the earth and all that Allah has created?* [7:185]

> *On the earth are signs for those of assured Faith, as also in your own selves: Will you not then see?* [51:20-21]

> *Soon will We show them Our Signs in the (furthest) regions (of the earth), and in their own souls, until it becomes manifest to them that this is the Truth…* [41:53]

> *Say: "I do admonish you on one point: that you do stand up before God—(It may be) in pairs, or (it may be) singly—and reflect (within yourselves)* … [34:46]

---

3. Narrated by Tirmidhī as acceptable.

'Standing up before God' in the above verse means to free the self from vain desires and sincerely seek true reality.

Standing up before God 'in pairs or individually' means being faraway from the influence of popular mentality and its persuasions. One can deliberate calmly when with his companion or in solitude with his own self, as if it were his intimate comrade.

Allah says:

> *Do they not consider the Qur'an (with care)? Had it been from other than Allah, they would surely have found therein much discrepancy.* [4:82]

> *(Here is) a Book which We have sent down unto you, full of blessings, that they may mediate on its Signs, and that men of understanding may receive admonition.* [38:29]

The Qur'an is the only revealed book that prescribes reflection, deliberation, reasoning and pondering, just like it has commanded worship and asceticism. No wonder that thinking is considered to be an Islamic obligation, as 'Abbās al-'Aqqād called it in the title of his book *al-Tafkīr Farīḍatun Islāmiyyah (Thinking, An Islamic Obligation).* It is also not surprising that Imam al-Ghazālī—in his luminous work *Iḥyā' 'Ulūm al-Dīn*—has considered contemplation to be one of "ten major saviours". He reports from the earlier sources that contemplation of an hour is better than standing in prayer by night. Some have even said that an hour's contemplation is better than a year of worship.

Muslims do not consider the intellect to be in contradiction with revelation; it is rather considered to be evidence for the genuineness of the revelation. Investigative Muslim scholars have always assumed the intellectual reasoning to be the basis of relying on previous sources. Had the intellect not been there, we would not have been able to perceive the existence of Allah nor would we have been able to substantiate it or to nullify the doubts of atheists and infidels; had the intellect not been there, the possibility of revelation and its occurrence would not have been established; it would not have been possible to validate the truthfulness of the prophets—Muḥammad (ṣ) being the last of them.

In spite of all this, the intellect has its own sphere, which it should not transgress or else it will go wandering in the valleys of delusion. Its sphere is the immense sphere of countless creatures and of endless creation. So far as the divine being of Allah and whatever is related to the venerability of His splendour is concerned, the intellect has no reign in this. It is only appropriate for it to submit to the divine revelation and seek from it, after having itself established its authenticity. After all, it is the intellect which substantiates the truthfulness of the revelation. Thereafter, as Imam al-Ghazālī has put it, it should take the back seat and seek from the revelation what does not come in the jurisdiction of its own specialisation—like the affairs of divinity, realms of the metaphysical and conditions of the hereafter. Allah says:

> *They ask you concerning the Spirit (of inspiration). Say: "The Spirit (comes) by command of my Lord: of knowledge it is only a little that is communicated to you, (O men!)"* [17:85]

A *ḥadīth* states, "Ponder over the creation of Allah, but do not reason about Allah Himself, lest you bring yourself to ruin."

By this submission, the human being saves his intellectual power and capabilities for study and exploration of what is more feasible and appropriate for him.

It is imperative upon every Muslim to seek useful knowledge and science from the relevant specialists. Seeking knowledge that is needed by the individual and by society at large, whether worldly or purely religious, is a religious obligation in Islam. Some of these obligations are absolute obligations on every individual (*farḍ 'ayn*), while some of it fall under collective obligation on the whole Islamic nation (*farḍ kifāyah*).

Knowledge needs to be sought and learnt. Allah has bestowed upon the human being tools and the means of seeking knowledge, and he should not waste them:

> *It is He Who brought you forth from the wombs of your mothers when you knew nothing; and He gave you hearing and sight and intelligence and affections: that you may give thanks (to Allah).* [16:78]

The Qur'an disparages the infidels and warns them that they shall become the fuel of the hellfire for squandering these gifts and means:

> *They have hearts wherewith they understand not, eyes wherewith they see not, and ears wherewith they hear not. They are like cattle,—nay more misguided...* [7:179]

The Qur'an demands restraint from pursuing what one does not have any evidence for:

> *And pursue not that of which you have no knowledge; for every act of hearing, or of seeing or of (feeling in) the heart will be enquired into (on the Day of Reckoning).* [17:36]

The guide to material and physical things are the senses, and that is why the Qur'an denounces the notion of those who say that the angels belonged to the feminine gender:

Did they witness their creation?... [43:19]

The guide to rational things is the intellect:

Say, "Produce your proof, if you are truthful!" [2:111]

Say, "Bring forth your argument, if you are telling the truth!" [27:64]

The guide to historical matters and the like is honest reporting:

Bring me a Book (revealed) before this, or any remnant of knowledge (you may have), if you are telling the truth! [46:4]

The guide to the metaphysical world and to religious concepts is the revelation:

Say: "Has Allah indeed permitted you, or do you invent (things) to attribute to Allah?" [10:59]

Tell me with knowledge if you are truthful. [6:143]

It is on such foundations that the Muslims established a great civilization, one which merged knowledge and faith to leave a lasting impression on human life in the form of the various sciences and eruditions that prevailed over the world for many centuries.

The human being of development and productivity

The Muslim is not a monk in a monastery. He is a person of toil and production contributing to life, to which he gives and from which he takes. Improvement of life to him is one of the purposes behind the creation of mankind and behind his appointment as the vicegerent of Allah on earth. Allah says through the address of Ṣāliḥ to his people:

> *"O my people! Worship Allah: you have no other god but Him. It is He Who has produced you from the earth and settled you therein..."* [11:61]

"Settled you therein" implies that He required them to cultivate the earth. A divine requirement is a commandment and in no way contradicts His worship. In fact, if development of the earth is rooted in the divine commandments and conforms to the teachings of the Sharī'ah, it in itself turns out to be a form of worship and thus a vehicle to endear the human being to the Almighty.

God has bestowed upon the human being intellect and knowledge, so as to enable him to function as His vicegerent on earth. He thus preferred him over the angels to whom He taught not what he taught Adam. He taught the father of the mankind names and characteristics. This preference meant that he had to use his intellect and knowledge to develop his abode, the earth; he had to benefit from all that Allah had created and subjugated to him therein, without arrogance and without perversion.

Allah made the earth as a cradle and expanse for the human being; it is his dwelling place and therein lie the requirements of his worldly life; He blessed it with amenities and appropriately provided what is required for the sustenance of humankind; He deposited therein the necessary means of livelihood to ensure continuity of mankind till the end of time.

There is not any creature on the earth but has its sustenance amply provided in this world.

But according to the divine law operating in the universe humans shall not get their share except by toil and struggle; he who makes an effort attains, and he who cultivates harvests.

Allah says:

> *It is He Who has made the earth manageable for you, so traverse you through its tracts and enjoy of the Sustenance which He furnishes: but unto Him is the Resurrection.* [67:15]

He who acts and puts in his effort gets his share; and he who sits and lingers without any excuse, and steals from those who put in their hard work and sweat does not deserve to eat.

The Islamic ritual acts of worship do not hinder the Muslim from working for his worldly life, as they do not require full-time devotion nor withdrawal from the normal life; it takes a matter of minutes to perform each of the five obligatory prayers spread throughout the day and night.

Friday, the day on which congregational prayers are obligatory, too, is not a day of relinquishing worldly actions like the Sabbath of the Jews. It is just like any other day of the week, and a Muslim is free to work or to relax, if he so desires.

The Qur'an says:

> *O you who believe! When the call is proclaimed to prayer on Friday (the Day of Assembly), hasten earnestly to the Remembrance of Allah, and leave off business (and traffic): That is best for you if you but knew! And when the Prayer is finished, then may you disperse through the land, and seek of the Bounty of Allah: and celebrate the Praises of Allah often (and without stint): that you may prosper.* [62:9-10]

Hence we see that the Muslim—as depicted by the Qur'an—keeps busy with the business of buying and selling and works according to his routine till he hears the call for prayers. Upon hearing the call, he halts and hastens to remembrance of Allah. As soon as the prayers are over, he returns to his work and continues to work for his livelihood; he disperses through the land seeking his share from the bounties of God.

"Seeking from the bounties of Allah" is a unique Qur'anic expression meaning to seek the gains such as from trade. It is an expression that has a special inspiration and impact on the heart and mind of the Muslim.

The Qur'an describes those who are punctual in attending prayers in mosques and are devoted to Him, saying:

> *In them is He glorified in the mornings and in the evenings, (again and again)—By men whom neither traffic nor merchandise can divert from the Remembrance of Allah, nor from regular Prayer, nor from the practice of regular Charity: their (only) fear is for the Day when hearts and eyes will be transformed (in a world wholly new)* [24:36-37]

Such devoted slaves of Allah are neither monks nor dervishes. They are people of business and wealth, but their mundane life does not distract them from their life hereafter; the share of their own selves does not engage them so much so as to disregard the rights of their Cherisher.

The Muslim is required to work for his worldly life through whatever field he can contribute in. It may be agriculture, industry, trade, cattle grazing, hunting, fishing, mining or anything else that is needed by people.

An authentic *ḥadīth* states,

> When a Muslim plants a seed or cultivates a plantation and a human being, a bird or any animal eats from its produce, it certainly amounts for him as a charity.

Another *ḥadīth*, narrated by Aḥmad and Bukhārī, states,

> If the Hour of Resurrection is about to breakout and at that time someone takes a seedling in his hand to plant, if he can afford [time] to plant it by the outbreak of the Hour then let him do so.

This means that the Muslim is called upon by obligation of his faith to work for his worldly life until his last breath, irrespective of whether anyone benefits from his work or not. He is required to work for the sake of work itself; for work is a form of worship.

A *ḥadīth* narrated by Bukhārī states,

> No one ever eats a better food than the one earned by one's own hands; Allah's prophet David used to eat out of his own labour.

Another *ḥadīth* reads, "A truthful trader shall be raised (on the day of resurrection) alongside the martyrs."

Muslim scholars have concluded from their debates about the occupation which is considered the best in the eyes of Allah. They concluded that the most favourable trade was one which people needed the most but shunned. If people eschew agriculture and pursue manufacturing and business for hefty earnings, even when they are in dire need of food and agricultural produce, agriculture in such times is considered superior and deserving of higher reward from Allah.

Likewise, if people desist from the manufacturing industry and become extremely dependent on non-Muslims, working in that field deserves a higher reward from Allah.

If people are in need of trade when there is a breakdown of roads and communication, grave economic dangers, low returns or monopoly by some individuals or groups over the markets in which prices are manipulated, the trade becomes a more noble profession than any other during such circumstances.

A RIGHTEOUS FAMILY

Since Islam views a righteous individual as the foundation of a righteous nation, it also aims at building a righteous family, since it is the first cell of a righteous society.

There is no disagreement that the institution of marriage—which binds man and woman with a sacred bond—is the ideal basis for the formation of a desired family. There is no way and place to establish a righteous family without marriage as prescribed by God.

Perverted notions of marriage

Humankind has known in the past and in recent times ideologies and groups that undermine the institution of marriage.

In pre-Islamic Persia, there was the philosophy of *Mani* which professed that the world was crammed with wickedness, which must become extinct, and that preventing marriages was the easiest and best way to accelerate this desired extinction.

In some shades of Christianity, the vehement concept of monasticism came into existence, which emphasises seclusion in monasteries and prohibition of marriage, believing that woman was the embodiment of desire and that since she is a satanic being in human form, any proximity to her was a sin which polluted the soul and distanced one from the kingdom of heaven.

In recent times, the West has seen pessimist philosophers, who inflict their wrath on womankind, saying that a woman is like a snake with a tender touch, whose venom is lethal; marriage gives her the opportunity to dominate man, to shackle him with obligations. Why then should man, by his own will, put the manacle around his neck when he was created free?

It is unfortunate that some of our 'modern' youth, allured by these notions, avert marriage, as it entails responsibilities, money and restrictions, while they fancy living in frivolities without any responsibility or liability. But if lust overpowers them and their sexual instinct summons them then they are found in the wicked houses of prostitution.

Islam encourages marriage

Islam rejects such devious notions and pessimist ideologies. The Messenger of Allah (ṣ) did not approve monasticism in Islam. He prohibited celibacy (*i.e.*, averting marriage to devote oneself to worship). He called upon the youth to marriage saying:

> O youngsters! Whosoever amongst you can afford to support a wife, should marry, for it is more (effective for) lowering the gaze and more (efficient) in protecting (chastity) of the private parts.[4]

4. Narrated by Bukhārī, through Ibn Mas'ūd, in the Book of Fasting and Book of Marriage.

Whenever he would notice from his companions anything suggesting their inclination to celibacy and asceticism, he would restrain them from overindulgence, direct them to adopt moderation and thus restitute them to the path of Islam. Indeed, his message is the embodiment of moderation and justice.

Both Bukhārī and Muslim, have narrated Anas reporting:

> A group of people came to the household of the Prophet of Allah (ṣ) enquiring about his (manner) of worship. When they were given answers (by some of his wives), they (as if) deemed their own worship to be little. They said, "We are no comparison to the prophet of Allah; Allah has forgiven him for his previous and later wrongdoings". One of them said, "I shall keep praying all through the night." Another one said, "I shall fast forever and never break it"; and the other said, "I shall dissociate myself from women and never marry". Meanwhile, the Messenger of Allah (ṣ) arrived and asked them, "Are you the people who said such and such? By Allah (the fact is that) I am the most God-fearing amongst you, the most pious of you, yet I fast and break fast, I pray and go to bed and I get married. Indeed, whosoever shun my practices, are not from me".[5]

Objectives of marriage in Islam

Nothing in the universe can discharge its duty alone. He has created everything dependent on another of its kind so as to complete and complement each other. Positive and negative

5. Unanimously agreed upon, as narrated in *al-Lu'lu' wa al-Marjān*.

come together to generate electricity and achieve their products of light, heat and motion. Likewise, in the world of the atom, it is inevitable for the electron to come in touch with the proton.

In the world of plants, it is essential that the male seeds unite with female seeds to result in crops and plants, and to produce grains and fruits. In the animal kingdom too, male and female must mate in order to breed and to produce milk to ensure continuity.

To this general law of the universe, the Qur'an has referred by saying:

> *And of every thing We have created pairs: that you may receive instruction.* [51:49]

> *Glory to Allah, Who created in pairs all things that the earth produces, as well as their own (human) kind and (other) things of which they have no knowledge.* [36:36]

In response to this law, Allah has prescribed for humankind a dignified way of union between man and woman which befits the status of the human being. That is what is known as "marriage".

Allah has created in men a desire for the opposite sex and lodged a similar desire in women. Each feel this need which is direr than the need for food and drink and which keeps on summoning them over and over again; each one feels a vacuum, which is not filled by anything other than this union based on the divine law of marriage. Only then does each of them attain peace of mind: they find peace in each other—overwhelming them and enlightening their life. This is one of the great signs of Allah, to which He has drawn our attention:

> *And among His Signs is this, that He created for you mates from among yourselves, that you may dwell in tranquillity with them, and He has put love and mercy between your (hearts): verily in that are Signs for those who reflect.* [30:21]

Marriage results in progeny, by which human existence spreads and its life extends; with it, the chain of righteousness links one generation to another generation. This is why God reminds His slaves of His favours:

> *And Allah has made for you mates (and companions) of your own nature, and made for you, out of them, sons and daughters and grandchildren, and provided for you sustenance of the best.* [16:72]

Zachariah prayed to Allah asking:

> *"O my Lord! Leave me not without offspring, though You are the best of inheritors"* [21:89]

> *"So give me an heir as from Yourself—(one that) will (truly) represent me, and represent the posterity of Jacob; and make him, O my Lord, one with whom You are well-pleased!"* [19:5-6]

Abraham supplicated to his Cherisher:

> *"O my Lord! Grant me a righteous (son)!". So We gave him the good news of a boy ready to suffer and forbear.* [37:100-101]

> *"Praise be to Allah, Who has granted unto me in old age Ismā'īl and Isaac: for truly my Lord is He, the Hearer of Prayer!"* [14:39]

While mentioning the characteristics of the servants of Allah, the Qur'an says:

> *And those who pray, "Our Lord! Grant unto us wives and offspring who will be the comfort of our eyes..."* [25:74]

With offspring, the nation of the believers expands and its numbers swell. They populate the earth, develop it and exploit its resources, and become capable of confronting the adversaries. There is no doubt that numbers are important in defining the balance of power on the earth. That is why Allah—in the words of Shu'ayb—hints to it as being a favour:

> *But remember how you were little, and He gave you increase.* [7:86]

The Messenger of Allah (ṣ) also said:

> Get Married. For I am going to show off the multitude of my nation to other nations; and do not be like the Christian monastic order (who shun marriage).[6]

Marriage preserves the existence of humankind until the time Allah has planned for its cessation. Allah says:

> *O mankind! Reverence your Guardian-Lord, Who created you from a single person, created, of like nature, his mate, and from them twain scattered (like seeds) countless men and women...* [4:1]

> *O mankind! We created you from a single (pair) of a male and a female, and made you into nations and tribes, that you may know each other (not that you may despise (each other)...* [49:13]

Another dimension of the institution of marriage is that it perfects the faith of the Muslim. It enables him to lower his gaze, to abstain from that which is forbidden, to satisfy his sexual appetite in the legitimate way, which saves him from the illicit path. This is why the Messenger of Allah (ṣ) said concerning marriage: "It is (more powerful than anything else)

---

6. Narrated by Bayhaqī in *Ṣaḥīḥ al-Jāmi' al-Ṣaghīr* (2941).

in enabling (one to) lower the gaze and protecting the vulva (*i.e.*, chastity)."

He further said:

> He who is blessed by Allah with a virtuous wife, surely, Allah helped him to perfect half of his faith; of the other half, he must take care of by fearing Allah.[7]

Marriage not only safeguards the religion of a person, it is also one of the ingredients for a harmonious life, which Islam encourages the believers to fulfil so as to release them for the dedication to what is higher in the form of elevating the soul and communion with the heavenly sphere. The Messenger of Allah (ṣ) said: "The worldly life is a temporary possession and the best worldly possession is a virtuous woman."[8]

He also said, "Four things belong to bliss: a virtuous woman, a spacious house, a righteous neighbour and a comfortable form of transportation"[9]

Sa'd ibn Abī Waqqāṣ reported that the Messenger of Allah (ṣ) said:

> A son of Adam is fortunate to have three things and miserable to have three; he is fortunate to have a virtuous wife, a decent house and a good mode of transport; and he is miserable if he has a bad wife, an awful house and an uncomfortable mode of transport.[10]

---

7. Narrated by Mundhirī in *al-Targhīb*—through Ṭabarānī and Ḥākim—as authentic. Also agreed on by Dhahabī: 2/161.
8. Narrated by Muslim.
9. Narrated by Ḥākim and Abū Na'īm in "*al-Ḥilyah*; Bayhaqī - through Sa'd - in "Shu'ab al-Imān" in "*Ṣaḥīḥ al-Jāmi' al-Ṣaghīr*" (887).
10. Haythamī. Narrated by Aḥmad, Bazzār and Ṭabarānī.

Marriage is the only way to raise a family; family is the kernel of society and the foundation of its structure. A noble society cannot come about unless a family is established. A family under the shades of motherhood, fatherhood, and brotherhood. A family where the pleasant emotions and noble affections of love, altruism, compassion, mercy and cooperation are inculcated.

With marriage, social bonds enhance, a person binds another clan with his own clan and another family to his own family, and they become in-laws, uncles and aunts of the children. Thus, the circle of intimacy, cordiality and social association expands. Allah values the bond of relationship by marriage just like the kinship by blood, when He says:

> *It is He Who has created man from water: then has He established relationships of lineage and marriage: for your Lord has power (over all things).* [25:54]

Marriage provides opportunity for the maturity of the human being. For the man it is a time to shoulder the responsibilities of a husband and father, and for the woman it is time to bear the responsibilities of a wife and a mother.

Many shun marriage, as mentioned above, because they want to live the whole of their life as immature adults, without any bond to bind them, without any home to hinder them and without any liability. Such people are not worthy of life nor does life benefit from their existence, whereas marriage is a strong and solemn covenant and implies shouldering of mutual responsibility between man and woman from day one. Allah says:

> *And women shall have rights similar to the rights against them, according to what is equitable; but men have a degree (of advantage) over them.* [2:228]

> *(Husbands) are the protectors and maintainers of women, because Allah has given the one more (strength) than the other, and because they support them from their means. Therefore, the righteous women are devoutly obedient, and guard in (the husband's) absence what Allah would have them guard.* [4:34]

The Messenger of Allah (ṣ) has said in separate *ḥadīths*:

> Each one of you is a shepherd and each one of you is accountable for his herd; it is sufficient as sin that a person neglect and mislay someone whom he supports; Allah is going to ask every responsible person about what he was made responsible for—whether he protected it or neglected and lost it; your spouse has a right on you.

Marriage enables a man to focus and devote himself for the perfection of his works outside the home, as he is assured that there is someone to look after the home, to protect his belongings and to bring up his children. It lends him a hand to be more efficient and productive at work, contrary to the case of someone who is otherwise perturbed, anxious and preoccupied and at odds between his profession and home, between his work and worries of food, drink and clothes at home. A poet once said:

> If in the house of a man, there was no noble spouse to manage it,
> Then to the wind would go the welfare of his house.

Recommendations for those who intend to marry

Islam strives towards establishing marriage on the solid foundations of mutual understanding and agreement between the two spouses and their respective families, so that it is rooted on firm ground and is not exposed to the gales and storms of life, whenever they occur and however strong they might be. This is why, from the very outset, it proposes some crucial recommendations.

Selecting the right life partner

The first of these recommendations is that both the parties make a right choice of a life partner. Appearance alone should not be the criteria, not only because appearance may be deceiving at times, but because a human being is not valued by appearance alone, rather by his or her character. Hence the Messenger of Allah (ṣ) has urged the man to choose a virtuous woman as a spouse in preference to a wealthy woman, a woman with captivating beauty or a woman of noble lineage. A virtuous wife is one who is religious and moral.

The Messenger of Allah (ṣ) has counselled in this regard through his famous sayings:

> A woman is married for four (motives): for her wealth and her descent, for her beauty and for her piety; be a conqueror of the one who is pious; your hands shall be filled with prosperity.[11]

---

11. Unanimously agreed upon; reported by Abū Hurayrah. Another narration, documented by Mundhirī in *al-Targhīb*, reads: "A woman is married for four (motives): for her wealth and her descent, for her beauty and for her piety; you should opt for the one who is religious and noble; your hands shall be filled with prosperity".

> Worldly life is a temporary possession and the best of all worldly possessions is a virtuous woman.[12]

Likewise, he has urged women and their guardians to opt for "a virtuous husband", not just one who is wealthy or who enjoys a high status.

A virtuous husband is one who is religious and pious.

In yet another *ḥadīth*, the Messenger of Allah (ṣ) advises:

> When someone, with whose piety and character you are satisfied with, comes to you (seeking the hand of a woman under your guardianship), marry her off to him. If you do not, there will be chaos in the earth and widespread depravity.[13]

Meeting the prospective spouse

Besides righteousness, it is important that both parties should be physically acceptable to each other as far as appearance is concerned. As perspectives vary from person to person, Islam has recommended looking at one's prospective spouse before marriage.

Once al-Mughīrah ibn Shu'bah told the Messenger of Allah (ṣ) that he had proposed to a woman. He asked al-Mughīrah whether he had seen her. Al-Mughīrah replied that he had not. The Messenger of Allah (ṣ) urged him to do so, saying: "Go and have a look at her; it is better for endurance (of love and affection) between you two".[14] The reason is that the eye is the messenger of the heart and if this takes place before marriage and if they feel acceptable to each other, their hearts

12. Narrated by Muslim through 'Abdullah ibn 'Amr.
13. Narrated by Tirmidhī, Ibn Mājah, Ḥākim and Bayhaqī.
14. Narrated by Aḥmad, Dārquṭnī, Ḥākim, Bayhaqī and Ṭabarānī.

may open up to each other. It is allowed for him to see her without her knowledge, so that her feelings are not hurt if he, for some reason, turns out not to have taken a liking to her. The woman too has the right to see her prospective husband. It is not sufficient to just have a glance at the prospective spouse. It is important that they talk to each other, so that they come to know each other's personality, even from a very basic conversation. Looking at someone does not reveal one's characteristics as much as a conversation does.

It is regrettable that many Muslims of our times have gone to extremes. There are those who reject outright that someone proposing to their daughter has any right to look at her. Some even disallow their daughters to be seen even after they have been bound in matrimony, except on the wedding night. The irony is that these girls have been going out and may even have travelled abroad and have been seen by everyone, except those who propose them for marriage!

On the other hand, there are those who allow the unmarried fiancé and fiancée to meet in privacy. They may even hang-out, hand in hand, at retreats and cinemas. Indeed piety and morality are caught in the middle of such extremism.

Importance of the girl's consent

It is not permissible for a father to give his daughter's hand in marriage to someone she disapproves. It is a must that she agrees explicitly or implicitly, *i.e.*, her consent can be implied in her positive silence, if she is too shy. The Messenger of Allah (ṣ) has said:

> A widow's authority over herself is higher than her guardian; a virgin must be asked about herself, and her (positive) silence implies her approval.[15]

Bukhārī has narrated through Khansā' bint Khaddām al-Anṣāriyyah that:

> Her father gave her in marriage against her will, while she was a widow; she went to the Messenger of Allah (ṣ), who annulled her marriage.[16]

Abū Dāwūd has reported through Ibn 'Abbās that:

> A maiden girl came to the Messenger of Allah (ṣ) complaining that her father had married her off against her will. After listening to her, he allowed her to opt (against or in favour of the marriage).[17]

The parents must not belittle and disregard their children's emotions when it comes to marriage. Ibn 'Abbās reported that a man came to the Messenger of Allah (ṣ) saying:

> We have an orphan girl with us; two men have proposed for her, one is penniless and the other is rich; she is in favour of the penniless and we prefer the rich man. He replied, "There is no marriage like the marriage of the two who feel affection for one another."[18]

Marriage should take place with the agreement of both families. That is why many Islamic jurists have made marriage

---

15. Narrated by Mālik and Aḥmad through Ibn 'Abbās; *Ṣaḥīḥ al-Jāmi' al-Ṣaghīr* (2809).
16. Narrated by Bukhārī in *Kitāb al-Nikāḥ*.
17. Narrated by Abū Dāwūd in the chapter of Marriage.
18. Narrated by Ibn Mājah and Ḥākim; *Ṣaḥīḥ al-Jāmi' al-Ṣaghīr* (5200); narrated by Ibn Mandah in *al-Amāli*; Albāni in *al-Ṣaḥīḥah* (624).

conditional upon the approval—and even presence—of the guardian, whereas some have deemed it to be desirable but not mandatory. Both have evidence from the Qur'an and the Sunnah, and is discussed at length in the books of jurisprudence.

It is more appropriate that a woman should not marry without the approval of her guardian, so that her husband does not exploit her later on and squander her rights, while she can't find anyone to defend her rights.

In fact it is even more fitting that the mother be consulted regarding the marriage of her daughter. A *ḥadīth* in this regard says, "Consult women regarding their daughters."[19] This is simply because mothers know their daughters more than the fathers do. Due to her disagreement with the marriage, she may embitter the married life of her daughter.

'Abd al-Ḥalīm Abū Shuqqah, in his voluminous book on the liberation of women in the Prophetic era, writes:

> Presence of the guardian at the marriage ceremony not only establishes the approval of the family to the marriage, but helps emphasise the fact that the marriage is not only a bond of intimacy between the man and the woman, but it is also a strong bond between the two families or the two clans. Like the presence of the guardian of the woman, the presence of the father of the man is also recommended, besides the presence of relatives from both sides, so that marriage marks the point of union between the two families.

In this context, Muḥammad 'Abduh writes:

---

19. Narrated by Aḥmad; although weak in its chain, some prophetic sayings do support this notion.

It goes without saying that the stipulations of the sacred Islamic Sharī'ah reveal to us that relations through matrimony is one of the types of kinship. It helps unite two tribes, otherwise distant in their descents. With it the bonds of affection and unity are given new life. Allah has forbidden man to marry his own mother or any other woman of her descent or anyone descending from her, as He has forbidden marriage to sisters or to women from one's own descent or to those descending from him.

Allah has also prohibited a woman to marry (after the death of her husband) with any man from the descent of the husband or with any man descending from him. Thus Allah has given to the branches and the roots of each one of the spouses the same status of the branches and the roots of the other. This profound sagacity has been established by the Sharī'ah as substantial evidence for the fact that the conjunction of one family with another through the relationship of matrimony is equivalent to the relationship by lineage in provisions, rights and reverence.

In fact, this is in line with the human nature. Whoever has a daughter inclines to her as a father to a child. The divine law of creation necessitates that someone from amongst the people will marry her. Since her happiness cannot exist without the well-being of the man she is married to, it is inevitable that the father is inclined to help him in making her happy and to complement her well-being. The same should be true of her relatives; they must be an embodiment of love for her husband as they are for her.

The rights of comradeship between husband and wife

Marriage is a solid contract and sacred companionship, which Islam wants to be lasting and unshakable. Thus, it has prescribed rights for both husband and wife, and imposed duties on both of them, in such a manner that if both sincerely adhere to them, they will enjoy a happy married life.

The essence of these rights and duties focuses on a single expression, *al-muʿāsharah bi al-maʿrūf* (amicable camaraderie). Allah says:

> *Live with them on a footing of kindness and equity...* [4:19]

> *And women shall have rights similar to the rights against them, according to what is equitable.* [2:228]

The expression used here—*bi al-maʿrūf*—means that which is endorsed by the positive convention of the time and to which the moderates and people of integrity are accustomed to and habituated with, like good companionship, desistance from harm, toleration of affliction and generosity. The beauty is that the latter verse makes rights and obligations mutually reciprocal between the two spouses, wherein every right is matched by a responsibility.

Ibn ʿAbbās has said:

> I like to embellish myself for my wife just as I want her to beautify herself for me, because Allah has prescribed: "And women shall have rights similar to the rights against them, according to what is equitable. [2:228]."

This represents an accurate comprehension of the implied meaning of the verse.

But the same verse gives men a degree of advantage or superiority over women; so let us try to understand this issue. Some interpreters of the Qur'an hold the view that this is the degree of guardianship and responsibility for the family and that this responsibility imposes more burden on men than on women. This is why while interpreting the following divine maxim, "...but men have a degree (of advantage) over them..." [2:228], Qurṭubī, the renowned interpreter of the Qur'an, has narrated through Ibn 'Abbās that the use of the word "degree" is an encouragement for men towards the graceful companionship and generosity of their women in expenditure and disposition. In other words, since he is 'superior', he has to exert himself more than her. Ibn 'Atiyyah described this a brilliant and sophisticated view.

Ṭabarī, the interpreter and historian, said that the most appropriate explanation of this verse is that the "degree" mentioned in the verse implies forbearance of the man towards his woman for some of her duties, bearing her patiently and fulfilling all his duties towards her so as to earn such a degree.

There are some common rights between the couple, like mutual respect and consultation about issues of significance regarding the family, as Allah has said about breast-feeding mothers:

> *If they both decide on weaning, by mutual consent, and after due consultation, there is no blame on them.* [2:233]

Among these rights is the right of sexual intimacy. That is a right of both to be fulfilled courteously according to their capability. Allah says:

> *Permitted to you, on the night of the fasts, is the approach to your wives. They are your garments and you are their garments.* [2:187]

The bond has been referred to as a "garment" for it means adornment, shield, intimacy and warmth.

These rights also include the right of cooperation on righteousness and piety—in happiness as well as in hardship. If such cooperation was desirable from all Muslims, it more so from husband and wife.

There is also the right of adornment for each other, as indicated by Ibn 'Abbās, saying: "I like to embellish myself for my wife just as I want her to beautify herself for me".

Rights of wife

Of the many rights which are obligatory upon the husband are the following:

Dowry

This is purely the right of the woman. A husband cannot delay its payment to his wife the moment she demands it; and after its payment, he cannot take it back, even partially. On the other hand, she may, out of her free will, give up a part of it. Allah says:

> *And give the women (on marriage) their dower as a gift; but if they, of their own good pleasure, remit any part of it to you, take it and enjoy it with right good cheer.* [4:4]

If the husband agrees to pay more than what had originally been agreed upon, it is fair. Allah says:

> *Give them their dowers (at least) as prescribed; but if, after a dower is prescribed, agree mutually (to vary it), there is no blame on you.* [4:24]

Maintenance

The wife is not obligated to spend on herself even if she happens to be rich. Spending on the wife is the obligation of the husband, because he is the custodian accountable for her, whereas she has come under his protection and is responsible for keeping his house, fulfilling his requests and taking care of their children.

To relinquish their maintenance is contradictory to the "amicable companionship" prescribed by Allah.

Allah says:

> *Let the man of means spend according to his means: and the man whose resources are restricted, let him spend according to what Allah has given him. Allah puts no burden on any person beyond what He has given him.* [65:7]

If the husband happens to be financially well-off but is miserly towards his wife and children, she is allowed to take his money without his permission, albeit in proportion to what is adequate for her and for their children's needs. Bukhārī and Muslim have narrated that Hind, the wife of Abū Sufyān, said:

> "O Messenger of Allah, Abū Sufyān is a miserly man; he does not provide for me and my child with sufficient sustenance." Upon hearing this the Prophet said to her, "Take courteously what genuinely suffices you and your children."[20]

20. Unanimously agreed upon; narrated through 'Ā'ishah, *al-Lu'lu' wa al-Marjān* (1115).

Thus the Messenger of Allah (ṣ) permitted Hind to take what was sufficient, without the permission of her husband, because the necessity called for that, simply because sustenance is something one could not survive without. Needs change with time; it is difficult to litigate before the courts every now and then to demand it. On the other hand, if a woman turns disobedient and rebels against her husband, her right lapses, because she fails to honour his rights over her and thus does not deserve from him.

If the husband is not capable of providing for the needs of his wife she has the right to demand termination of the marriage, because life cannot be maintained and continued. Allah says:

> *After that, the husbands should either retain wives on equitable terms or let them go with kindness.* [2:229]

When holding together on equitable terms becomes impractical it is incumbent to release her graciously because the *ḥadīth* prescribes "no damaging and no harming (is allowable to the self or to others)".[21] If the wife can endure, that is worthier of her, because that conforms with noble character.

Kindness and cordiality

The needs of the wife from her husband are not confined to her material requirements; she also has psychological and emotional needs from him such as her conjugal rights.

One should not assume that this is inconsistent with the dignity of the man and belittles his prestige. The greatest man

21. Narrated by Aḥmad and Ibn Mājah through Ibn 'Abbās, *Ṣaḥīḥ al-Jāmi' al-Ṣaghīr*" (7517q).

of all times used to be playful with his wife 'Ā'ishah; sometimes she would overtake him in a race and at times he would leave her behind and exclaim that it was in requital of that.[22]

> And 'Ā'ishah said: "I used to play with my dolls in presence of the Messenger of Allah (ṣ) in his house. I had friends who used to play with me; when the Messenger of Allah (ṣ) would enter, they would hide from him (in veneration of his aura) and then tiptoe towards me and (continue to) play with me".[23]

> 'Ā'ishah also said:

> "The Messenger of Allah (ṣ) would give me cover with his attire while I watched the Abyssinians performing in the mosque till I overstrained him; thus you may well imagine how long a young girl eager for amusement (might have watched the sport)."[24]

The Messenger of Allah (ṣ) listened to 'Ā'ishah narrating about eleven women and what each one had said about her respective husband. This is according to a well known narration called Ḥadīth of Umm Zar'.[25]

Guarding her honour

The husband must recognise the honour of his wife and protect it. He should not offend her for some of her actions or utterances. He must not reveal to others their mutual secrets

---

22. Ibn Mājah (No. 1979); Companionship of Women (57).
23. Unanimously agreed upon; narrated through 'Ā'ishah, *al-Lu'lu' wa al-Marjān* (1581).
24. Narrated by Muslim, "'Īd Prayers", No: 892.
25. Unanimously agreed upon; narrated through 'Ā'ishah; *al-Lu'lu' wa al-Marjān* (1590).

or disparage her family. He should not spy on her nor be vindictive. This is why the Messenger of Allah (ṣ) prohibited someone from travelling to return to his family unawares at night time, so that it was not seen as if he was mistrusting them or trying to find some fault with them, because such conduct implies distrust and ruins a cordial relationship.

It is the right of the husband to be ardently vigilant regarding his wife, but there should not be an imbalance in it to the extent that because of it, she starts getting suspicions and ultimately get accused of indecency. Virtue is in moderation; anything exceeding its own limits, turns against itself. A *ḥadīth* says:

> Some of ardent vigilance is dear to Allah; some of ardent vigilance is abhorred by Allah. The ardent vigilance liked by Allah is that which is out of suspicion; the ardent vigilance abhorred by Allah is that which is not out of suspicion (but out of mistrust).[26]

The word used here *rībah* (suspicion) implies that a man notices about the behaviour of his woman and evidences indicating misgivings and suspicions. In such a situation, one must be vigilant and not ignore it and thus become a *dayyūth* (cuckold).

Forbearance and endurance

The woman is not an angel. She is a human being who does good and commits bad and who errs and accomplishes good too. The man has to be patient and endure to save the edifice of marriage from collapsing.

---

26. Abū-Dāwūd through Jābir ibn 'Atīk; No: 2659.

The Messenger of Allah (ṣ) says: "Be advised of righteousness with regard to women".[27] "For the woman is like a rib (*i.e.*, with a curve); if you force her to straighten, if you can enjoy her, you shall benefit from her in spite of her crookedness."[28] The curve or crookedness in a woman refers to the emotional aspect of her personality more than that of man. For the sake of lasting companionship, there is no alternative to coaxing her and being patient with her; straightening her will be realised only by breaking her, and that is not something desirable.

In another *ḥadīth*, the subject occurs as: "A faithful man does not hate a faithful woman; if he is resentful of any of her characteristics, he may like another one of her characteristics".[29] He, thus, looks to her fair-mindedly, keeping in mind her virtues as he tolerates her shortcomings; after all, who is ever free from shortcomings?

A true Muslim man is one who puts reality above guesswork and turns to intellect in matters of emotion, to such an extent that despite his feelings of abhorrence, he arduously constrains himself. All this is done so as to make the household intact and thriving, in compliance with the divine directive of:

> *Live with them on a footing of kindness and equity. If you take a dislike to them it may be that you dislike a thing, and Allah brings about through it a great deal of good.* [4:19]

---

27. Unanimously agreed upon; narrated through Abū Hurayrah; *al-Lu'lu' wa al-Marjān* (934).
28. Unanimously agreed upon; narrated through Abū Hurayrah; *al-Lu'lu' wa al-Marjān* (933).
29. Narrated by Aḥmad and Muslim through Abū Hurayrah; *Ṣaḥīḥ al-Jāmi'* (7741).

Rights of husband

The husband too has his rights on the wife which she must fulfil, so that the amicable companionship is accomplished alongside the divine directives. The most important among these are the following:

Constructive obedience

Every establishment must have its head. Since man has been nominated by nature, as well as by his obligation, to provide for the family. He has also been elected as the leader of the family and enjoys the right of obedience. Allah says:

> *Men are the protectors and maintainers of women, because God has given the one more (strength) than the other, and because they support them from their mean...* [4:34]

This dependability and responsibility mark the degree of privilege that has been given to man instead of woman.

> *And women shall have rights similar to the rights against them, according to what is equitable; but men have a degree (of advantage) over them...* [2:228]

The woman is forbidden to disobey her husband or to desert him without a reason acceptable to the Sharī'ah. The *ḥadīth* states: "If a woman spends her night staying away from the bed of her husband, the angels keep cursing her till she returns back".[30] Islam has emphasised this right of the man and it is not permissible for her even to offer voluntary prayers or fast without his permission while he is present. The Messenger

30. Unanimously agreed upon; narrated through Abū Hurayrah; *al-Lu'lu' wa al-Marjān* (912).

of Allah (ṣ) says: "It is not permissible for a woman to fast while her husband is present, except with his permission." [31]

Guarding herself and his assets during his absence

Allah says:

> *Therefore, the righteous women are devoutly obedient, and guard in (the husband's) absence what Allah would have them guard.* [4:34]

An authentic *ḥadīth* states that "the woman, in her husband's house, is a shepherdess and is accountable for her herd."[32]

Guarding herself means guarding his secrets and not letting anyone he dislikes to enter his house. Among the attributes of a virtuous wife, the Messenger of Allah (ṣ) mentioned, "When he is away from her, she guards herself and his possessions for him."[33]

Guarding his possessions means being thrifty while spending his money. It is alright to give in charity from his wealth what is usually given; thereupon she will be his partner in sharing the reward from Allah for that. The *ḥadīth* states:

> If a woman spends from the house of her husband without being a profligate, she merits reward for that and he too deserves similar reward for having earned it.[34]

---

31. .Unanimously agreed upon; narrated through Abū Hurayrah; *al-Lu'lu' wa al-Marjān* (604).
32. Unanimously agreed upon; narrated through Ibn 'Umar; *al-Lu'lu' wa al-Marjān* (1199).
33. Narrated by Ibn Mājah through Abī Umāmah (1857).
34. Unanimously agreed upon; narrated through 'Ā'ishah; *al-Lu'lu' wa al-Marjān* (603).

Positive Cooperation

Many of the great jurists hold the view that it is not obligatory upon the woman to serve her husband, cook his food, wash his clothes and carry out other household chores, although it is more appropriate for her to do what the common practice is. But Ibn Taymiyyah holds that it is incumbent upon her to positively reciprocate with cooperation from her side. Although positive cooperation is prescribed to be desirable in all situations, it is all the more appropriate and corroborated among the couple and that this was the requisite of the following divine declaration:

> *And women shall have rights similar to the rights against them, according to what is equitable.* [2:228]

Disciplining upon disobedience or for disregarding obligations

Allah says:

> *O you who believe! Save yourselves and your families from a Fire whose fuel is Men and Stones.* [66:6]

> *Enjoin prayer on your people, and be constant therein.* [20:132]

As long as the man is the leader of the household, accountable to Allah and responsible to society, it is his right to restrain the woman from committing the forbidden, disregarding the obligations or undermining spousal rights, so that the family does not collapse. However, this should take place without undermining the dignity of the woman.

BUILDING A RIGHTEOUS SOCIETY

Islam aims at building a righteous society as it aims at building a righteous individual and a righteous family. The latter two provide solid foundations for a righteous society.

The righteous society pursued by Islam is one whose individual members and families are attached to the peaceful values of Islam and its exemplary principles, and which realises these values and principles as the mission of its life and pivot of its existence.

Rallying around belief

Islamic society is neither a nationalistic nor a regional society. It is an ideological society, one which is based on concepts and beliefs; its belief system and ideological foundation is Islam.

The members of this society consist of different races and colours, and come from various parts of the world, speak different languages or belong to different groups, but all these differences fade away in the face of the unity of belief that "there is no god, but the One and only God; and Muḥammad is His Messenger". This is the common faith which binds all peoples together in the genuineness of its universal brotherhood, as outlined by the Qur'anic maxim:

> *The believers are but a single brotherhood.* [49:10]

Should we need to describe this society with an outstanding attribute which makes it distinct from all other societies, we can say that it is a society grounded on faith or the society of the faithful, those whom Allah describes in the beginning of Sūrah al-Baqarah:

> *Who believe in the Unseen, are steadfast in prayer, and spend out of what We have provided for them; And who believe in the Revelation sent to you, and sent before your time, and (in their hearts) have the assurance of the Hereafter. They are on (true) guidance, from their Lord, and it is these who will prosper.* [2:3-5]

The Islamic faith is not mere slogan nor is it bigotry against others; it is a reality that settles deep in the core of one's personality, from which spout its behaviour to be substantiated by positive, righteous deeds. This is why the Qur'an has always personified faith in the form of deeds and morals, for example in the beginning of the Sūrahs al-Anfāl and al-Mu'minūn and at the end of Sūrah al-Ḥujurāt.

Veneration of righteous deeds

From here emanates the importance of another of the values on which the righteous society is established. This value is the veneration of righteous deeds to the extent of sanctification. These deeds could be purely of a religious nature, like in case of prayers, fasting, hajj, 'Umrah (lesser pilgrimage), glorification of Allah, recitation of the Qur'an and supplications, or of a worldly nature, like striving to earn livelihood, cultivating the land through agriculture, industrial activity and other professional pursuits such as working for whatever is in the interests of the people and endeavouring towards their benefit. This is the established and recognised principle that the Qur'an regards to be a pillar of every religion and comes coupled with faith in God and in the Day of Judgement. Allah says:

> *Those who believe (in the Qur'an), and those who follow the Jewish (scriptures), and the Christians and the Sabians—any who believe in Allah and the Last Day, and work righteousness, shall have their reward with their Lord; on them shall be no fear, nor shall they grieve.* [2:62]

There are more than seventy instances where the Qur'an has connected labour with faith, for instance:

> *As to those who believe and work righteousness, verily We shall not suffer to perish the reward of any who do a (single) righteous deed.* [18:30]

It goes without saying that establishing the rites prescribed by Allah and performing the major obligations (congregational prayers, paying *zakāh*, fasting during Ramadan and performing hajj) are the foremost applications of righteous deeds. There is no worthier deed for the human being than recognising his creator, serving the cause of his cherisher and devoting his service to Him alone. By doing so, he expresses his gratitude to Him and honours the right of His divinity. In the chapter "The Constituents of Islam", we have seen how worship encompasses the whole of one's life and existence, to the extent that every useful act is considered an act of worship.

Call to righteousness

Calling to righteousness, enjoining good and forbidding evil stand unequivocally distinct from among the fundamentals of Islam. According to Islamic logic, it is not sufficient that a person be righteous when he is alone and at the same time totally indifferent to the evil surrounding others; pious indeed is he who reforms himself and endeavours to reform others by calling them to righteousness, enjoining virtue and forbidding vice, as Allah says:

> *Let there arise out of you a band of people inviting to all that is good, enjoining what is right, and forbidding what is wrong: They are the ones to attain felicity.* [3:104]

This distinguishes the Islamic nation from all other nations:

> *You are the best of peoples evolved for mankind, enjoining what is right, forbidding what is wrong, and believing in Allah.* [3:110]

This explains the rationale of the two outstanding Messengers of Allah, David and Jesus cursing the Children of Israel, who kept silent over wrongdoings and did not forbid iniquities. This has been registered by the Qur'an thus:

> *Curses were pronounced on those among the Children of Israel who rejected Faith, by the tongue of David and of Jesus the son of Mary: because they disobeyed and persisted in excesses. Nor did they (usually) forbid one another the iniquities which they committed: evil indeed were the deeds which they did.* [5:78-79]

Jihād (struggle) in the cause of Allah

Jihād (struggle) for the cause of Allah, that is, to defend truth, to consolidate virtue, to remove obstacles in the path of the Call, to prevent sedition, to stop invaders in their aggression, to discipline renegades and to defend the downtrodden, is a primary Islamic principle, which no Muslim refutes nor pretends to ignore its significance and worthiness. No one claims ignorance about what Allah has promised to those who struggle for His cause, let alone denies its legitimacy. Allah says:

> *O you who believe! what is the matter with you, that, when you are asked to go forth in the Cause of Allah, you cling heavily to the earth? Do you prefer the life of this world to the Hereafter? But little is the comfort of this life, as compared with the Hereafter. Unless*

you go forth, He will punish you with a grievous penalty, and put others in your place; but Him you would not harm in the least. For Allah has power over all things. [9:38-39]

And why should you not fight in the cause of Allah and of those who, being weak, are ill-treated (and oppressed)?—Men, women, and children, whose cry is: "Our Lord! Rescue us from this town, whose people are oppressors; and raise for us from You one who will protect; and raise for us from You one who will help!" [4:75]

Fight in the cause of Allah those who fight you, but do not transgress limits; for Allah loves not transgressors... And fight them on until there is no more tumult or oppression, and there prevail justice and faith in Allah; but if they cease, Let there be no hostility except to those who practise oppression. [2:190-193]

O you who believe! Take your precautions, and either go forth in parties or go forth all together. [4:71]

Against them make ready your strength to the utmost of your power, including steeds of war, to strike terror into (the hearts of) the enemies, of Allah and your enemies, and others besides, whom you may not know, but whom Allah does know. Whatever you shall spend in the Cause of Allah, shall be repaid unto you, and you shall not be treated unjustly. [8:60]

Reinforcing virtues

Reinforcing, corroborating and guarding all moral virtues in various aspects of life. These virtues include justice, honesty, uniting the bonds of kinship, cooperation in beneficence and piety, discipline, truthfulness and chastity, honouring trusts and covenants, fidelity in privacy as well as in public, sincerity, moderation in poverty as well as in affluence, patience in suffering, adversity and agony through thick and thin, refraining from harming others with one's hands and tongue, and purifying the heart from all spiritual diseases like malice, jealousy, pretence, hypocrisy and love for worldly life. All these are the pillars of morality, without which the Muslim society does not rise nor stand.

Brotherhood and love

Brotherhood and affection are among the columns and pillars of Muslim society and indeed among the exigencies of the faith that unite the faithful with a strong bond of belief and declare them as brothers and sisters:

> *The believers are but a single brotherhood.* [49:10]

History and reality bear witness to the fact that there is no bond stronger than the bond of belief and that there is no belief more robust than Islam.

The lowest rank of the Islamic brotherhood is having hearts and minds free from jealousy and hatred, which have been considered by the *ḥadīth* as the "disease of nations" and "severers" (since jealousy and hatred sever piety from the individual). Allah praises the generation succeeding the companions of the Messenger (ṣ), saying:

> *And those who came after them say: "Our Lord! Forgive us, and our brethren who came before us into the Faith, and leave not, in our hearts, rancour (or sense of injury) against those who have believed. Our Lord! You are indeed Full of Kindness, Most Merciful."* [59:10]

The deeper the faith, the wider and stronger the brotherhood tends to be; having its shade and fruits within the self and in life. Along with this, the self is liberated from egocentricity and aspires to give rather than waiting for someone to offer, and to sacrifice rather than being opportunistic. The *ḥadīth* states: "One of you does not enjoy faith till he likes for his brother what he likes for himself."[35]

A strong fraternity can elevate one to the ranks of altruism, the quality with which Allah has labelled the society of the companions of the Messenger (ṣ) saying:

> *But those who before them, had homes (in Madīnah) and had adopted the Faith—show their affection to such as came to them for refuge, and entertain no desire in their hearts for things given to the (latter), but give them preference over themselves, even though poverty was their (own lot). And those saved from the covetousness of their own souls,—they are the ones that achieve prosperity.* [59:9]

Empathy and kindness

Empathy and mutual kindness are nothing but the fruits of a deeply bound brotherhood. The *ḥadīth* has portrayed this with brilliant eloquence:

> Notice the affection, empathy and mercifulness amongst the Muslims, as if they were one single body; that when any of its organs complained, all the other organs reciprocated to this pain with malaise and restlessness.[36]

---

35. Unanimously agreed upon; narrated through Anas; *al-Lu'lu' wa al-Marjān* (28).
36. Unanimously agreed upon; narrated through Nu'mān ibn Bashīr; *al-Lu'lu' wa al-Marjān* (1671).

Another *ḥadīth* puts it thus:

> The merciful are bestowed with mercy by the Most Merciful and the Exalted; be kind to those on the earth, and you shall be shown mercy by the One Who is in the heavens.[37]

Sympathy and mercy are even more desirable towards the weak such as orphans, the underprivileged, the stranded travellers, servants and the disabled. That is why the Qur'an has branded the people who ignore them and leave them hungry, unclothed and isolated, as manifestations of infidelity (towards humanity) and disbelief in the Day of Judgement:

> *See you one who denies the Judgement (to come)? Then such is the (man) who repulses the orphan (with harshness), And encourages not the feeding of the indigent.* [107:1-3]

In the same context, the Qur'an condemns pagan society, saying:

> *Nay, nay! But you honour not the orphans! Nor do you encourage one another to feed the poor!* [89:17-18]

The Qur'an depicts for us a scene of the Day of Judgement, wherein someone is receiving his book of deeds in his left hand; the wealth he had owned is of no benefit to him nor is the power he had possessed able to protect him; he is being humiliated and exposed:

> *(The stern command will say): Seize you him, and bind you him, and burn you him in the Blazing Fire. Further, make him march in a chain, whereof the length is seventy cubits! This was he that*

---

37. Narrated by Aḥmad, Abū Dāwūd, Tirmidhī and Ḥākim through Ibn 'Amr.

> *would not believe in Allah Most High. And would not encourage the feeding of the indigent!* [69:30-34]

Companionship and cooperation

Companionship and cooperation are the practical manifestation of brotherhood and mutual kindness. As elaborated by the Qur'an, the domain of Islamic cooperation consists of the deeds rooted in piety and devoutness, not in sin and aggression:

> *Help you one another in righteousness and piety, but help you not one another in sin and rancour.* [5:2]

This is the reason of prohibition of practices like usury and hoarding of goods through which the strong exploit the weak and the rich drain out the poor.

The Messenger of Allah (ṣ) has exemplified the Islamic concept of solidarity and cooperation through his magnificent saying:

> (The example of) one faithful to another faithful is that of an interlaced structure; (to illustrate this) he crossed his fingers.[38]

This includes cooperation between members of the public and its various groups as well as between the public and the ruler, just as the Qur'an has described the collaboration between Dhū al-Qarnayn and the community menaced by Gog and Magog:

38. Unanimously agreed upon; narrated through Abū Mūsā; *al-Lu'lu' wa al-Marjān* (1670).

He said: "(The power) in which my Lord has established me is better (than tribute); Help me therefore with strength (and labour): I will erect a strong barrier between you and them". [18:95]

Solidarity and mutual care

Solidarity and mutual care (so that the rich come forward to help and assist the downtrodden) are the characteristics of a society in which such people are not ignored. The least of this is giving out the obligatory dues of *zakāh*—the third pillar of the Islamic faith, which is protected by three things: first is the protection afforded by the conscience of the Muslim, that is his faith; the second is the protection of society in general, that is the Muslim public consensus; the third is the protection of the state which is in the form of law and authority. Allah says:

Of their goods, take alms, so that you might purify and sanctify them. [9:103]

In wealth, there are other rights too besides *zakāh*, especially the rights of the neighbour. This is in the form of moral protection which society vouchsafes for every neighbour during hardships and ease.

A *ḥadīth* emphasises this right by declaring: "He is not faithful who goes to bed with a full stomach while his neighbour is hungry."[39]

Islamic solidarity encompasses all aspects of life—material and abstract—including economics, education, science, literature and military, among others. The subject has been

39. Narrated by Bukhārī in *al-Adab al-Mufrad*, Ṭabarānī in *al-Kabīr*, Ḥākim in *al-Mustadrak* and Bayhaqī in *al-Sunan* through Ibn 'Abbās. Also narrated by Suyuṭī in *al-Jāmi' al-Ṣaghīr* (7583).

elaborated at length by Dr Muṣṭafā al-Sibā'ī in his book *Ishtirākiyyah al-Islām* (The Socialism of Islam).

Mutual guidance and advice

Mutual guidance and advice represent the moral solidarity of the Muslim society, which makes every Muslim responsible for the members of his or her society. Among the Muslims, there is no one who cannot be advised; there is also no one too small that makes him not eligible to give advice.

> *By (the Token of) Time (through the Ages), verily man is in loss, except such as have Faith, and do righteous deeds, and (join together) in the mutual teaching of Truth, and of Patience and Constancy.* [103:1-3]

> *The believers, men and women, are protectors of one another, they enjoin what is just, and forbid what is evil.* [9:71]

Likewise the *ḥadīth* says: "Religion is sincerity to Allah, to His Book, to His Messenger, and to the leaders and laymen of the Muslim community."[40] In another *ḥadīth*, it is stated: "A faithful person is the mirror of another faithful person."[41]

Chastity and moral pre-eminence

The Muslim society is one which is based on cleanliness, chastity and immaculate presentation. It forbids fornication, both open and hidden, and considers intoxicants and gambling as Satan's deeds; it ordains the faithful men and women to lower

40. Narrated by Muslim through Tamīm al-Dārī.
41. Narrated by Ṭabarānī in *Awṣaṭ* through Anas in *Ṣaḥīḥ al-Jāmi' al-Ṣaghīr* (6655).

their gaze and protect their private parts; it forbids shameless behaviour and seduction, whether verbal or physical, so that the sickness of heart does not ravage and revel in indecency without care for morality or religion.

Islamic society is not a society of infallible human beings, but when a Muslim is punished for wrongdoing, the shame humbles him so that he does not dare to boast about it or publicise it. Thus, fallout of his misconduct is contained and its sparks are not scattered. Having slipped, he is asked to repent with sincerity:

> *Allah loves those who turn to Him constantly and He loves those who keep themselves pure and clean.* [2:222]

Justice

Justice includes being just with fellow human beings while dealing with them in the affairs of life. Justice is an Islamic obligation and being unjust is forbidden, as the *ḥadīth qudṣī* (sacred saying) states, "O my slaves, I have denied injustice to myself and forbidden it amongst you, so do not be unfair between yourselves."[42]

Justice includes economic and social justice, which stands in the face of the wealthy so that they are restrained from oppressing the weak. It is instrumental in containing the transgression of the rich as much as it uplifts the poor by defining their rights in wealth—*zakāh* being the first, not the last.

Justice includes legal and judicial justice, so that every human being gets his due, even if it was from the most

42. Narrated by Muslim.

powerful. Even if a culprit happens to be the son of the caliph, he will be punished. The Messenger of Allah (ṣ) say: "By Allah, even if Fāṭimah, the daughter of Muḥammad, has committed theft, I would chop off her hand."[43]

An advanced society

Among the most important attributes of society which Islam establishes is that it is an advanced society.

This needs further elucidation. The word "advancement" or "progress" is a subjective term. Western civilisation today claims to be the civilisation of progress and that its societies are advanced societies, and that the Muslim societies and those of the so called "third world" are backward societies. At times they become somewhat polite and instead of labeling "backward", they label them "developing".

It is inevitable that we respond candidly to this fabrication by defining our stance with regard to progress, or, in other words, the stand of Islam regarding technological advancement.

The answer to this question demands that we first define advancement, because passing a judgement in favour of something or against it is the outcome of a definition of that thing.

Advancement in the ordinary usage implies someone being ahead of someone else; on the contrary, backwardness means being behind someone.

Advancement and backwardness are relative terms. You may be considered to be in the front in relation to a person behind you; you may be considered to be lagging behind in

43. Unanimously agreed upon.

respect of the person in front of you; you may even be in front of a group of the retarded persons, in which case, you are in forefront of the retarded!

Correlation of advancement and the goals of life

Advancement may be measured by correlating a goal that a person wants to achieve. Every movement towards the goal is considered as progress. This is in contrast to any movement in the opposite direction of the goal, because that, for sure, will only take one backwards.

Similarly, the stagnation of someone without moving forwards or backwards, is in itself backwardness, because it gives another person the chance to move forward, while the former is static. This means that he is being left behind by those who continue to step forward. This is especially true in this context, because human beings are a dynamic species.

The question may be asked: what is the goal or goals which humans should strive to succeed in their lifetime, so that proximity to such goals or distances thereof can be taken as the yardstick of progress or backwardness?

Basic goals of human life

Islam sets some basic goals for human existence on earth. The salient features among these goals, as the Qur'an defines, are three. These have been mentioned by Imam Rāghib al-Aṣfahānī in his brilliant book *al-Dharī'ah ilā Makārim al-Sharī'ah* (The Means Towards the Noble Deeds of Sharī'ah):

> Worship of Allah: This has been referred to and elucidated by the divine saying:

I have only created Jinns and men, that they may serve Me. [51:56]

Vicegerent of Allah on earth: This has been referred to and elucidated by the divine saying:

I will create a vicegerent on earth... [2:30]

...and make you inheritors in the earth; that so He may try you by your deeds. [7:129]

Development of the earth: This has been referred to and elucidated by the divine saying:

O my people! Worship Allah: You have no other god but Him. It is He Who has produced you from the earth and settled you therein... [11:61]

Comprehensive advancement

The advancement envisioned by Islam is holistic and comprehensive. It is spiritual and material, moral and civilised, worldly and otherworldly, and scientific and religious, yet instead of conflict between these contradictions, Islam combines them with a beautiful balance and congruity.

It is advancement in goals and objectives, and progress in means and methods at the same time. Islam is keen about the means as it is about the end. In no way does it accept reaching a noble end through unethical means; it, rather, rejects outright the notion of reaching truth by way of untruth; it rejects the use of illicit money and usury, for example, in the construction of mosques and schools, because Allah accepts nothing but good.

In light of such a comprehensive concept of advancement, stood the towering edifice of Islamic civilization, combining the material marvels, in the form of dazzling architectural wonders and artistic innovations, and the religious and moral notions that were the real propellant behind these innovations. In fact, faith and morality were the bolsters of that civilization, the manifestations and achievements of which continue to strike awe in people and who exclaim: this is nothing but a divinely inspired civilization, revolving around faith and morality.

BUILDING A RIGHTEOUS NATION

Among the objectives of Islam is to build a nation of excellence that implements its message, establishes its life on the basis of its belief and Sharīʿah, brings its generations to its guidance and reaches with its message the whole world, carrying along with it the mercy, the light and the beneficence for the whole mankind. Allah says:

We sent you not, but as a Mercy for all creatures. [21:107]

Given the well known circumstances in which Islam emanated, building such a nation was not an easy task. Islam was born in the Arabian peninsula, where life rested on tribal partisanship. The tribe was the basis of allegiance and loyalty; it was the source of pride and affiliation; there was no place for the son of the tribe except within the fold of the tribe; rather, one did not exist except with it. The tribe was one's lineage and descent; it was its power and strength; it was the economy and the polity. With its pleasure, one was pleased; with its anger or with the annoyance of one of its chieftain, one could be ostracised . One would side with his tribesman irrespective of whether he was right or wrong; the motto and the slogan was: "Help your brother—*i.e.*, the fellow tribesman, whether he is wrongful or the aggrieved." It is said that the chieftain of a large tribe was described as: "The man that when he is enraged, with him are enraged a hundred thousand swords; and none questioned what enraged him!"

Every tribe used to try to rise above the other tribe and attempted to clip its wings. This was the reason aggressions on each other had remained unabated. A poet said:

> At times we would attack even our brother tribe Bakr,
> When we found none other than our brother to invade.

Then when Islam came, it brought with it a paradigm shift, a transformation of their conscience and a turning point in the state of their affairs. Islam freed them from the prison of tribalism to the open sphere of a Nation of Faith; it admonished prejudices and negative partisanship, especially those of tribalism. Muḥammad the Messenger of Allah (ṣ) said:

> He does not belong to us, the one who calls to tribal bigotry or fights for that or dies for that...[44]

> ... who fights under the banner of blindness (of prejudice), infuriated by bias of his clan, or calls to tribal bigotry or supports someone on such a pretext and gets killed, his death is the death of paganism.[45]

---

44. Narrated by Abū Dāwūd in "*al-Adab*", 1521, through Jubayr ibn Muṭ'im; although a week narration, it has been cited by Muslim who came after him.
45. Narrated by Muslim in "*al-Imārah*", 1848, through Abū Hurayrah.

When asked what "bigotry" was, he replied, "(It means) that you support your people on injustices."[46] Indeed, he interpreted it in light of its influence on the prevailing situation of his own pagan society, where a bigot would side with his tribe even if it oppressed and perpetrated injustice, and would be against its opponents even if they were righteous or were the victims. This was against the spirit of Islam, which came to establish justice:

> *O you who believe! stand out firmly for justice, as witnesses to Allah, even as against yourselves, or your parents, or your kin...* [4:135]

> *And let not the hatred of others to you make you swerve to wrong and depart from justice. Be just: that is next to piety: and fear Allah.* [5:8]

In some moments of human weakness, the tribal inclination surfaced with some of the Companions and they addressed fellow tribesmen with "O the sons of so and so". Hearing this the Messenger of Allah (ṣ) was furious and said, "(How come) there is a call of paganism, while I am in the midst of you?!"[47] This was the occasion when he uttered his unequivocal statement about tribal bigotry "Give it up, it is a vile stuff."[48]

Islam aims at building a nation on the basis of belief and ideology, not on any material or earthly basis. This is unlike what humans, who build nations on the basis of race, colour, language or region, where humans have neither a choice nor preference and have been imposed upon from birth; no one

46. Narrated by Abū Dāwūd in "*al-Adab*", 5119, through Wāthilah bin al-Asqa'; also narrated by Ibn Mājah in *al-Fitan*, 3949.
47. Mentioned by Ibn Kathīr in his interpretation of the Qur'an through Ibn Isḥāq; 1/389.
48. Narrated by Bukhārī.

selects his race or colour or language or the land he is born in; everyone inherits such circumstances.

As far as belief is concerned, it essentially falls within the scope of human choice. In fact, acceptance of blind faith is open to doubt; such faith is actually invalidated by many authentic Muslim scholars.

Islam desires that the Muslim be the nation affiliated with the Truth, and not personality. The Islamic nation does not rise on the basis of race, colour or class. It is the nation of belief and a message.

This is the nation of Islam, or the nation of the Muslims. As Allah says:

> *It is He Who has named you Muslims, both before and in this (Revelation); that the Messenger may be a witness for you, and you be witnesses for mankind!* [22:78]

That is the nation of faith or the nation of the faithful. That is why it is always addressed by the Qur'an as "O you who believe!"

Depiction of the Islamic nation in the Qur'an

The outstanding attributes which distinguish this nation from all others are the following:

Divine nation

First of all, it is divine because of its divine source and subsequently divine course. It is the nation established by revelation from Allah, His guidance and instructions tended to it until its religion was perfected and thus His benefaction on it completed.

Allah says:

This day have I perfected your religion for you, completed My favour upon you, and have chosen for you Islam as your religion [5:3]

Allah is the maker of this nation, He says:

Thus, have We made of you an Ummah justly balanced. [2:143]

The expression "We made" denotes that God is the Maker, Moulder and Designer of this nation. Respectively Allah says:

You are the best of peoples, evolved for mankind. [3:110]

The expression "evolved" indicates that there is an Evolver who evolved this nation. It did not appear randomly and aimlessly, nor was it like a wild plant that grows without the care of a cultivator. It was a desired plant that enjoyed protection and care. The one, who evolved this nation, cultivated it and prepared it for its eternal message and marvellous mission, is none other than God Himself.

This is the nation, whose source is divine and whose course too is divine, because it lives for Allah and for His worship, and for the actualisation of His divine order on the earth. Indeed, it comes from Allah and will return to Allah,[49] as Allah instructs His Messenger:

Say: "Truly, my prayer and my service of sacrifice, my life and my death, are (all) for Allah, the Cherisher of the Worlds: No partner has He: this am I commanded, and I am the first of those who bow to His will. [6:162-163]

---

49. Please refer to the chapter "Rabbāniyyah" in my *al-Khaṣā'iṣ al-'Āmah fī. al-Islām.*

Moderate nation

The second attribute, moderation, qualifies the Muslim nation for acting as a witness over all people and for assuming the status of teacher for humankind. In this regard Allah says:

> *Thus, have We made of you an Ummah justly balanced, that you might be witnesses over the nations, and the Messenger a witness over yourselves.* [2:143]

This moderation is comprehensive and all-embracing: moderation of belief and concept, rituals and worship, morals and behaviour, systems and legislation, and thought and emotion.

This also applies equilibrium and the harmony between spirituality and materiality, idealism and realism, and individualism and collectivism.[50]

Indeed it is the nation that represents the straight path in the midst of zigzag routes and tortuous tracks. It is the path of Allah, Who holds the sovereignty of the heavens and the earth; it is the path of those bestowed with His favours, from the prophets, the truthful, the martyrs and the righteous; it is not the path of those whose portion is wrath or of those who go astray.

Nation of the Call (Daʿwah)

Muslims are the nation of the divine call and heavenly mission; not a nation cocooned within itself or who have a monopoly over truth, righteousness and guidance, not to spreading them to their fellow human beings. Indeed calling (to Islam)

---

50. Please refer to the chapter "Waṣaṭiyyah" in my *al-Khaṣā'iṣ al-ʿĀmah fī al-Islām*.

being obligatory, enjoining virtue and forbidding vice, along with faith in Allah, form the basis and is the reason why it is preferred over all other nations. This is affirmed by Allah saying:

> *You are the best of peoples evolved for mankind, enjoining what is right, forbidding what is wrong, and believing in Allah.* [3:110]

Certainly, it did not outweigh other nations in the divine balance, due to some material or racial merit. How could that be so when this nation is comprised of people of diverse races who embrace the religion of Allah from amongst Arabs and non-Arabs?!

The nation of Islam has outweighed others, in the divine balance, due to its capacity of enjoining virtue and forbidding vice. Preceding the above Qur'anic verse, another verse states:

> *Let there arise out of you a band of people inviting to all that is good, enjoining what is right, and forbidding what is wrong: They are the ones to attain felicity.* [3:104]

The verse has been interpreted in two ways. According to one, it commands Muslims to transform themselves into the Nation of the Call who enjoin the right and forbid the wrong, which would qualify them exclusively for the attainment of felicity. This interpretation is inclusive and makes the whole nation responsible for the Mission.

Another interpretation sees it as a representative obligation, in the sense that Muslims collectively must delegate the duty of the Call and of enjoining the right and forbidding the wrong to a section of capable and competent people from amongst them.

The message of Islam is universal; it is for the people of all races, colours, regions, groups, languages, and classes. God says:

> *We sent you not, but as a Mercy for all creatures.* [21:107]

> *Blessed is He who sent down the criterion to His servant, that it may be an admonition to all creatures.* [25:1]

> *Say: "O men! I am sent unto you all, as the Messenger of God...* [7:158]

It is incumbent upon the nation of Islam to call the whole of humankind towards Islam in their respective languages to manifest to them the truth of Islam and to fulfil the duty of reaching out and leaving no plea for anyone to remain in darkness; it is essential to enjoin virtue and forbid vice lest they (Muslims) shall be cursed like those who were cursed before them for neglecting and abandoning this duty. Allah says:

> *Curses were pronounced on those among the Children of Israel who rejected Faith, by the tongue of David and of Jesus the son of Mary: because they disobeyed and persisted in excesses. Nor did they (usually) forbid one another the iniquities which they committed: evil indeed were the deeds which they did.* [5:78-79]

Nation of unity

The nation that Islam seeks to build is a united nation, whatsoever may be its constituents in terms of race, colour or class. Islam fuses all these differences into its melting pot and binds them together with a most trustworthy and unbreakable bond. Allah says:

Verily, this brotherhood of yours is a single brotherhood, and I am your Lord and Cherisher: therefore serve Me (and no other). [21:92]

And verily this Brotherhood of yours is a single Brotherhood, and I am your Lord and Cherisher: therefore fear Me (and no other). [23:52]

Allah has unified its belief and Sharī'ah, unified its purpose and unified its course. Allah says:

Verily, this is My way, leading straight: follow it: follow not (other) paths: they will scatter you about from His (great) path... [6:153]

A nation whose God is the One and only God, whose messenger is Muḥammad (ṣ), whose Book is the Qur'an, whose direction of prayer is the Ka'bah, whose law is the Sharī'ah of Islam, whose homeland is the vast House of Islam and whose leadership personifies the political unity of the Islamic nation.

For this reason, Islam disapproves that there be two leaders for the Muslims at the same time, with the purpose of upholding the unity of the Nation and preventing disunity and discord within it.

The Nation of Islam is one nation, as ordained by Allah, rather than being scattered nations, as desired by the imperialists. God says:

And hold fast, all together, by the rope which Allah (stretches out for you), and be not divided among yourselves... [3:103]

Be not like those who are divided amongst themselves and fall into disputations after receiving Clear Signs: For them is a dreadful penalty. [3:105]

The Qur'an has warned against the plots of some People of the Book, who work hard to break the unity of the Muslims and instigate sectarian feuds. Allah has warned:

> *O you who believe! If you listen to a faction among the People of the Book, they would (indeed) render you apostates after you have believed!* [3:100]

The context of revelation of this and subsequent verses implies that they would indeed divide Muslims into factions after having been united by Islam and into enemies after having been brethren.

The unity of the nation makes it obligatory upon the Nation of Islam to uphold the Islamic brotherhood above all partisanships and biases, as Allah regards it as an indicator and embodiment of faith:

> *The Believers are but a single Brotherhood...* [49:10]

The Messenger of Allah (ṣ) says:

> A Muslim is the brother of another Muslim; he does not harm him nor does abandon him.[51]

Another *ḥadīth* confirms and emphasises the same:

> The Muslims are equal with respect to blood. The lowest of them are entitled to give protection on behalf of them, and the one residing far away may give protection on behalf of them. They are like one hand against all those who are outside the community...[52]

---

51. Unanimously agreed upon; narrated through Ibn 'Umar, *Ṣaḥīḥ al-Jāmi' al-Ṣaghīr.*
52. Narrated through 'Abdullah ibn 'Umar, by Abū Dāwūd in chapter "al-Jihād" (2751); by Ibn Mājah (2852); translation of Prof. Ahmad Hasan at http://www.masmn.org/documents/hadith/sunan_abu_dawud/014.htm.

Islam warns Muslims against harbouring mutual enmity to the extent that it leads to infighting as in the case of pre-Islamic pagan tribes. The Messenger of Allah (ṣ) says: "Do not revert as infidels beheading each other",[53] and "insulting a Muslim is dissoluteness and fighting him is infidelity".[54]

Faith in the Nation does not negate peculiarities of groups

It will be useful to caution about something relevant in this regard. Faith in the Nation established on the basis of the Islamic belief and on the brotherhood of faith that embraces all the Muslims under its magnanimity, wherever they may be, does not negate the fact that there are cultural peculiarities in every people, of which they feel proud, which they preserve and about which they cannot be remiss. There is no problem with this as long as these cultural peculiarities do not assume the form of ethnic bigotry resisting Islamic brotherhood or do not grow into egotistic separatism threatening the solidarity of the state of Islam.

The Messenger of Allah (ṣ) did allow the tribes to fight under their respective tribal banners operating under the general Islamic command, as did the Rightly Guided Caliphs, so that it can be a source of enthusiasm and encouragement because they would not like to let down their tribes and kinsfolk.

> Certainly, the love of a person for his people and kinsfolk, his desire to earn benefit for them and to ward off vice from

---

53. Unanimously agreed upon; narrated through Jarīr Ibn 'Abdullah (as in *al-Lu'lu' wa al-Marjān*, 44); through 'Abdullah ibn 'Umar (45).
54. Unanimously agreed upon; narrated through Ibn Mas'ūd (as in *al-Lu'lu' wa al-Marjān* (43).

them is a natural instinct that is not unpleasant and there is no danger hidden therein, just as there is no peril in his love and care for his family. No wonder that the Messenger of Allah (ṣ) directed his companions to gain knowledge of lineage of their tribes, because it implied uniting the bonds of kinship even if they seemed distant. He said, "Know about your lineage to be able to unite the bonds of your kinship"[55].

Another *ḥadīth* reads:

The best amongst you is the defender of his clan, as long as he does not commit sin.[56]

The lies in the situation whereby his clan takes a hostile position against Islam. In such a situation loyalty is forbidden, however close may be the kinship. Allah says:

You will not find any people who believe in Allah and the Last Day, loving those who resist Allah and His Messenger, even though they were their fathers or their sons, or their brothers, or their kindred... [58:22]

O you who believe! Take not for protectors your fathers and your brothers if they love infidelity above Faith: if any of you do so, they do wrong. Say: If it be that your fathers, your sons, your brothers, your mates, or your kindred; the wealth that you have gained; the commerce in which you fear a decline: or the dwellings in which you delight—are dearer to you than Allah, or His Messenger, or

---

55. Narrated by Tirmidhī through Abū Hurayrah, saying that it was amazing from this aspect (1980); Also narrated by Aḥmad: 2/374, as well as by Ḥākim; Considered genuine by Dhahabī 4/161.
56. Narrated by Abū Dāwūd through Surāqah bin Mālik (in "al-Adab", 5120).

the striving in His cause;—then wait until Allah brings about His decision: and Allah guides not the rebellious. [9:23-24]

There is nothing wrong to be devoted to one's family, tribe or clan, as long as it does not conflict with the adoration of Allah and devotion to His Messenger (ṣ), as a poet once said:

My pedigree is Islam and none except Islam
If they boast of their lineage to Qays or Tamīm!

In such a state the Muslim says the same as what Salmān al-Fārisī said. When asked, "Whose son are you?" he replied, "I am the son of Islam!"

Nationalism according to Ḥasan al-Bannā

This meaning was very clear to Ḥasan al-Bannā. He did not reject 'nationalism' outright nor did he accept it unqualified. His stance regarding it was unequivocal just like his stance on patriotism. He said:

If those who are proud of the ideology of 'nationalism' intend with it that the successors must follow the path of the ancestor towards attaining the heights of glory and magnificence and conquering the orbit of excellence and exuberance; if they want to follow their footsteps as being their virtuous models; if they mean that the glory of the father is adored by his son, because—due to bond of blood and heredity—he finds in it zealousness and benevolent exhilaration, then that is a worthy and handsome purpose and we support and espouse it. Certainly our stock-in-trade for awakening the aspirations of the living generation is to stimulate them with the glory of their ancestors. Perhaps there is a hint to this in the saying

> of the Messenger of Allah (ṣ) when he said: "People are minerals; the best of them during the days of paganism will be the best of them in Islam, provided they comprehend".[57] Here we see that Islam is not averse to nationalism per se in this virtuous noble sense.

If nationalism means that a clan or tribe is more deserving of one's generosity and benevolence and more entitled to his kindness and struggle, this meaning too is correct. Who does not view his kinsfolk, among whom he was raised, worthier of the fruits of his hard labour? A poet once said:

> Certainly the tribe of a person remains the most deserving
> than anyone else,
> Even after they might have reached the heights of glory
> because of him.

If by nationalism people mean that when all of us have been afflicted, we are called upon to strive and struggle and that every group has to do its best and achieve the target, then blessed is such a division of labour. We are indeed in need of someone who can drive forward the nations with their resources, until all of us converge in prosperity, crowned with freedom and liberty.

Such forms and shades of nationalism are not disdained by Islam. Islam being our yardstick and touchstone, our hearts open to such notions and causes.

On the other hand, there is nationalism which seeks to restore pagan customs, to revive bygone memories, to restore a prosperous civilisation that once settled and sought

57. Unanimously agreed upon through Abū Hurayrah as in *Ṣaḥīḥ al-Jāmiʿ al-Ṣaghīr*".

to disentangle from Islam, all on the pretext of ethnic pride. Some countries, out of their overzealousness, destroyed all manifestations of Islamic and Arab unity; they got rid of Arabic names, the Arabic script and vocabulary, and revived pagan customs. Such notions of nationalism are deemed abhorrent, its consequences are noxious and its outcome is vice. It shall lead it to disaster, where it will lose its heritage; with it, it shall fall from grace and forfeit its most prominent characteristics and the most sacred manifestations of its nobility. Certainly the religion of Allah shall not be harmed by this:

> *If you turn back (from the Path), He will substitute in your stead another people; then they would not be like you!* [47:38]

If nationalism means to take pride in ethnicity to the extent that it leads to the disparagement of other communities, to aggression against them and to their immolation for the sake of honour and to preserve the purity of a certain race, just as Germany and Italy called to that end or as do all those nations which consider themselves superior to others, then such an obnoxious notion of nationalism has nothing to do with humanness; it means that humankind wrangles for the sake of an unholy fantasy.

The Islamic brotherhood does not believe in such nationalism or philosophies; it does not call itself as Pharaoic, Arab, Phoenician or Syrian nor associate itself with any such names and titles with which people identify themselves. The Prophet (ṣ) has said:

> Allah has driven away the arrogance of the (pre-Islamic) days of ignorance and the vainglory of pedigree; the ancestry of all people goes back to Adam, and Adam was (created) from

> clay; an Arab enjoys no superiority over a non-Arab, except by piety.[58]

How beautiful are these words, declaring that all human beings belong to Adam, that all equally belong to this (lineage), and that superiority is qualified through noble actions, thus they must compete through righteous deeds. Indeed, these are the two such strong pillars that if the edifice of humanity was raised on such concepts, humanity would rise on them to reach the skies. People descend from Adam, thus they are brethren, hence they must cooperate and become reconciled with each other; they must be merciful to each other; they must guide each other to righteousness. Superiority is based on deeds; they all must strive from their respective positions for the elevation of humanity at large. Is there anything loftier than this exaltedness?

Peculiarities of Arab culture

Ḥasan al-Bannā says further:

> In spite of this, we do not negate specialities of different peoples and their distinctive natural characteristics. We are conscious that every people have their own distinctions and shares of nobility and morality; certainly there is respective variance and (degrees of) superiority; we believe that the Arab character has been blessed more amply and abundantly, but this does not mean that people should make their characteristics the pretext for antagonism against

58. Narrated by Abū Dāwūd in "al-Adab", 5116; Tirmidhī in "al-Manāqib", 3950; Aḥmad and Bayhaqī through Abū Hurayrah; also refer to my *al-Muntaqā min al-Targhīb wa al-Tarhīb* (No. 1792).

> others; instead, they should utilise their advantages as means of achieving the mission assigned originally to every people, *i.e.*, to endeavour for advancement of humankind. You may perhaps not come across in whole of the history any people who might have realised this reality as did that Arab group, the noble companions of the Messenger of Allah (ṣ).

This means that Imam al-Bannā did not see any sense in erecting a superfluous barrier of inconsistency between the Arab character and Islam.

BUILDING A RIGHTEOUS STATE

Just as Islam seeks to establish a righteous nation to uphold the mission of godliness, humanism, morality and universalism, it also seeks that this nation should rule a state which will achieve its goals, advance its characteristics, uphold its message and strive to inculcate it within and to promote it outside.

The imperialism that subjugated most parts of the Muslim world managed to inculcate in many Muslims an alien notion suggesting that Islam is a religion and not a state; in other words it is a 'religion' in the Western sense of the word having nothing to do with the affairs of the state, because these are regulated by human reasoning in light of its continued experiments and ever changing circumstances.

The imperialists wanted to impose upon Islam in the East that which was imposed upon Christianity in the West. They believed that since their own renaissance was not accomplished except after liberation from the ascendancy of religion, it was imperative that the renaissance of the Islamic East too must be on the rubbles of religion.

This is in spite of the fact that religion to them meant the church and the papal authority, and despotism of the clergy over consciences and souls; whereas there is nothing like that in Islam—no pope or priesthood nor despotism over consciences and souls.[59]

However, colonialism has been able to hatch groups that believe that religion has no role in regulating the state and that religion and politics are different. They believe this notion of theirs applies to Islam as it applied to Christianity. Among the misguiding slogans that were spread, was the slogan that "religion is for God and the homeland is for all!". This is a slogan of truth coined for falsehood, as it can be turned on any side; one can say, "Religion is for God and the homeland too is for God" or "The religion is for all and the homeland too is for all" or "The religion is for all and the homeland is for God."

What they intend from the slogan '"Religion is for God", is that religion is merely between the conscience of a person and his God and there is no place for Him in the system of life and society.

The most famous example of this notion was the 'secular state' which Mustafa Kamal established in Turkey and imposed with an iron fist on the Muslims in Turkey after having demolished the Ottoman caliphate. This was the last political bastion left for Islam after centuries-old conflict with the Crusaders and the international Jewry.

---

59. Refer to the chapter "Religion and State" in Muḥammad al-Bahī, *al-Fikr al-Islāmī al-Ḥadīth wa ṣilatuh bi al-Isti'mār al-Gharbī*. Also, please refer to the chapter "Dawlah Islāmiyyah lā Dawlah Dīniyyah" of my *Bayanāt al-Ḥall al-Islāmī wa Shubuhāt al-'Ilmāniyyīn wa al-Muttagharibīn*.

Since then governments in the Muslim countries have imitated Turkey with varying degrees. Islam was excluded from administration and legislation and was secluded to what was named 'personal law'; it was also barred from influencing cultural, educational and social life, except to trivialities. The gates were set wide open for Western-style orientation, for Western culture and customs.

One outstanding manifestation of the Western cultural attack was that of the 'secular ideology', which kept religion free from the affairs of the state. The secular ideology influenced even those who studied at al-Azhar, the seat of Islamic learning.

It was imperative to emphatically stand in the face of secularism, its precursors and its justifications, by asserting the comprehensiveness of Islam and to expose this living dimension of its teachings and commandments, *i.e.*, the dimension of state and ethics. It was all the more essential to declare that politics is part and parcel of the system of Islam.

Basis in Islamic texts

This was not an innovation by the Islamic movement and its thinkers. It was rather what the texts of Islam, its history and its mission elucidate unequivocally.

From its source texts, it is sufficient to cite just two verses of Sūrah al-Nisā':

> *Allah does command you to render back your trusts to those to whom they are due; and when you judge between man and man, that you judge with justice: verily how excellent is the teaching which He gives you! For Allah is He Who hears and sees all things.*

> *O you who believe! Obey Allah, and obey the Messenger, and those charged with authority among you. If you differ in anything among yourselves, refer it to Allah and His Messenger, if you do believe in Allah and the Last Day: That is best, and most suitable for final determination.* [4:58-59]

The address in the first verse is to the rulers and the judiciary. They are required to safeguard trusts and judge with justice, because squandering trusts and undermining justice will destroy the state. The Messenger of Allah (ṣ) has warned:

> When trusts are squandered, people should expect the (nearness of) the Day of Judgement. (When asked how these could be squandered, he replied): When affairs are entrusted to those who are inappropriate then expect (the nearness of) the Day of Judgement.[60]

The address in the second verse is to the subjects of the state. They are asked to obey "those charged with authority" provided they are "from amongst them". Their obedience has been mentioned next after obedience to Allah and His Messenger. They are also commanded that in case of a dispute, they must refer their differences to Allah and His Messenger (the Qur'an and the Sunnah). All this implies that Muslims must have their own state which should be obeyed, else such commandments would be absurd.

In light of the above verses, Ibn Taymiyyah penned his famous book *al-Siyāsah al-Shar'iyyah fī Iṣlāḥ al-Rā'ī wa al-Ra'iyyah* (Sharī'ah Based Politics Towards Reformation of the Ruler and the Ruled). The subject matter of the work is based on these verses.

---

60. Narrated by al-Bukhārī, through Abū Hurayrah, in the Book of Knowledge (Ḥadīth 59, al-Fatḥ:1/141); repeated in the Book of Slaves.

When we look into the Sunnah, we find the Messenger of Allah (ṣ) saying, "He who dies without having the pledge of allegiance tied to his neck, dies the death of paganism."[61] Certainly, it is illegitimate for the Muslim to pledge allegiance to any ruler who does not adhere to Islam. In light of the *ḥadīth*, only that pledge of allegiance can save him from sin, if pledged to one who rules by the divine revelation. Until then, Muslims are committing sin; with the establishment of the Islamic rule, the desired pledge of allegiance becomes a reality. The Muslims cannot be saved from this sinfulness but by two things: first, by renunciation—even if it is with the heart and mind—of the situation that is deviant to the Sharī'ah of Islam; secondly, by their endeavour for the revival of the Islamic way of life, guided by genuine Islamic government.

In fact there are many *ḥadīths* on governance, judiciary, leadership and its attributes, responsibilities in the form of establishing the Islamic penal code, safeguard of civil rights, taking the righteous as advisors, establishing prayers, paying *zakāh*, enjoining virtue and forbidding vice, and many other subjects of governance and administration.

This is why affairs of the Muslim state and government have been described in the books about beliefs and doctrines of faith as well as in works of jurisprudence. There are books about the constitutional, administrative, financial and political affairs of the state, for example: *al-Aḥkām al-Sulṭāniyyah* (The Laws of Governance) by al-Māwardī and Abū Ya'lā, *al-Ghiyāthī* (The Succouring) by Imam al-Ḥaramayn, *al-Siyāsah al-Shar'iyyah fī Iṣlāḥ al-Rā'ī wa al-Ra'iyyah* (Sharī'ah Based Polity Towards

61. Narrated by Muslim through Ibn 'Umar, in the book of *al-Imārah*, No. 1851.

Reformation of the Ruler and the Ruled) by Ibn Taymiyyah, *Taḥrīr al-Aḥkām* (Writing the Laws) of Ibn Jamā'ah, *al-Kharāj* (The Tribute) by Abū Yūsuf and Yaḥyā ibn Ādam, and *al-Amwāl* by Abū 'Ubayd and Ibn Zanjuwayh. Likewise there are works that were intended to serve as books of references for judges, and rulers, like *al-Ṭuruq al-Ḥukmiyyah* (Methods of Governance), *al-Tabṣirah* (The Enlightenment) and *Mu'īn al-Aḥkām* (Assistant to Adjudications).

Historical basis

As far as the history of Islam is concerned, it conveys to us that the Messenger of Allah (ṣ), supported by the revelation, strived with all his power and intellect to establish an Islamic State and a homeland for the Islamic call, purely for the faithful, wherein there shall be no authority over them except the Sharī'ah. To achieve this goal, he first invited different Arab tribes to believe in him, defend him and protect his mission, until Allah blessed his supporters of Madīnah, those of Aws and Khazraj tribes, with faith in his message and mission. When Islam began to spread among the people of Madīnah, a delegation comprising 73 men and women came to Makkah during the hajj season. They pledged their allegiance to him, to defend him and obey him, and to enjoin virtue and forbid vice. After their pledge of allegiance, the Migration (*Hijrah*) took place. The migration to Madīnah was solely to establish the distinguished Islamic society overseen by the Islamic state.

Madīnah became the *Dār al-Islām* (House of Islam) and base of the new Islamic state headed by the Messenger of Allah (ṣ). He was the commander and supreme leader of the Muslims, as well as the Prophet and Messenger of Allah (ṣ).

Joining this state, supporting it, living in its shade and fighting under its banner were an obligation upon whosoever embraced Islam at that time. One's faith was not complete without migrating to the House of Islam, abandoning the House of *Kufr* (disbelief), falling in line with the party of faith and struggle, against which all worldly forces converged. Allah says:

> *As to those who believed but came not into exile, you owe no duty of protection to them until they come into exile.* [8:72]

> *But take not friends from their ranks until they flee in the way of Allah (from what is forbidden).* [4:89]

The Qur'an also condemns those who chose to live in the House of Kufr without being able to establish their religion and fulfil their obligations and rites. When the angels take the souls of those who die in sin against their souls:

> *Say: "In what (plight) were you?" They reply: "Weak and oppressed were we in the earth." They say: "Was not the earth of Allah spacious enough for you to move yourselves away (from evil)?" Such men will find their abode in Hell—what an evil refuge! Except those who are (really) weak and oppressed—men, women, and children—who have no means in their power, nor (a guide-post) to their way. For these, there is hope that Allah will forgive: For Allah does blot out (sins) and forgive again and again.* [4:97-99]

At the time of the death of the Messenger of Allah (ṣ), the foremost issue that occupied his Companions was to appoint the supreme leader for themselves. They prioritised this even over his burial. Thereupon they proceeded to pledge allegiance to Abū Bakr entrusting him to look after their affairs. This continued afterwards. Keeping in view such historical consensus from the times of the Companions and the generation succeeding them, the scholars of Islam have derived that it is mandatory to appoint an Imam, because he symbolises the Islamic state.

Throughout their history, Muslims did not know of a schism between religion and state. This is an innovation of secularism in this age and has been forewarned by the Messenger of Allah (ṣ), saying (as reported by Mu'ādh):

> Behold! The wheel of Islam is spinning; keep revolving around the axis of Islam; the Qur'an and the ṣulṭān (*i.e.*, the religion and the state) are going to break off; thereupon, do not part with the Book. (Time will come when) there will be rulers over you, who will prescribe for themselves contrary to what they will enjoin upon you; if you will disobey them, they will kill you, and if you will obey them, they will lead you astray.

When asked for guidance during such times, he replied,

> Do as the companions of Jesus, the son of Mary, did; they were sawn with saws and hung on the gallows. Death in obedience of Allah is better than a life of disobedience to Him.[62]

---

62. Narrated by Isḥāq bin Rāhawayh in his *Musnad* through Suwayd bin 'Abd al-'Azīz (who is a weak reporter); also narrated by Aḥmad bin Manī' through reliable reporters (as opinioned by al-Buṣayrī in *al-Itḥāf*). Please refer to *al-Maṭālib al-'Āliyah* by Ibn Ḥajar (Vol. 4; *ḥadīth* no: 4408, edited by Shaykh Ḥabīb al-Raḥmān al-A'ẓamī, published by Awqāf, Kuwait). Also narrated by Ṭabarānī.

Basis in Islamic nature

The composition of Islam and its message is a universal religion and comprehensive code of conduct. Due to this composition, it is destined to penetrate all aspects and dimensions of life. It is unimaginable that it could have overlooked governance and left it to the whims and fancies of the dissolute or to the labyrinths of philosophical thought.

Likewise, the religion of Islam calls for structuring and designation of responsibility; it abhors disturbance and disorder. During the congregational prayers, the Messenger of Allah (ṣ) teaches us that we must straighten the rows and that the most knowledgeable should lead the prayers. Even when travelling, he instructs us saying, "Choose one of you as your leader."

Ibn Taymiyyah writes in his book *al-Siyāsah al-Shar'iyyah* (Sharī'ah Based Politics):

> It must be known that custodianship of the peoples' affairs is one of the greatest obligations of the religion; In fact, religion and worldly life have no standing except with it. The well-being of humans cannot be realised except with social cooperation, because of their need of each other. Hence, when they get together, there has to be a head. The Messenger of Allah (ṣ), said: "If three persons embark on travel, they must choose one of them as their leader"[63]. Imam Aḥmad narrates through 'Abdullah ibn 'Amr that the Messenger of Allah (ṣ) said: "It is not allowed for three to be present in any part of the globe without having elected one of them as a leader." Thus he made it obligatory to choose a

63. Narrated by Abū Dāwūd through Abū Sa'īd and Abū Hurayrah; also narrated by Ṭabarānī (*Majma' al-Zawā'id*; 5/249).

> leader even during an incidental gathering while on travel, cautioning thereby about the necessity of leadership in all social situations.
>
> Since Allah the Almighty has made enjoining virtue and forbidding vice obligatory, and that this obligation cannot be accomplished without power and position just as all other obligations like *jihād*, justice, celebrating and facilitating hajj, Friday prayers and Islamic festivals of Eid, championing the cause of the oppressed and implementing penalties cannot be accomplished without power and position. It has been narrated that "verily the position of authority is Allah's shade in the earth." This was the reason that our pious predecessors like al-Fuḍayl ibn 'Iyāḍ and Aḥmad ibn Ḥanbal used to say: "If we had a supplication granted (by Allah), we would pray for authority."[64] This is simply because with the righteousness of authority, Allah reforms masses of people.

Moreover, the nature of Islam being a system that required to rule, lead, move life, govern the society and steer the course of human life along the path of divine guidance, it is unthinkable that rhetoric, exhortation and moral discourse would suffice as its mission, or that it can leave its commandments, precepts and directives for diverse aspects of life to the people's conscience alone, so that when these consciences weaken or perish, the commandments and percepts also weaken and perish alongside it. The third Rightly Guided Caliph, 'Uthmān has summarised this by saying, "Certainly Allah restrains with the authority of power what is not be held back with the Qur'an."

---

64. *Al-Siyāsah al-Shar'iyyah* (included in the *Fatāwā* of Ibn Taymiyyah; 28/390-391).

Among the people, there are those who attain guidance from the book and the criterion, and among them, there are those who cannot be deterred except by strict means. Allah says:

> *We sent aforetime our apostles with Clear Signs and sent down with them the Book and the Balance (of Right and Wrong), that men may stand forth in justice; and We sent down Iron, in which is (material for) mighty war, as well as many benefits for mankind.* [57:25]

Ibn Taymiyyah says further:

> He who deviates from the Book, is treated with iron; this is the reason that the religion very much requires both—the Book and the sword.[65]

According to al-Ghazālī:

> Life in this world is the farm of the life hereafter; religion is not consummated except with worldly life; authority and religion are inseparable. Religion is the foundation and authority is the guard; anything that does not have foundations is (bound to be) demolished; anything that does not have a guard is (bound to) vanish. Possession and control are not achieved except with authority.[66]

Had the Islamic texts not been explicit about the obligation of establishing the Islamic state, and had the history of the Messenger of Allah (ṣ) and his companions not been a witness to implementation on the ground of these texts, the nature of the Islamic mission by itself would have made it inevitable that Islam should have its state or home, with its own beliefs,

---

65. *Fatāwā*, 28/264.
66. Imam Ghazālī, *Iḥya' 'Ulūm al-Dīn*: 1/71, "Book of Knowledge".

practices, guidance and concepts, morals and virtues, and with its traditions and jurisprudence.

Hence it is always imperative for Islam to have its dependable state. There is an even greater need of such a state especially in our times, in which the 'ideological state' came into being, where states adopt an ideology, on which it bases its complete structure, covering education, culture, legislation, judiciary, economy and other social and political institutions. This is especially evident in the case of the socialist and communist states. Through technological advancement, modern science provided so much in the service of the state that the state has become immensely capable of influencing the beliefs, emotions, inclinations and behaviours of society. We can say that the state, with its state of the art apparatuses, has become capable of not only changing values and ideals, but of re-defining them unless there is stronger resistance to withstand it.

The Islamic state is an 'ideological state' founded on belief and method. It is not a mere 'security apparatus' to protect people from internal transgression or from external aggression. Its task, rather, is deeper and more profound. Its mission is to educate the nation and guide it on the basis of Islamic principles, to construct a positive environment and appropriate milieu for translating Islamic beliefs, concepts and instructions into practical reality, so that it can manifest itself as the beacon for all those who seek the right path and exemplify cogent guidance in the face of those who insist on treading the path of doom.

That is why Ibn Khaldūn defines the caliphate as an institution established to encourage people to conform to the requirements from the perspective of the Sharī'ah about their interests of the life hereafter followed by the worldly life attributed to it, because the worldly affairs are weighed by the Sharī'ah in light of the interests of the life hereafter. In fact, the caliphate is the representation of the Supreme Lawgiver in guarding the religion and in managing the worldly affairs with it.[67]

Indeed that is how Allah describes the responsibility of the faithful to their empowerment by Allah in the land. In other words, when they are bestowed with authority, they are:

> *...those who, if We establish them in the land, establish regular Prayer and give regular Charity, enjoin the right and forbid wrong: with Allah rests the end (and decision) of (all) affairs.* [22:41]

The mission statement of the Islamic state is the one pronounced by Rub'ī bin 'Āmir while addressing Rustam, the commander of the Persians:

> Allah has sent us to liberate the people from worship of the slaves (of Allah) to the worship of Allah alone, from melancholy of worldly life to its abundance, and from the tyranny of other religions to the justice of Islam.

Moreover this 'ideological state' is not of local nature. It is, rather, a state with a universal mission, because Allah has entrusted the nation of Islam with the duty to call humankind towards the guidance and the light that they possess. He has commissioned it by them being witnesses over humankind and with the leadership of edifying the nations. The Islamic nation did not come into being on its own, nor for its own sake; it was

---

67. *Muqaddimah*, 2/518, edited by Dr 'Alī 'Abd al-Wāḥid Wāfī.

evolved for the benefit of mankind; it was brought into being by Allah, Who accorded it the status of the 'best of peoples' and addressed it saying:

> *Thus, have We made of you an Ummah justly balanced, that you might be witnesses over the nations.* [2:143]

Hence we see that after the signing of the treaty of Ḥudaybiyah, the Messenger of Allah (ṣ) was given the opportunity. He wrote to kings and governors in various parts of the world calling them to Allah and to join him under the banner of the One and only God. He placed upon them the responsibility for their subjects if they failed to join the community of the faithful. He concluded all such letters with the Qur'anic verse:

> *Say: "O People of the Book! Come to common terms as between us and you: That we worship none but Allah; that we associate no partners with him; that we erect not, from among ourselves, Lords and patrons other than Allah." If then they turn back, say you: "Bear witness that we (at least) are Muslims (bowing to Allah's Will)".* [3:64]

Our need for a state valuing Islam

The foremost need of the Islamic mission in our times is the emergence of a *Dār al-Islām* (abode of Islam) or *Dawlah al-Islām* (state of Islam) that can adopt the message of Islam as its faith and system, and as its way of life and civilization. It is required to base its whole life, material as well as moral, on the basis of this comprehensive message, and to open its doors for every faithful who wishes to migrate from the lands of darkness.

The existence of such state is an Islamic requirement. It is also a human need because it will present to humankind a living example of a fusion of religion and state, union between physical matter and soul, and harmony between the progress of civilisation and nobility of character. That shall be the cornerstone of establishing the greater Islamic state that will unite the Muslim nation under the banner of the Qur'an and in the shade of caliphate of Islam. But the forces hostile to Islam are desperate to hamper the establishment of such a state on any land, howsoever small in size and thinly populated that might be.

The West may allow a Marxist state and the socialists may tolerate a liberal state, but neither of them allows the establishment of a true Islamic state. There is nothing strange when we find them aiming their guns against Sudan, when it declared Sharī'ah as its law. A similar case happened to Algeria where the Islamic party was prevented from coming to power, even though it won with a clear majority in the democratic elections.

Whenever a successful Islamic movement emerges and they fear that it might hold the reigns of power, it will be a target of attacks by the enemies of Islam. This is done in the form of displacement, sanctions, torture and genocide, and through distortion and misinformation. As soon as the victim is about to recover from a blow, they stun it with another volley of strikes, in such a manner that it is kept ever busy with his agony and far away from its aspirations.

THE WELFARE OF MANKIND

From the Islamic mission to establish a nation that is distinguished by its objectives and values, and from its championing a message that is distinct with its values, ideals and characteristics, it should not be misunderstood that Islam is a reclusive religion and lives in isolation, without concern for others, whether they are righteous or depraved, whether they take the right path or go astray.

Certainly that is not the case. Indeed Islam, since the inception of its call, has a universal message, a call for the whole of mankind and a mercy for all human beings. It is for all peoples in the East and West.

In verses of the Qur'an, revealed prior to the Migration to Madīnah, we come across numerous verses that clearly show the universality of the message of Islam. For example:

> *We sent you not, but as a Mercy for all creatures.* [21:107]

> *Blessed is He who sent down the criterion to His servant, that it may be an admonition to all creatures.* [25:1]

> *This is no less than a Message to (all) the worlds. And you shall certainly know the truth of it (all) after a while.* [38:87-88]

> *Say: "No reward for this do I ask of you: This is no less than a Message for the nations."* [6:90]

> *Say: "O men! I am sent unto you all, as the Messenger of Allah..."* [7:158]

> *We have not sent you but as a universal (Messenger) to men, giving them glad tidings, and warning them (against sin).* [34:28]

The nation of Islam is tasked with conveying this universal message to the whole world. They ought not to monopolise this divine blessing. It is imperative that, after having found the guidance with the divine light, they guide others to it; after having been reformed by faith and righteous deeds, they are obliged to strive for reforming all other nations and to call them to the very grace bestowed upon them by Allah.

Allah has characterised the Muslim ummah as the best of nations:

> *You are the best of peoples evolved for mankind, enjoining what is right, forbidding what is wrong, and believing in Allah.* [3:110]

"Evolved" indicates that there is someone who has evolved this blessed nation. Indeed, that Evolver is none other than Allah. This nation did not grow like wild vegetation; it was brought forth by the Cultivator Who strewed its seed and took care of it.

It did not evolve by itself, but was evolved for mankind, for guiding it, benefiting, reforming and liberating it from darkness to light.

In other words, the nation of Islam, in the first instance, is the nation with a mission and a message, and it has been delegated with the same mission with which its Messenger was sent to mankind. The Prophet (ṣ) said: "You have been commissioned as facilitators; you have not been sent as impeders."[68] In the same vein the Qur'an asserts:

> *Let there arise out of you a band of people inviting to all that is good, enjoining what is right, and forbidding what is wrong: They are the ones to attain felicity.* [3:104]

68. Narrated by Bukhārī, Tirmidhī and al-Nasā'ī in the Book of Cleanliness, through Abū Hurayrah.

"Out of you" in the above verse is meant to be inclusive, implying that all of us, as a nation, must call to virtue; on the other hand, it is meant to be selective, implying that it is imperative that there be a group from amongst us dedicated to calling to righteousness and virtue. In both cases, the Islamic nation is responsible for the mission and for enjoining virtue and forbidding vice. The whole nation bears the responsibility to constitute the dedicated group, to strengthen it, provide for its requirements, prepare it for the mission and monitor its performance; hence it has been ordained collectively with this mission.

This is how the noble Companion, Rib'ī bin 'Āmir comprehended the message. When the commander of the Persians asked him at the battlefield of Qādisiyyah, "Who are you people?", 'Āmir replied passionately:

> We are a nation ordained by the Almighty to liberate His slaves from the worship of His slaves towards the worship of Him alone; from the melancholy of the world to its abundance, and from the tyranny of religions to the justice of Islam.

Thus did the noble Companion—no graduate of any university—summarise the major objectives of Islam in these words. Indeed he had acquired this knowledge and wisdom from the school of Muḥammad (ṣ), which produced the finest people of piety called the Companions, the like of which the world has not witnessed since.

The universal message of Islam is an open mercy and a call to the welfare of the whole of mankind. This mercy is evident in a number of fundamental values to which Islam calls. The foremost among these are as follows:

Liberation of man from servitude of fellow humans

Islam, by its call to belief in the absolute unity of Allah and by its resistance to polytheism, in all its forms, liberated human beings from the servitude of other human beings, just as it liberated them from the worship of objects, false impressions and hedonism.

Islam brought down the false deities that were sanctified as gods besides Allah, whether from amongst the clergy or powerful figures. Alluding to this fact Allah mentions the state of the People of the Book:

> *They take their priests and their anchorites to be their lords in derogation of Allah, and (they take as their Lord) Christ the son of Mary; yet they were commanded to worship but One God: there is no god but He. Praise and glory to Him: (far is He) from having the partners they associate (with Him).* [9:31]

The Qur'anic verse with which the noble Messenger of Allah (ṣ) concluded his letter to the rulers, like Heraclius, Chosroes II, Muqawqis, Negus and other Christian rulers and chieftains, was:

> *O People of the Book! Come to common terms as between us and you: that we worship none but Allah; that we associate no partners with Him; that we erect not, from among ourselves, Lords and patrons other than God.* [3:64]

The expression "that we erect not, from among ourselves, Lords and patrons other than God" is tantamount to a new birth for humankind. It means that no human being should deify himself for others, that they should not bow to each other and that one should not prostrate to another fellow human being. With it the foreheads ascended so high that they would kneel to none other than their Creator; the backs straightened so that they would not bend in front of anyone other than their Designer; with it humans became venerable that they would not humble themselves before anyone other than the One and only God, the Omnipotent.

In Islam the hearts and minds turn towards God alone in hope and with fear. "They are hopeful of his mercy and fear his punishment." To Allah alone hands are stretched; Him alone do the tongues ask in supplication; He alone possesses the power of awarding and dispossessing, of lowering and elevating, and of life and death.

By virtue of having created them and providing them with incalculable amenities, Allah alone possesses the absolute right of legislation over humans; He possesses the unqualified right to pronounce the lawful or unlawful for them; He is "the one wielding the rule" and "to Him belong the creation and the command":

> *Say: "Shall I seek for judge other than Allah?—when He it is Who has sent unto you the Book, explained in detail."* [6:114]

Brotherhood and equality of humans

From the fruits of Islamic belief in the absolute unity of Allah comes the brotherhood of man. Of the prerequisites of such brotherhood is the equality of humans. It is based on two factors:

Firstly, by virtue of the call to the belief in the unity of Allah, all humans are slaves of the same Lord; He created them and made them equals, so they enjoy equality in the status of servitude to Allah.

Secondly, they all are children of the same father. However their skin colours differ or wherever their homelands are, or their tongues vary or their classes disparate, they still remain the children of Adam. They are on par in their status of affiliation to Adam.

This is what the Messenger of Allah (ṣ) communicated to his nation on the occasion of the Farewell Pilgrimage. In his sermon to the large congregation, he said,

> O people, the Lord of all of you is one; the father of all of you is one; all of you belong to Adam; Adam was created from dust; an Arab has no superiority over a non-Arab nor does a non-Arab have any superiority over an Arab except by way of piety.[69]

Allah says:

> *O mankind! We created you from a single (pair) of a male and a female, and made you into nations and tribes, that you may know each other (not that you may despise each other). Verily the most honoured of you in the sight of Allah is (he who is) the most righteous of you. And Allah has full knowledge and is well acquainted (with all things).* [49:13]

Imam Aḥmad has narrated through Zayd ibn Arqam that the Messenger of Allah (ṣ) used to invoke Allah after every congregational prayer with the following three supplications:

---

69. Narrated by Aḥmad in his *Musnad*: 5/411, through Abū Naḍrah; considered authentic by Albānī.

> O Allah, our Lord and the Lord and Owner of everything, I bear witness that You are the One and only God who has no associate.

> O Allah, our Lord and the Lord and Owner of everything, I bear witness that Muḥammad is your slave and Your messenger.

> O Allah, our Lord and the Lord and Owner of everything, I bear witness that all humans are brethren.

These noble, triple supplications imply three fundamental witnesses. Firstly, witness to the unity of Allah. Secondly, witness to Muḥammad (ṣ) being the slave and the Messenger of Allah. Thirdly, witness to the bond of brotherhood of the whole of mankind. This brotherhood is the broad brotherhood of man. And certainly, it embodies the three elements of love, equality and cooperation.

It may be pointed out that Allah says in the Qur'an "the Believers are but a single brotherhood" and that His Messenger Muḥammad (ṣ) has said, "A Muslim is the brother of another Muslim", which means that the basis of brotherhood is nothing but religion and faith.

We say that the religious brotherhood based on faith is special and the deepest of ties, but it does not conflict with other forms of brotherhood, like national or ethnic brotherhood, as mentioned in the following Qur'anic verses:

> *To the 'Ād People (We sent) Hūd, one of their own brethren.* [11:50]

> *To the Thamūd people (We sent) Ṣāliḥ, one of their own brethren.* [11:61]

> *To the Madyan people (We sent) Shu'ayb, one of their own brethren.* [11:84]

> *Behold, their brother Nūh said to them: "Will you not fear (Allah)?"* [26:106]

> *Behold, their brother Lūt said to them: "Will you not fear (Allah)?"* [26:161]

Thus, the Qur'an confirms the existence of brotherhood between those Messengers and their peoples, even though they rejected them and rebelled against them, they still belonged to them and were not alien to them. That is the ethnic brotherhood.

There is also the bond of human brotherhood among the descendants of Adam in general. This has been mentioned above in the light of the prophetic supplications.

Justice for all people

Islam calls towards welfare of mankind, the establishment of justice between all peoples being one example. Justice in Islam is not for Arabs alone; it is for all the peoples of the world without any exception.

While mentioning the objectives of revealed religions, Allah says:

> *We sent aforetime our messengers with Clear Signs and sent down with them the Book and the Balance (of Right and Wrong), that men may stand forth in justice...* [57:25]

Thus it stands established that the deputation of the Messengers and revelation of the books were aimed at achieving a basic objective, so that the people will accomplish justice, in other words, fairness to ensure that everyone, without exception, gets his rights. Allah says:

> *Allah does command you to render back your trusts to those to whom they are due; and when you judge between people, that you judge with justice.* [4:58]

The command is lucid in its message that when you judge between "people", not only Muslims, that you judge with complete justice. In fact Allah revealed nine verses of Sūrah al-Nisā' admonishing His noble Messenger (ṣ) when he was about to defend some of the hypocritical Muslims who had accused a Jew of stealing. The accused had not stolen; the accusers themselves had stolen. Allah said:

> *We have sent down to you the Book in truth, that you might judge between men, as guided by Allah: so be not (used) as an advocate by those who betray their trust; but seek the forgiveness of Allah; for Allah is Oft-Forgiving, Most Merciful. Contend not on behalf of such as betray their own souls; for God loves not one given to perfidy and crime.* [4:105-107]

Allah has commanded the believers to stand firmly for justice. They should not be dissuaded by affection for kins or by hatred of others. Justice is above the emotions of love and hate; it must be for Allah alone. Allah says:

> *O you who believe! Stand out firmly for justice, as witnesses to Allah, even as against yourselves, or your parents, or your kin.* [4:135]

This is the justice towards loved ones, whether it is towards family members or even one's own self. Allah also says:

> *O you who believe! Stand out firmly for Allah, as witnesses to fair dealing, and let not the hatred of others to you make you swerve to wrong and depart from justice. Be just: that is next to piety: and fear Allah. For Allah is well-acquainted with all that you do.* [5:8]

In spite of dislike or hatred to certain people, Muslims are not supposed to commit transgression, because Allah does not like those who depart from justice nor does He guide them to the right path, as such people never succeed in this world or the hereafter.

Muslims apply justice with all peoples; they applied it in the lifetime of the Messenger (ṣ), during the era of the Rightly Guided Caliphs and the early centuries of Islam.

We know of ʻUmar ibn al-Khaṭṭāb ordering the aggrieved Coptic Egyptian to seek retribution from the son of the governor of Egypt, ʻAmr ibn al-ʻĀṣ. History then registered his famous statement: "O ʻAmr, when did you begin to enslave the people when they were born free?"

This spontaneous statement of ʻUmar became the opening statement of the formal documents of human rights and constitutions of advanced countries in modern times.

What must be lauded here is that Islam made the masses perceive that justice is an obligation which endures no remissness or lenience and that the aggrieved will, for certain, retrieve his due from the perpetrator. There is nothing strange that one would travel all the way from Fusṭāṭ to Madīnah, bearing all the hardship of the long journey, to claim his due. In the Roman empire, the oppressed were robbed of their possessions and honour and they could not raise their voice. There was no one in the wilderness to listen to his cry. In contrast, during the caliphate of 'Alī ibn Abī Ṭālib, the judge appointed by him passed his verdict against 'Alī himself, the Commander of the Faithful, in favour of a Christian subject, because 'Alī could not refute the claim against him. Upon seeing this fairness of Islamic justice, the Christian could not resist to declare publicly his faith in Islam and to confess that 'Alī was right and had been framed, adding that such verdicts were nothing less than prophetic.

Such examples are ample in history books.

Universal peace

Among other gains which Islam calls to is peace between humans instead of wars and conflicts.

This may sound strange to some as Islam is the religion of *jihād* in the path of Allah, and that in Islam, *jihād* is the best of all righteous acts, to the extent that even one who fasts all his life and devotes to worship throughout the night for the rest of his life does not deserve the reward of a *mujāhid* in the path of Allah.

Jihād in Islam has been prescribed to defend the Islamic mission from being obstructed; it has been ordained to fight those who fight Muslims and enjoined to defend the oppressed against transgressors. *Jihād* has not been ordained against the innocent and peaceful who do not harm Muslims or fight them or aid their enemies.

This is evident in the Qur'an:

> *Fight in the cause of Allah those who fight you, but do not transgress limits; for Allah loves not transgressors.* [2:190]

And fight them on until there is no more tumult or oppression, and there prevail justice and faith in Allah; but if they cease, let there be no hostility except to those who practise oppression. [2:193]

And why should you not fight in the cause of Allah and of those who, being weak, are ill-treated (and oppressed)?—Men, women, and children, whose cry is: "Our Lord! Rescue us from this town, whose people are oppressors; and raise for us from You one who will protect; and raise for us from You one who will help!" [4:75]

...Therefore if they withdraw from you but fight you not, and (instead) send you (guarantees of) peace, then Allah has opened no way for you (to war against them). [4:90]

Will you not fight people who violated their oaths, plotted to expel the Messenger, and took the aggressive by being the first (to assault) you? [9:13]

But if the enemy incline towards peace, do you (also) incline towards peace, and trust in Allah: for He is One that hears and knows (all things). [8:61]

The history of the Islamic mission attests to the fact that during the thirteen years of the nascent period in Makkah, Islam enjoined upon its followers to be patient in the face of persecution; they were always soothed and told to address their oppressors:

To you be your way, and to me mine. [109:6]

My work to me, and yours to you! [10:41]

This was in spite of the fact that they were being told by their oppressors, "Our religion is to us and you don't have a religion; to us is our work and your deeds are in vain." Muḥammad (ṣ) and his Companions were persecuted with the worst kinds of torture and anguish; their loved ones and their belongings were harmed. After that long torment, Islam permitted its followers to defend themselves:

> *To those against whom war is made, permission is given (to fight), because they are wronged;—and verily, Allah is most powerful for their aid;—(They are) those who have been expelled from their homes in defiance of right,—(for no cause) except that they say, "Our Lord is Allah."*... [22:39-40]

The raids and expedition that were carried out by the Muslims were out of compulsion; they were drawn to react reluctantly. Allah says:

> *Fighting is prescribed for you, and you dislike it. But it is possible that you dislike a thing which is good for you, and that you love a thing which is bad for you. But Allah knows, and you know not.* [2:216]

Allah depicts the state of the Muslims during the battle of Badr, saying:

> *Just as your Lord ordered you out of your house in truth, even though a party among the Believers disliked it.* [8:5]

The Muslims were not bloodthirsty, as the enemies of Islam have painted them to be; on the contrary, they were defenders of the creed whose sanctities were desecrated, whose followers were driven away from their homeland, whose possessions were impounded, who were invaded in their own land like the instance at Uḥud and Khandaq. Despite all that, the Qur'an comments on the battle of Khandaq as follows:

And God turned back the Unbelievers for (all) their fury: no advantage did they gain; and enough is Allah for the Believers in their fight. And Allah is full of Strength, able to enforce His Will. [33:25]

The Qur'anic observation "...and enough is God for the believers in their fight..." demonstrates the great favour of Allah to the believers in the form of turning back their enemy from them without achieving their obnoxious goal. Allah sufficed the faithful in fighting the intruding enemy and freed them from the consequences of war, without having to fight one.

Similarly, following the expedition of Ḥudaybiyah and the resulting treaty between the Muslims and the Makkan polytheists, Allah revealed Sūrah al-Fatḥ (The Victory):

Verily We have granted you a manifest victory. [48:1]

When some of the companions sceptically asked the Messenger (ṣ), whether the apparently humiliating treaty was a victory, he replied with an unambiguous 'yes'. In this context, Allah mentions His favour to the Muslims:

And it is He Who has restrained their hands from you and your hands from them in the midst of Makkah, after that He gave you the victory over them. And God sees well all that you do. [48:24]

Here, one must ponder over how Allah deals with restraining the hands of the faithful from their enemy and the hands of their enemy from them as a favour to the faithful. Can there be a better confirmation of the fact that Islam regards peace in itself as a blessing from Allah, which is promoted by the Qur'an as a favour?

The least that can be cited in this regard is what the Messenger of Allah (ṣ) said, "The ugliest names are *ḥarb* and *murrah*" (*i.e.*, war and bitter).[70] This indicates that he hated even the word 'war', whereas in pre-Islamic Arabia people used to name their sons as *harb*. Muḥammad (ṣ) cautioned them against even such names. It is obvious that such an attitude could not be expected from a warmonger, as alleged by those who follow their fancies instead of objectivity.

Tolerance towards non-Muslims

The principles and values Islam enjoins in this regard are not only tolerance towards non-Muslims, but in the manner of interacting with them with respect, without prejudice and malice towards those who differ with Muslims.

This is true for non-Muslims, nevertheless there is a special treatment for the People of the Book, *i.e.*, Jews and Christians, for they share the revealed religion and belong to Abraham, the common Patriarch. The Qur'an calls them the "People of the Book", permitted Muslims to eat the meat slaughtered by them and to marry their daughters. Allah says:

> *This day are (all) things good and pure made lawful unto you. The food of the People of the Book is lawful unto you and yours is lawful unto them. (Lawful unto you in marriage) are (not only) chaste women who are believers, but chaste women among the People of the Book, revealed before your time…*[5:5]

Marital bond is one of the primary bonds that connects humans. Allah says:

---

70. Narrated by Abū Dāwūd in "Adab" through Abū Wahab al-Jashmī (4950); referred also to al-Nasā'ī. Imam al-Kaṭṭābī reasons it to the odious consequences of war.

> *It is He Who has created man from water: then has He established relationships of lineage and marriage: for your Lord has power (over all things).* [25:54]

One must remember that according to the Qur'an, marriage stands on the foundations of tranquillity, affection and mercy. It reads:

> *And among His Sign s is this, that He created for you mates from among yourselves, that you may dwell in tranquillity with them, and He has put love and mercy between your (hearts): verily in that are Signs for those who reflect.* [30:21]

The marriage of a Muslim man with a Christian or Jewish woman means that his in-laws, the maternal grandparents of his children, their maternal uncles, aunts and cousins are from amongst them too. Certainly such kith and kin enjoy the rights of "the bond of kinship" enjoined by Islam.

Indeed there is no wider or higher horizon of tolerance with non-Muslims than the horizon of the Islamic Sharī'ah.

With regard to treatment of non-Muslims, the Qur'an has lucidly distinguished between their two categories. One are those who wage war against Muslims and drive them away from their lands or are accomplices to that. The other are those who reconcile and live peacefully with Muslims and not hostile to them. This is found in two noble verses of the Qur'an considered to be the rock-solid ground and guiding principles for the bonding with non-Muslims. Allah says:

> *Allah forbids you not, with regard to those who fight you not for (your) Faith nor drive you out of your homes, from dealing kindly and justly with them: for Allah loves those who are just. Allah only forbids you, with regard to those who fight you for (your) Faith, and*

> *drive you out of your homes, and support (others) in driving you out, from turning to them (for friendship and protection). It is such as turn to them (in these circumstances), that do wrong.* [60:8-9]

As narrated in the books of *tafsīr,* these two verses were revealed concerning the idol-worshipping polytheists. It follows from here that the People of the Book are entitled to an even higher degree of kindness and justice.

There are two types of people who have treaties with Muslims. The first are those who sign a temporary treaty with the Muslims. With them, the terms are fulfilled till the end of the treaty. The other are those who enjoy a permanent and eternal covenant with Muslims. These are the people known by Muslims as *Ahl al-Dhimmah* or People under Protection, and are under the protection of God, His Messenger (ṣ) and Muslim society at large. Regarding this category of people, the Islamic jurists stipulate: "For them is what is for us, upon them is what is upon us." This is their status in general, except where the nature of our creeds call for variation.

'People under Protection' are citizens of the State of Islam. 'People under Protection' is not derogatory expression or a form of disparagement, as may be misconceived by some. In fact it implies the obligation of protection and fulfilment of it as part of a religious duty and obedience to the Sharī'ah.

If Christians take this expression as offensive, it can be changed or dropped, because our devotion to God is not through words. In fact the second Rightly-Guided Caliph 'Umar ibn al-Khaṭṭāb, once did away with something more significant than this: he dropped the word Jizyah (tribute) in spite of the fact that it is mentioned in the Qur'an. He did so in response to the petition of Christians from the Arab tribe of Banī Taghlīb. The scorned the imposition of 'tribute' and, instead petitioned that whatever was collected from them be collected in the name of charity, even if it was double the due amount. Upon this 'Umar granted their appeal. 'Umar did not see any harm in this and said, "These people are foolish; they accepted the implication and rejected the name."[71]

This was an allusion from 'Umar to an important principle, *i.e.*, the importance of considering the objectives and meanings, not just terminology, and to reflect on the substance. It is not necessary to use the word 'tribute', which offends Christians in Islamic countries, where they have become a part of the national fabric. It is sufficient that they pay a tax similar to *zakāh* and that they participate in nation-building.

Imam al-Awzā'ī had stood up along with a group of such "protected citizens" in Lebanon against the 'Abbāsid prince, who happened to be a kin of the Caliph.

Similarly, Ibn Taymiyyah addressed Emperor Timur regarding the release of the captives taken by his men. When the emperor offered to release the Muslim prisoners only, he rejected the offer unless 'the protected' were also released along with the Muslims.

Islam and tolerance

Religious and intellectual tolerance has levels and degrees. The lowest allows the opponent freedom of religion and faith. The intermediate level allows the right to believe in the religion and creed of one's choice. After that one should not be pressured into abandoning his belief and do what he believes to be impermissible. For example, if a Jew believes that Saturday

71. See my *Fiqh al-Zakāt*, vol. 2, p. 708.

is a day of rest, it is not acceptable to assign him a job on a Saturday, because if he is forced, he will do so with a feeling of guilt to his faith.[72]

If a Christian believes that it is obligatory to attend church on Sunday, one must not stop him from doing so.

Another degree of tolerance is not to prohibit on others what is permissible to them.

When the Muslims attain a high degree of magnanimity, they characterised that superior level of moderation with others from amongst the non-Muslims under them.

A Muslim respects the non-Muslim's right to what is permitted by his religion; he gives them space and does not harass him with bans, although he could do so on the pretext of respect to the law and religion of the state, where he would be accused of intolerance. He also could have used the argument that whatever is permitted by a certain religion is not necessarily obligatory upon its followers to practise.

If the religion of a Christian permits the eating of pork, he can survive all his life without eating it and eat beef, mutton and poultry. The same is true about wine. If Christianity permits it, it is not among the obligations of the Christians to drink wine, especially when some Christians believe that it is prohibited.

Had Islam asked such people to give up wine and pork to respect their Muslim brethren, there is absolutely no religious reservation for them from doing so, simply because by giving

---

72. According to the book *Ghāyah al-Muntahā* and its commentaries belonging to the Ḥanbalī school of jurisprudence, "It is prohibited to call a Jew on his Sabbath; this prohibition remains effective with regard to him; he is exempted from work on a holiday. This is in light of the *ḥadīth* narrated by al-Nasā'ī and Tirmidhī, which reads: 'You are Jews and it is especially important for you not to violate the Sabbath'" (Vol. 2, p. 604).

up these things, the non-Muslims would not have violated any of their religious obligations. In spite of this, Islam does not exert pressure on non-Muslims regarding something they believe is permissible. Instead, it tells Muslims to leave them with what they believe.

Muslim spirit of tolerance

There is another thing that does not fall under the jurisdiction of the state, "the spirit of magnanimity" mirrored in good social relations, polite interaction, good neighbourly ties and human affection such as kindness, mercy and beneficence. These qualities are requisites of daily life and cannot be regulated by law.

This magnanimity is evident from the Qur'anic edict regarding a polytheist's parents who might seek to bring their Muslim child back to polytheism. Here the Qur'an guides by saying:

> *...yet bear them company in this life with justice (and consideration)* [31:15]

In Sūrah al-Mumtaḥanah, God instructs Muslims to show beneficence and justice towards opponents who are not hostile.

> *Allah forbids you not, with regard to those who fight you not for (your) faith nor drive you out of your homes, from dealing kindly and justly with them: for God loves those who are just.* [60:8]

This is also manifest from the verse in Sūrah al-Insān describing the righteous servants of Allah:

> *And they feed, for the love of Allah, the indigent, the orphan, and the captive.* [76:8]

It is worth mentioning that at the time this verse was revealed, there were no captives other than polytheists.

Similarly, this is obvious from the response of the Qur'an to the reservation of some Muslims about giving charity to their relatives and neighbours from amongst the polytheists:

> *It is not required of you (O Messenger), to set them on the right path, but Allah sets on the right path whom He pleases. Whatever of good you give benefits your own souls, and you shall only do so seeking the 'Face' of Allah. Whatever good you give, shall be rendered back to you, and you shall not be dealt with unjustly.* [2:272]

Muḥammad ibn al-Ḥasan, a disciple of Imam Abū Ḥanīfah and inscriber of his school of jurisprudence, has narrated that "the Messenger of Allah (ṣ) sent relief to the people of Makkah who were facing drought to be distributed to the poor".[73] This was despite all the torment and ordeal that he had suffered at the hands of the Makkans.

Aḥmad, Bukhārī and Muslim narrated through Asmā', the daughter of Abū Bakr:

> My mother, who was a polytheist, came to Madīnah during the period of the treaty of the Quraysh (with the Muslims).[74] Following that, I came to the Messenger (ṣ) and asked whether I should welcome her when it was apparent that she was keen. He said, "Yes, unite the bonds of kinship with your mother."[75]

Islamic generosity is manifested also in how the Messenger (ṣ) used to deal with Jews and Christians. He used

---

73. *Sharḥ al-Sayr al-Kabīr*, Vol. 1, p. 144.
74. *i.e.*, Ḥudaybiyah.
75. *Tafsīr Ibn Kathīr*, Vol. 4, p. 349.

to visit them and treat them hospitably, visit their sick and carry out transactions with them.

Ibn Isḥāq writes:

> When a delegation of (the Christians of) Najrān came to see the Messenger of Allah (ṣ) in Madīnah, they called on him in his mosque just after the 'Aṣr prayers. It happened to be their prayer time. They stood to pray in the mosque itself. People sought to prevent them from doing so. The Messenger of Allah (ṣ) said: "Leave them alone." They then stood facing the East and prayed in their own way.

Intellectual basis for Muslim tolerance

The Muslims' tolerance towards the opponents of their religion is deep rooted in the coherent concepts embedded in Islam as well as in their hearts and minds. The most important among these is the belief of every Muslim in the dignity of the human being irrespective of religion, gender or colour. Allah says:

> *We have honoured the sons of Adam.* [17:70]

This honour bestowed by the Almighty on man makes the right to dignity and protection indispensable.

From the practical examples we can quote the narration of al-Bukhārī through Jābir ibn 'Abdullah. Once a funeral passed by the Messenger of Allah (ṣ), he stood up in respect. Upon this some of the companions exclaimed saying, "O Messenger of Allah, it is the funeral of a Jew." To this he responded, "Isn't he a human being?" Certainly in Islam every soul has honour and dignity. How beautiful is this attitude and how wonderful is this interpretation and explanation!

The disagreement of people over religion is a reality intended by Allah. It is He who, amongst all His creatures, gave the humans the freedom and choice to do or not to do a certain act.

> *Let him who will believe, and let him who will, reject (it).* [18:29]

> *If your Lord had so willed, He could have made mankind one people: but they will not cease to dispute.* [11:118]

A Muslim knows for certain that God's plan cannot be thwarted or criticised and that He does not devise for anything other than with wisdom, whether or not people comprehend it. From this standpoint, a Muslim never contemplates compelling people to believe in Islam. How can it be otherwise when Allah enlightened His noble Messenger (ṣ) saying:

> *If it had been your Lord's will, they would all have believed,—all who are on earth! Will you then compel mankind, against their will, to believe!* [10:99]

A Muslim is not obligated to call the non-Muslims to account for being disbelievers or to punish people for their depravity. They will be called to account on the Day of Resurrection:

> *If they do wrangle with you, say, "Allah knows best what it is you are doing. Allah will judge between you on the Day of Judgement concerning the matters in which you differ."* [22:68-69]

God further elaborates the Islamic outlook to His noble Messenger (ṣ), with regard to the People of the Book:

> *Now then, for that (reason), call (them to the Faith), and stand steadfast as you are commanded, nor follow you their vain desires; but say: "I believe in the Book which Allah has sent down; and I*

am commanded to judge justly between you. Allah is our Lord and your Lord: for us (is the responsibility for) our deeds, and for you for your deeds. There is no contention between us and you. Allah will bring us together, and to Him is (our) Final Goal. [42:15]

With this perspective, the conscience of the Muslim rests and he does not find any conflict between his own conviction, the non-Muslims and the Islamic requirement of beneficence and justice, while believing in the truth of the Islamic faith.

The Islamic conviction that Allah ordains justice, and calls for the highest moral standards even towards the polytheists. He abhors injustice and castigates those who tyrannise, even if injustice was inflicted on a non-believer by a Muslim. Allah the Almighty says:

And let not the hatred of others to you make you swerve to wrong and depart from justice. Be just: that is next to piety: and fear Allah... [5:8]

Muḥammad (ṣ) the Messenger has said:

The invocation of the oppressed, even if he was an infidel, is barred by no barrier (from reaching Allah).[76]

The tolerance and magnanimity of Islam towards non-Muslims have no parallel in history, especially with regards to the People of the Book, and more specifically to the citizens of the Islamic state. ۞

76. Narrated by Aḥmad in his *Musnad*.

CHAPTER 5

The Sources of Islam

THE QUR'AN AND THE SUNNAH

Islam is the religion of God; with it He revealed His last book. In order to convey the message, He sent His last Messenger (ṣ), so that with His blessing he would guide mankind to the divine path.

The tenets of Islam consist of a set of commandments and obligations which the Messenger of Allah (ṣ) called the people to observe. He conveyed to his nation what Allah revealed to him concerning the realities of existence and of the metaphysical realms relating to divinity, prophecy and the Hereafter. He also revealed to them all that Allah had enjoined, forbidden and permitted to His servants with regard to their religious and worldly affairs.

The tenets of Islam are not confined to the practical and legal aspects of worship and dealings, as is dealt by the science of jurisprudence (*fiqh*), nor are they confined to aspects of theory and doctrine, as dealt by scholastic theology. They are also not confined to spiritual and ethical matters, as is dealt by the branches of Islamic mysticism and ethics. In fact, the tenets of Islam encompass all these aspects in a wonderfully balanced, comprehensive and synergetic manner.

The Qur'an and the Sunnah (traditions of the Prophet (ṣ) and his Companions) are the two indispensable and impeccable sources of Islam, from which all the Islamic tenets are derived. The Qur'an is the primary source and the Sunnah follows suit.

IJMĀ' AND QIYĀS

It may be asked: why have *ijmā'* (consensus) and *qiyās* (juristic reasoning) not been listed as sources of knowledge concerning the tenets of Islam?

The first answer to this question is that these two sources are also sources of reference alongside the Qur'an and Sunnah when it comes to "the many practical tenets" dealt by *fiqh* (jurisprudence). But here we are discussing the Islamic tenets as a whole, which, along with the juristic regulations, includes beliefs, morals, world view and ethics. All these depend essentially on the two basic, indispensable sources of Islam, the Qur'an and the Sunnah.

Secondly, these two sources, *ijmā'* and *qiyās*, are corroborated by the Qur'an and the Sunnah. It is with this corroboration only (*i.e.*, with the Qur'an and not independently) that their authority is validated. So this implies that the basic sources of derivation and inference are the Qur'an and the Sunnah.

Thirdly, the Qur'an and Sunnah are categorically regarded as the two impeccable sources of Islam and no devout Muslim questions their ultimate authority. This is unlike the consensus (*ijmā'*) and juristic reasoning (*qiyās*), topics on which a lot has been mentioned in the study of *fiqh*, although the average Muslim nevertheless holds them in high esteem.

There are some issues with regard to *ijmā'*, such as its feasibility, its pertinent occurrence, appropriate knowledge regarding its subject if its course is chosen, and knowledge of it once it has been implemented.

There are also issues related to *qiyās* such as its proper application and its conditions of acceptance. The contentions of the Ẓāhiriyyah (a juristic school opposed to analogical reasoning) and others regarding such a well-known concept as *qiyās* is really incomprehensible.

The sources of Islamic knowledge regarding the rulings of Islam have now been clearly defined. In other words, the principal authorities of Islam have been specified.

The principal authority of Islam does not belong to any religious body or school, as is found in Christianity in the form of their holy establishments.

Its principal sources of reference are not to a religious head, whatever may be his status in terms of knowledge and piety. Simply put, Muslims do not have a pope-like authority attributed with holiness and a sense of infallibility.

Islam's principal references are not determined by any particular academic institution, by any one of the Islamic schools of thought, nor are they determined by any kind of religious fraternity whose followers blindly follow the doctrine of the order.

What we find in the history and heritage of Islam is that the independent judgements (*ijtihād*) of man in Islamic law are not infallible and are therefore liable to error in their understanding and application. We take what is beneficial from them and do away with the things that are not of benefit. If a jurist makes a correct decision then he is worthy of two rewards and if he makes an incorrect ruling then he is worthy of one reward. This is so as long as these rulings were based on his community within a specific context and were accompanied by sincere intentions.

The highest principles of reference in Islam go back to two divine and infallible sources, the Qur'an and the Sunnah, which we have been commanded to follow and refer to in those matters in which we differ.

One can say that both these represent a single source or a single reference since they both stem from the divine revelation, irrespective of whether it is an unequivocal revelation as in the case of the Qur'an or an equivocal revelation as sometimes in the case of the Sunnah.

As far as the contribution of the Islamic scholars in interpreting the Qur'an, explaining the Ḥadīth and the derivation of laws (*aḥkām*) is concerned, it is not infallible. Yet, on the whole, it is an essential guide when deciphering the myriad of problems. The intellect illuminates the path and guides us towards a correct understanding. It allows us to make the correct derivations and diligent interpretations (*ijtihād*), so that there are no slips and misunderstandings.

Why did Allah reveal the Qur'an?

God, did not reveal the Qur'an to mankind merely to be recited and to receive its blessings, nor did He reveal it simply to be used as decoration on walls or to be recited on solemn occasions such as death in the hope that God will have mercy on the deceased.

He revealed His book for regulating the course of human life, to rule by it by what Allah has revealed of guidance and the religion of truth, guide mankind to the correct path and take them away from darkness.

Certainly, Allah did not reveal the Qur'an only to be recited for the dead; He sent it down so that the living can be guided. He did not reveal it to decorate walls with its verses, but to embellish human lives.

The blessings from the Qur'an are derived by following it and acting according to it. Allah says:

> *And this is a Book which We have revealed as a blessing: so follow it and be righteous, that you may receive mercy:* [6:155]

In fact the Qur'an itself clearly outlines its own objectives for which Allah has sent it down, *i.e.*, to be an effective living reality in the lives of the people. It says:

> *We have sent down to you the Book in truth, that you might judge between men, as guided by Allah.* [4:105]

> *O mankind! Verily there has come to you a convincing proof from your Lord: for We have sent unto you a light (that is) manifest. Then those who believe in Allah, and hold fast to Him—soon will He admit them to mercy and grace from Himself, and guide them to Himself by a straight way.* [4:174-175]

> *There has come to you our Messenger, revealing to you much that you used to hide in the Book, and passing over much (that is now*

unnecessary). There has come to you from Allah a (new) light and a perspicuous Book—wherewith Allah guides all who seek His good pleasure to ways of peace and safety, and leads them out of darkness, by His will, unto the light; guides them to a path that is straight. [5:15-16]

To you We sent the Scripture in truth, confirming the scripture that came before it, and guarding it in safety: so judge between them by what Allah has revealed, and follow not their vain desires, diverging from the Truth that has come to you. [5:48]

And this (He commands): Judge you between them by what Allah has revealed, and follow not their vain desires, but beware of them lest they beguile you from any of that (teaching) which Allah has sent down to you. [5:49]

We have sent it down as an Arabic Qur'an, in order that you may learn wisdom. [12:2]

A Book which We have revealed unto you, in order that you might lead mankind out of the depths of darkness into light—by the leave of their Lord—to the Way of (Him) the Exalted in Power, Worthy of all Praise! [14:1]

Verily this Qur'an does guide to that which is most right (or stable), and gives the Glad Tidings to the Believers who work deeds of righteousness, that they shall have a magnificent reward; And to those who believe not in the Hereafter, (it announces) that We have prepared for them a Penalty Grievous (indeed). [17:9-10]

So that we are guided by the Qur'an, it is important that we are aware of what God intends for us from His book. This depends on our correct understanding of the Book and on the sound interpretation of its verses and commandments, so that we do not attribute to it whatever is not originally intended. We should also be careful of adding, omitting, or prioritising certain passages by re-arranging verses. There is a set of rules and regulations which guards the Qur'an from being manipulated by liars, from the misinterpretation of the ignorant and the distortion of those who have gone astray.

Believing in parts of the book

There are some Muslims who say that they believe in the Qur'an and submit to its commandments, but only in certain aspects. Such people would accept the Qur'anic commands in the aspects of creed, rituals and ethics, but would refuse to accept those aspects pertaining to such matters as legislation, economy and politics.

Some people accept its laws, but only where family matters and personal affairs are concerned. Their scope of belief does not involve the Qur'an's guidance pertaining to society, governance, polity, economy and international relations.

Strangely, such statements come from those who claim to belong to the creed of Islam, who profess that they accept Allah as their Lord, Islam as their religion, Muḥammad (ṣ) as the final Messenger and the Qur'an as their guide.

How can this come from one who believes that the Qur'an is the Book of God and that whatever it contains is nothing but the word of Allah?

Do they mean to correct their Lord? Or do they claim to be more knowledgeable than Him concerning the interests of His own creation, or attempt to act in a kinder manner to themselves than their Creator and Cherisher?

Do such people think that they are rivals to Allah, so that they can compete with Him regarding His own creation and enter into partnership with Him? How evil is their Judgement!

How can the created be a rival to the Creator? How can the created, feeble, mortal with limited capabilities, be a challenger to the Supreme One, Who is timeless and eternal, Who is the Omnipotent and holds the ultimate will, and Who is not curtailed by anything earthly or heavenly?

We have seen those who argue that only those portions of the Qur'an revealed in Makkah are obligatory to be followed, and the portions revealed in Madīnah are non-binding, claiming that the latter contradict our present environment, which, as they claim, should not be allowed to be stagnated by the Qur'an and the Sunnah.

Similar behaviour by the Children of Israel is vehemently condemned by Allah. They have been strongly reprimanded for having been selective with regard to the Torah which was revealed to Moses. They would pick and choose commandments which appealed to them and disregard anything that did not please them. The Qur'an says:

> *Then is it only a part of the Book that you believe in, and do you reject the rest? But what is the reward for those among you who behave like this but disgrace in this life?—and on the Day of Judgement they shall be consigned to the most grievous penalty. For God is not unmindful of what you do. These are the people who buy the life of this world at the price of the Hereafter: their penalty shall not be lightened nor shall they be helped.* [2:85-86]

Allah warned His Messenger (ṣ)—and this by default is a warning to his nation—against any inclination to such people lest they allure him away from the teachings of the Qur'an and as a result he might not rule by it and fail to comply with it:

> *And this (He commands): Judge you between them by what Allah has revealed, and follow not their vain desires, but beware of them lest they beguile you from any of that (teaching) which Allah has sent down to you.* [5:49]

The Qur'an also sharply disparages a category of the hypocrites who disregard the law of Allah and His Messenger (ṣ), except when it suits their personal interests. It emphatically refutes their claim of being faithful. Allay says:

> *They say, "We believe in Allah and in the Messenger, and we obey": but even after that, some of them turn away: they are not (really) Believers. When they are summoned to Allah and His Messenger, in order that He may judge between them, behold some of them decline (to come). But if the right is on their side, they come to him with all submission. Is it that there is a disease in their hearts? or do they doubt, or are they in fear, that Allah and His Messenger will deal unjustly with them? Nay, it is they themselves who do wrong. The answer of the Believers, when summoned to Allah and His Messenger, in order that He may judge between them, is no other than this: they say, "We hear and we obey": it is such as these that will attain felicity.* [24:47-51]

The faithful, when summoned to submit to the rule of Allah and His Messenger (ṣ), submit to it without hesitation and obey it without any apathy. "It is such as these that will attain felicity."

The covenant of faith in Allah as the Lord, Muḥammad (ṣ) as the final Messenger and the Qur'an as the guide, requires and implies gratification and contentment with what Allah and His Messenger ordain, or else faith becomes meaningless rhetoric and pretention:

> *It is not fitting for a believer, man or woman, when a matter has been decided by Allah and His Messenger to have any option about their decision.* [33:36]

On the other hand, and in contrast with the believers, there are those who do not submit to the law of Allah and His Messenger (ṣ), except when it suits their desires. Such people have disease in their hearts.

> *They are (no better than) wrong-doers.* [5:45]

> *...they are not (really) Believers.* [24:47]

The Qur'an as indivisible entity

The Qur'an is a single, indivisible entity; its teachings and rulings are interrelated and integrated. This correlation is similar to that of the different organs of the body. So just as one part affects the other parts, it is then not possible to separate one part of the body from its other constituent parts.

Belief nourishes worship and worship nurtures morals. Together they feed the practical and statutory aspects of life.

It does not make sense if a Muslim reads the divine command about fasting (in Sūrah al-Baqarah) and declare his submission to it, but he disobeys the divine ruling about the retribution for murder in the same chapter. The two verses are:

> *O you who believe! Fasting is prescribed to you as it was prescribed to those before you, that you may (learn) self-restraint.* [2:183]

> *O you who believe! The law of equality is prescribed to you in cases of murder.* [2:178]

When questioned about their selective behaviour, they argue that the first verse deals with the acts of worship, whereas the second is to do with legal penalties!

This means that the human being is taking up the role of a reviewer of the divine law where they adopt certain aspects and leave out others, according to their whims. The truth is that no one can review what Allah decrees.

Likewise, such people may accept the following verse from Sūrah al-Baqarah:

> *Allah! There is no god but He—the Living, the Self-Subsisting, Eternal. No slumber can seize Him nor sleep…* [2:255]

At the same time they discard the following verse in the same chapter:

> *O you who believe! Fear Allah, and give up what remains of your demand for usury, if you are indeed believers. If you do it not, take notice of war from Allah and His Messenger: But if you turn back, you shall have your capital sums: Deal not unjustly, and you shall not be dealt with unjustly.* [2:278-279]

Another example of such a warped understanding can be accepting the following verse from Sūrah al-Mā'idah:

> *O you who believe! When you prepare for prayer, wash your faces, and your hands (and arms) to the elbows, rub your heads (with water), and (wash) your feet to the ankles.* [5:6]

and rejecting the following verse in the same chapter:

As to the thief, male or female, cut off his or her hands: a punishment by way of example, from Allah, for their crime: and Allah is Exalted in power. [5:38]

Such people, upon hearing the following command of Allah:

So establish regular Prayer, give regular Charity... [22:78]

may say that they accept prayers (*ṣalāh*) but ignore charity (*zakāh*), because the former one is purely a spiritual ritual whereas the latter one is an obligation related to wealth and economics.

How astonishing is such attitude! Can a creation of God become more knowledgeable than his Creator?

With such an attitude and behaviour, a person not only becomes a rival to Allah, but also attempts to be the supreme authority, revoking from the commandments of Allah whatever that his intellect or whims cannot accept.

What is certain, and this is unanimously agreed by the scholars of Islam, is the fact that all the Qur'anic teachings must be implemented. In this regard, there is no divisions of the 'spiritual' and 'material', 'religious' and 'worldly', or 'individual' and the 'societal'.

Such labels do not exist in the Holy Book of Allah. There are no significant differences between them as long as they fall within the purview of the divine commandments and regulations.

In the first chapter, Sūrah al-Fātiḥah followed by the second chapter, al-Baqarah, one finds in the very beginning the description of the pious people guided by the Book as those:

> *Who believe in the Unseen, are steadfast in prayer, and spend out of what We have provided for them.* [2:3]

At the outset, the Book binds the dimension of belief ("faith in the Unseen"), the dimension of rituals ("being steadfast in prayers") and the economic dimension ("spending out of what is provided by the Allah"). This is how the faithful, the pious and the benevolent are described by the Qur'an. There is no differentiation between these aspects of the Muslim character. Further lucid and precise examples can be found in the Sūrahs al-Anfāl, verses 2-5, al-Mu'minūn: 1-11; al-Shu'arā: 36-39; al-Furqān: 63-76 and al-Dhāriyāt: 15-19.

There are similar examples regarding commands and prohibitions, for example the ten commandments given in Sūrah al-An'ām:

> *Say: "Come, I will rehearse what Allah has (really) prohibited you from": Join not anything as equal with Him; be good to your parents; kill not your children on a plea of want—We provide sustenance for you and for them; come not near to shameful deeds—whether open or secret; take not life, which Allah has made sacred, except by way of justice and law, thus does He command you, that you may learn wisdom. And come not near to the orphan's property, except to improve it, until he attain the age of full strength; give measure and weight with (full) justice—no burden do We place on any soul, but that which it can bear; whenever you speak, speak justly, even if a near relative is concerned; and fulfil the Covenant of Allah: thus does He command you, that you may remember. Verily, this is My way, leading straight: follow it; follow not (other) paths, they will scatter you about from His (great) path: thus does He command you, that you may be righteous.* [6:151-153]

Similar are the wise commandments given in Sūrah al-Isrā':

Your Lord has decreed that you worship none but Him, and that you be kind to parents. Whether one or both of them attain old age in your life, say not to them a word of contempt, nor repel them, but address them in terms of honour. And, out of kindness, lower to them the wing of humility, and say: "My Lord! bestow on them your Mercy even as they cherished me in childhood." Your Lord knows best what is in your hearts: If you do deeds of righteousness, verily He is Most Forgiving to those who turn to Him again and again (in true penitence).

And render to the kindred their due rights, as (also) to those in want, and to the wayfarer: But squander not (your wealth) in the manner of a spendthrift. Verily spendthrifts are brothers of the Evil Ones; and the Evil One is to his Lord (himself) ungrateful. And even if you have to turn away from them in pursuit of the Mercy from your Lord which you do expect, yet speak to them a word of easy kindness. Make not your hand tied (like a niggard's) to your neck, nor stretch it forth to its utmost reach, so that you become blameworthy and destitute. Verily your Lord does provide sustenance in abundance for whom He pleases, and He provides in a just measure. For He does know and regard all His servants. Kill not your children for fear of want: We shall provide sustenance for them as well as for you. Verily the killing of them is a great sin. Nor come near to adultery: for it is a shameful (deed) and an evil, opening the road (to other evils). Nor take life—which Allah has made sacred—except for just cause. And if anyone is slain wrongfully, we have given his heir authority (to demand qiṣāṣ or to forgive): but let him nor exceed bounds in the matter of taking life; for he is helped (by the Law).

Come not near to the orphan's property except to improve it, until he attains the age of full strength; and fulfil (every) engagement, for (every) engagement will be enquired into (on the Day of Reckoning). Give full measure when you measure, and weigh with a balance that is straight: that is the most fitting and the most advantageous in the final determination. And pursue not that of which you have no knowledge; for every act of hearing, or of seeing or of (feeling in) the heart will be enquired into (on the Day of Reckoning). Nor walk on the earth with insolence: for you cannot rend the earth asunder, nor reach the mountains in height. Of all such things the evil is hateful in the sight of your Lord. These are among the (precepts of) wisdom, which your Lord has revealed to you. Take not, with Allah, another object of worship, lest you should be thrown into Hell, blameworthy and rejected. [17:23-39]

All these verses contain belief, worship, ethics and conduct. Obviously, these are related to the religious as well as worldly affairs. They relate to the individual, the family and to society. They fall under the same context with no disparity.

Many a time the Qur'an uses the same diction to command what might be considered as different fields. The examples are:

...the law of equality is prescribed to you in cases of murder... [2:178]

It is prescribed, when death approaches any of you, if he leave any goods that he make a bequest to parents and next of kin, according to reasonable usage; this is due from the God-fearing. [2:180]

Fasting is prescribed to you as it was prescribed to those before you, that you may (learn) self-restraint, [2:183]

Fighting is prescribed for you, and you dislike it... [2:216]

This single Arabic diction *kutiba 'alaykum* ("prescribed for you") is used as a command and denotes an obligation and decree. It is used with regards to retribution which comes under criminal justice, and with regards to the will of the deceased which comes under personal law and family affairs. It is also used in relation to fasting which is an act of worship and with regards to fighting, which is a part of international relations. All these have been "prescribed" and ordained upon the faithful by Almighty Allah.

Authority of the Sunnah in legislation and guidance

The Sunnah of the Prophet (ṣ) is a detailed course of Islamic teachings. It tells how to implement its teachings and build the Ummah based on these teachings. The Qur'an states:

> *Allah did confer a great favour on the believers when He sent among them an messenger from among themselves, rehearsing unto them the Signs of Allah, sanctifying them, and instructing them in Scripture and Wisdom, while, before that, they had been in manifest error.* [3:164]

The Sunnah is exemplified by the sayings, deeds and affirmations of Prophet Muḥammad (ṣ), the final Messenger of Allah. It is the second authority in Islam after the Qur'an.

The Qur'an is the constitution that contains the essentials and fundamentals of Islam such as matters related to belief, worship, morality, dealings and etiquettes.

The Sunnah is the theoretical description as well as practical implementation of the Qur'an in all these areas. Following the

Sunnah is mandatory, as is obeying the Prophet (ṣ), just as he is obeyed in regards to what was revealed through him in the form of Qur'anic verses.

This is established by the Qur'an. This is established by the Sunnah itself, by the consensus of the Ummah, and by the intellect.

This has been mentioned in detail in our various other books with ample evidence.

No Qur'an without the Sunnah

In spite of all this, Muslims have been smitten both in the past and present by a small but noisy group ill-equipped with regard to specialised knowledge. This group purports that we are not in need of the Sunnah, that the Qur'an suffices for us without the Sunnah and that Qur'an alone is the source of the religion along with its beliefs, laws, concepts, values, morals and ethical compartment.

Doubts of the adversaries of the Sunnah

Adversaries of the Sunnah—not unlike any innovator of heresy and aberration—resort to doubts as evidence to support their arguments. These misgivings have been rebuffed cogently by Muṣlim scholars of all backgrounds.

These adversaries of the Sunnah or the so-called *Ahl al-Qur'ān* (followers of the Qur'an, as they identify themselves) have argued based on these verses:

> *Nothing have we omitted from the Book.* [6:38]

> *We have sent down to you the Book explaining all things.* [16:89]

They argue that Allah has undertaken to preserve the Qur'an when He says:

> *We have, without doubt, sent down the Message; and We will assuredly guard it (from corruption).* [15:9]

However, on the other hand, Allah has not undertaken to preserve the Sunnah.

The Messenger of Allah (ṣ) was merely assigned the job of writing down the revelations from Gabriel, as a "scribe of the revelation". He did not do so for the Sunnah; he rather said, "Do not write from me anything other than the Qur'an."

For the above reasons, the Sunnah has been penetrated by abomination, fabrication and what certainly is not rooted in the Ḥadīth (sayings of the Prophet). This is besides those weak and unsound narrations, which are not worth contending with. In other words there is utter chaos in the Ḥadīth literature since there is no way of verifying the genuine and fake *ḥadīths.*

Rebuttal by scholars of Ḥadīth

None of the above misgivings could withstand the scientific examination by scholars of Ḥadīth, based on the following points.

The Qur'an clearly defines the fundamentals and the Sunnah elaborates them:

This is in so far as the divine saying goes:

> *We have sent down to you the Book explaining all things...* [16:89]

This basic rule implies the fundamentals upon which the religion of Islam, its beliefs and laws, stand. One of these fundamentals is that the Messenger is the beacon of light appointed by God to elucidate all that was revealed to him. In other words, the Sunnah elaborates the Qur'an. The Qur'an ascertains this, saying:

> *We have sent down unto you (also) the Message; that you mayest explain clearly to men what is sent for them.* [16:44]

None amongst the first generation of the faithful or their successors understood that the elucidation by the Qur'an was elaborate. For example, acts of worship such as the five daily prayers have not been detailed in the Qur'an. Its schedule, its tenets, etiquette and rules are not detailed in the Qur'an itself, but by the Sunnah, which is inextricably part of the religion.

Preservation of Qur'an necessitates preservation of Sunnah

> *We have, without doubt, sent down the Message; and We will assuredly guard it (from corruption).* [15:9]

Imam al-Shāṭibī interpreters the word 'guard' to imply preservation of the Qur'an by way of its clear guidance, as well as the preservation of the Sunnah by way of inclusion. Indeed the preservation of the Qur'an necessitates the preservation of that which further elucidates it (*i.e.*, Sunnah), since it is an act of preserving both the Qur'an and Sunnah.

Hence, we can say that preservation has two aspects. Firstly, the material aspect, meaning preservation of the words and syntax from being forgotten, omitted or distorted. Secondly, the preservation of the abstract dimensions of the Qur'an, such as the preservation of its meanings from corruption or distortion.

As for previous revealed books, Allah did not guarantee their preservation. Their preservation was entrusted to their receivers. These books have undergone two types of corruption. Firstly, the syntactical corruption, whereby words were replaced and in some instances, omitted. Secondly, the intellectual distortion, whereby the interpretation was rendered irrelevant to the source.

Allah has guarded the Qur'an from both corruption and distortion. In fact, the prophetic elucidation of the Qur'an through the Sunnah was the intended will of God in order to preserve His book. This amounts to the confirmation of His promise to this effect:

> *...more, it is for Us to explain it (and make it clear)* [75:19]

Certainly, Islamic sciences and its strict methodology of verification affirm the truth of the preservation of the Sunnah just as Allah preserves His book.

Scholars continued this tradition, passing on this legacy from generation to generation as torch bearers of the faith, vindicating prophethood and the glad tidings brought by Muḥammad (ṣ), who said:

> In every generation there will be those who shall ward off deviation from this [religious] knowledge and who shall defend it against distortion of the radicals, pretence of the fraudsters and interpretation of the ignorant.

Phases of recording the Sunnah

It is true that the Messenger of Allah (ṣ) did not appoint scribes for recording the Sunnah, as he did in the case of the Qur'an.

He had even prohibited recording anything other than the Qur'an. There were very few who could write and writing materials were scarce. As such, this initial prohibition was to encourage those who could write to prioritise recording the Qur'anic verses in order to avoid any confusion. Nevertheless, he did ensure that such important matters as charity and blood money be written down. He also allowed companions like 'Abdullah ibn 'Amr and others to record his sayings. He emphasised the importance of accurately conveying his sayings to others. This is evident in his famous discourse, wherein he says:

> May Allah make him flourish (and to be radiant), that person who hears my talk and then comprehends it and then communicates it (exactly) as he heard it; for many a recipient is more perceptive than the original message-bearer.

Today, it has been established with certainty by researchers that the recording of the Sunnah did not commence after the first century of Hijrah, as was once understood. The recording of the Sunnah has had many phases, commencing during the life of the Messenger (ṣ) himself, and continued through the times of his companions and their successors.

Efforts of Muslim scholars in purifying the Sunnah

There have been people who attributed fabrications to the Messenger of Allah (ṣ) with different motives and intentions. By doing so, they only ensured for themselves the wrath of God. Yet, this is not surprising: there are those who fabricate even against Allah Himself; some even claim to have received divine revelation. History has witnessed the ardent stance of prudent scholars in guarding the Sunnah, and sifting through every narrated *ḥadīth* to intercept such frauds and impostors, unmask them and expose their lies. When Imam 'Abdullah ibn Mubārak was asked about the existence of such fabrications, he replied, "For (countering) it (*i.e.*, such lies), great scholars of authority exist!"

Indeed great scholars of authority have laid down their lives for this cause and pursued the fabricators, like money experts who detect counterfeit notes from the real ones. Such counterfeits may change hands among the public without being noticed by the authorities, but the fraud is ultimately exposed.

Scholars of Ḥadīth set up stringent rules and established various sciences of Ḥadīth with its terminology and stipulated the criterion for the acceptance of a *ḥadīth*. The procedure is so rigorous that throughout its history, mankind has not seen such a methodology that preserves the heritage of a man (the Prophet) from distortion.

With regard to the allegation that the Ḥadīth has become dubious because of its being mixed up with the weak narrations, let it be clear that it is nothing but the pretentious views held by those who are not expert in the science of Ḥadīth or fail to explore its depths. There are those who have not even familiarised themselves with the great endeavours of scholars and intellectuals of the past, who devoted themselves to this service and dedicated their lives in order elucidate it and defend it with amazing veracity: those who established the disciplines of scientifically scrutinising the biographies of the narrators of Ḥadīth (*'Ilm al-Rijāl*), their rankings (*Ṭabaqāt*) and chronologies (*Tawārīkh*) and categorised *ḥadīths* into levels of trustworthy, acceptable, weak or questionable. They founded around ninety branches of sciences that collectively came to be known as the sciences of Ḥadīth (*'Ulūm al-Ḥadīth*).

These sciences formed the touchstone for Ḥadīth verification. Consequently, they sifted through the whole anthology of Ḥadīth literature and separated the authentic from the weak. They paid great attention to investigating *ḥadīths* related to rules and regulations and wrote exhaustively about *ḥadīths* classified as weak, giving detailed criticism of their flaws.

The efforts of the followers of the final Messenger (ṣ) to preserve his legacy are unprecedented in the history of mankind. Existence of some fraudulent *ḥadīths* does not necessitate discarding the entire Ḥadīth literature. Is that not like calling for the incineration of all the currency in circulation and banning its use just because some swindlers floated counterfeit notes?

Rejecting Sunnah is against the Qur'an

Those who reject the Ḥadīth and confine themselves to the Qur'an alone are in gross contradiction with the Qur'an in the first place.

The Qur'an orders the faithful to obey the Messenger of Allah (ṣ) along with their obedience to Him. This is emphasised in various places in the Qur'an.

The Qur'an regards the obedience to the Messenger of Allah (ṣ) as obedience to Allah Himself, just as it deems the pledge of allegiance to the Messenger (ṣ) as allegiance to Allah Himself. Here are some examples:

> *He who obeys the Messenger, obeys Allah.* [4:80]

Verily those who plight their fealty to you do no less than plight their fealty to God. [48:10]

Obey Allah, and obey the Messenger, and beware (of evil): if you do turn back, know you that it is Our Messenger's duty to proclaim (the message) in the clearest manner. [5:92]

O you who believe! Obey Allah and His Messenger, and turn not away from him when you hear (him speak). [8:20]

Say: "Obey Allah, and obey the Messenger: but if you turn away, he is only responsible for the duty placed on him and you for that placed on you. If you obey him, you shall be on right guidance. The Messenger duty is only to preach the clear (Message). [24:54]

He that obeys Allah and His Messenger, has already attained the highest achievement. [33:71]

So obey Allah, and obey His Messenger: but if you turn back, the duty of Our Messenger is but to proclaim (the Message) clearly and openly. [64:12]

O you who believe! Obey Allah, and obey the Messenger, and those charged with authority among you. If you differ in anything among yourselves, refer it to Allah and His Messenger, if you do believe in Allah and the Last Day: That is best, and most suitable for final determination. [4:59]

Had obedience to the Messenger been limited to compliance with the Qur'an alone, there was no need for the coordinating conjunction (obey God and obey the Messenger). The conjunction requires variation. By demanding obedience to Allah and obedience to the Messenger at various places, the Qur'an implies their variation.

Majority of juristic regulations based on Sunnah

Most of the regulations, which form the axis of various significant schools of jurisprudence, are based on the Sunnah.

Whoever studies Islamic jurisprudence knows that if the Sunnah, its branches and derivatives, are taken out from our juristic legacy, there would be hardly anything left!

This serves as the rationale for the study of the Sunnah since it is a guide to the Qur'an and has engaged and engrossed scholars of significant schools of jurisprudence and has been a prime preoccupation of the scholars in their studies on the fundamentals of jurisprudence. As is known to the students of Islam, these studies deal with authority of the Sunnah, its veracity, qualifications for its acceptance, denotations and other details.

This, as mentioned above, is true about all the schools of Islamic jurisprudence, from the school of Dāwūd and Ibn Ḥazm—which reject the concept of *qiyās* (juristic reasoning) and *ta'līl* (justification)—to the schools Abū Ḥanīfah and his disciples—known as "the opinionative school" of Islamic jurisprudence.

Between Sunnah and Qur'an

Although both the Qur'an and Sunnah form the sources of divine guidance and legislation, both are not of the same status and that there are basic differences between the two.

The Qur'an is conclusively authentic, because it was transmitted from generation to generation with unquestionable consistency. As far as Sunnah is concerned, less of it is established on consistent narrations and more of it is based on independent narrations.

The Qur'an was revealed through manifest revelation, wherein the Spirit of Faith and Truth (*i.e.*, the Archangel Gabriel) came down with the revelation of the divine word and planted it upon the heart and mind of the Messenger (ṣ). The Qur'an unequivocally says:

> *With it came down the spirit of Faith and Truth—to your heart and mind, that you may admonish.* [26:193-194]

So far as Sunnah is concerned, a part of it is based on the inspiration sent to the spirit of the Prophet, while the remaining is founded on his true visions (*ru'yā*); however, both these types of inspiration do not amount to revelation. The Sunnah also includes what was established through diligence, which has been endorsed by Allah and is termed as the "hidden revelation". Certainly Allah does not endorse wrong, so that people do not go astray.

The Qur'an, its letters and meaning, are from God. As far as Sunnah *i.e.*, its verbal part, is concerned, it is from the Prophet (ṣ). This is the reason that unlike Ḥadīth and Sunnah, the Qur'an being the unmediated divine word must be narrated verbatim.

The Qur'an is guarded and preserved by Allah. Allah says:

> *We have, without doubt, sent down the Message; and We will assuredly guard it (from corruption).* [15:9]

So far as Sunnah is concerned, it has been preserved by default due to the divine preservation of the Qur'an, since it acts as the elucidator of the Qur'an. It is only logical that one which elucidates the Qur'an must also by default be divinely preserved.

The Qur'an is unique with regard to its inimitability. It is the greatest miracle of Muḥammad (ṣ). The Sunnah, although represents the eloquence of human expression, cannot be compared to the divine word as such.

The authentic Sunnah should not contradict the Qur'an. Hence, the Sunnah is either the elucidator of the Qur'an, complements it or assumes the role of a legislator with regards to certain regulations within its framework of objectives and fundamentals; it is not and cannot be in contradiction with the Qur'an. It must be emphasised that there cannot be an authentic Sunnah that contradicts the Qur'an. Whatever may be found otherwise is either something which is authentic but incomprehensible (in the present moment in time of our understanding of such a Sunnah) or it may be comprehensible but unauthentic. The key is that the unauthentic tradition has no significance, whereas an incomprehensible tradition must be interpreted accordingly so that it complies directly with the Qur'an. The Qur'an is the root of the sources and that which stems from the root cannot divert from it.

It is appropriate to cite here Ibn al-Qayyim who has mentioned in his book *I'lām al-Mūqi'īn* regarding the relation of the Sunnah with the Qur'an. According to him, this relation has three aspects.

Firstly, the Sunnah must conform with the Qur'an in all aspects with regards to any particular regulation so that there is an absolute concurrence between the two sources based on the synergy of the two criteria.

Secondly, the Sunnah must be an elucidation and interpretation of what the Qur'an intends to originally convey.

Thirdly, the Sunnah should either enjoin a regulation the obligation of which the Qur'an has remained silent; or it should prohibit something about which the Qur'an has also remained silent. The Sunnah must not go beyond this and contradict the Qur'an in any way.

Whatever is in excess of what is in the Qur'an is legislation introduced by the Messenger of Allah (ṣ), in which he must be obeyed. This in no way means preferring the Sunnah over the Book of Allah. Rather it implies the submission by the believers to Allah's command to obey His Messenger. If the Messenger was not to be obeyed in this aspect then obedience to him is pointless and then supposedly specific obedience to him too would become null and void. Since obedience to him has been commanded insofar as it conforms with the Qur'an, not in anything else, that means there is no specialised obedience specific to him. Allah says:

He who obeys the Messenger, obeys Allah. [4:80]

The authority of Sunnah derived from Qur'an

The status of the Sunnah is that it is the elucidator and the Qur'an is the elucidated; the Qur'an is the source text and the Sunnah explains and explicates it; everything found in the Sunnah draws on the Qur'an in one way or another. In his book *Al-Muwafiqāt,* Imam al-Shāṭibī illustrates this fact with sufficient evidences.

For example, the prohibition of a man marrying a woman, and her paternal or maternal aunt at the same time, is a kind of *qiyās* (juristic reasoning) based on the Qur'anic commandment forbidding joining two sisters in wedlock to one man. This reasoning in turn is based on the prophetic warning against joining two sisters wherein the logic of the forbiddance has been mentioned as severing the bonds of kinship. The *ḥadīth* says: "If you do so, you shall be severing the bonds of your kinship."

Likewise, bequeathing to the grandmother the portion of the mother upon death of the mother is based on the juristic reasoning of treating her as mother; since the grandmother is in a sense regarded as a mother.

As suggested by Imam al-Shāfi'ī, the prohibition of eating beasts of prey which have fangs is the implementation of the Qur'anic corroboration that one of the assignments of the Messenger of Allah (ṣ) is to prohibit that which is harmful:

> *...and prohibits them from what is bad (and impure)...* [7:157]

Prohibition of eating and drinking in utensils made of gold or silver or similar precious metals is based on condemnation by the Qur'an of extravagance and self-indulgence and for considering lavishness among the reasons of moral deterioration and the decadence of nations which eventually lead to their ultimate destruction.

Prohibition of being alone with an unmarried woman is again an implementation of the Qur'anic edict against going near adultery.

> *Nor come near to adultery: for it is a shameful (deed) and an evil, opening the road (to other evils).* [17:32]

This is because "nor come near to adultery" implies prohibition from preludes to the act of adultery.

Similarly the Messenger of Allah (ṣ) while cursing drunkards, also cursed nine other supporting professions, because he considered them contributing to the same satanic abomination, from which Allah commands to disdain.

> *...an abomination,—of Satan's handwork; eschew such (abomination)...* [5:90]

This is because the Qur'an uses the command "eschew", which is more eloquent an expression than "quit". In other words, Allah commands turning away from intoxicants instead of commanding not to consume it. With this reasoning, the Messenger of Allah (ṣ) cursed, along with those who consume it, nine others who support this vice, including those who press it, those who serve it, those who carry it, those who trade in it, and so on.

According to Ibn Barrajān, whatever the Prophet (ṣ) has said can be found in the Qur'an. In fact, the Sunnah is rooted in the Qur'an itself, directly and indirectly, and it is comprehensible to those who strive to understand it. Allah the Almighty says:

> *Nothing have we omitted from the Book.* [6:38]

Certainly there is nothing in the Sunnah that might be impertinent to the Qur'an, let alone something that might deviate from it or contradict it. In it is to be found the elucidation of what is found in the Qur'an; it specifies what is generic in the Qur'an and it qualifies what is unconditional in the Qur'an.

Praise be to Allah, the Cherisher and Sustainer of the worlds.

Index

'Abd al-Ḥalīm Abū Shuqqah 274
'Abd al-Ḥalīm Maḥmūd, 34
'Abduh, Muḥammad 21, 23, 25, 274
'Abdullah Darrāz, Muḥammad 1, 19, 35, 36
'Abdullah ibn 'Amr 271, 326, 377
'Abdullah ibn Mas'ūd 42
Abraham, prophet 4, 44, 74, 265, 347
Abū Bakr, caliph 122, 153, 157, 158, 325, 353
Abū Hurayrah 90, 91, 117, 163, 270, 283, 284, 285, 303, 313, 315, 317, 321, 326, 334
Abū 'Ubayd 323
Abū Ya'lā 322
'Ad 44, 339
Adam, prophet 40, 44, 72, 74, 127, 130, 157, 184, 245, 257, 267, 316, 317, 338, 340, 354
  children of 338
adhān 193, 213
aḥkām 360
Ahl al-Qur'ān 373
Ahriman 195
Aḥzāb, the battle of 221
'Ā'ishah 92, 157, 158, 163, 279, 281, 285
Al-Azhar, University 34, 320
al-Bukhārī 241, 321, 354
'Alī, caliph 222, 330, 343
Allah
  belief in 45–59
  First Cause 45, 56
  Prime Mover 56
'Amr ibn al-'Āṣ 342
'Aqqād, 'Abbās Maḥmūd al- 27, 194, 253
Aristotle 56, 203

Ashbāh wa al-Naẓā'ir, al- 165
Ashja'ī, Na'īm bin Mas'ūd al- 221
Aws 323

Banī Ādam 184
Banī Makhzūm 189
Banū Qurayẓah 221
Banū Thaqīf 222, 223
barzakh 8
Bayhaqī, al- 240
Bible 3, 44, 128, 129, 195
bigotry 70, 288, 303, 304, 312
Brahmanism 137
Brail, Dr 16
breast-feeding 277
brotherhood 19, 53, 147, 152, 186, 187, 190, 214, 268, 287, 292, 292–293, 293, 295, 310, 311, 312, 316, 337, 339, 340
  Islamic 292, 311, 312, 316
Buddhism 3, 176, 201
Bukhārī, Imam al- 91, 103, 117, 158, 163, 165, 166, 198, 241, 260, 262, 263, 273, 279, 296, 304, 321, 334, 353, 354

Carnegie, Dale 16
Carrel, Alexis 33
Chaldeans 24
chastity 297
Children of Israel 197, 206, 247, 290, 309, 364
Christian 4, 67, 112, 123, 124, 137, 177, 201, 266, 336, 343, 348, 351
Christianity 3, 25, 67, 123, 124, 127, 137, 176, 177, 195, 204, 261, 318, 319, 351, 359
Companions vii, 81, 137, 144, 177, 190, 216, 304, 324, 325, 335, 345, 358

Dār al-Islām 323, 331. *See also* Islam, House of
da'wah 307
dawlah al-Islām 331
Day of Judgement vii, 43, 58, 108, 116, 118, 157, 173, 191, 197, 217, 239, 240, 288, 294, 321, 355, 364
Day of Resurrection 44, 117, 216, 355
dayyūth 282
dhikr 238
Dhū al-Qarnayn 295
Divine
  legislation 179
  morality 178
Dubos, René Jules 33

Egyptians 24, 63
empathy 293–295
enjoining virtue and forbidding vice 289, 308, 322, 327, 335

farḍ 'ayn 255
farḍ kifāyah 212, 255

Fāṭimah 117, 189, 299
fatwā 229
fiqh 180, 357, 358, 359
fiṭrah 73, 171
freedom
of belief 208
to criticise 208
furūḍ al-kifāyah see *farḍ kifāyah*

Ghassānide 189
Ghatafān, tribe of 221
Ghazālī, al- 81, 253, 254, 328
Gog and Magog 295
Gospel 25, 43, 163
Greeks 24
Greek Stoicism 137

hajj 83, 88, 97, 110, 146, 186
ḥalāl 154, 188
ḥalāl wa al-ḥarām, al- 154
Ḥamzah ibn 'Abd al-Muṭṭalib 39
Ḥanafī 165, 226
ḥarām 154, 159, 188
Ḥasan al-Bannā 190, 314, 317
Heavenly Kingdom 137
Hereafter 2, 10, 18, 45, 63, 102, 137, 138, 147, 149, 152, 153, 161, 171, 174, 183, 197, 247, 287, 290, 357, 362, 364
Hijrah 230, 323, 377
Hinduism 3
hippies 30
Ḥudaybiyah, treaty of 118, 222, 331, 346, 353
Hūd, prophet 44, 49, 60, 74, 339
ḥudūd 148, 151, 155
human existence 300

Ibn 'Abbās 273, 276, 277, 278, 280, 296
Ibn 'Ābidīn, hanafite 230, 231
Ibn 'Atiyyah 277
Ibn Jamā'ah 323
Ibn Khaldūn 329
Ibn Nujaym al-Ḥanafī 165
Ibn al-Qayyim 81, 95, 193, 217, 218, 229, 230, 231, 383
Ibn Taymiyyah 76, 77, 82, 83, 84, 85, 95, 100, 286, 321, 323, 326, 327, 328, 350
Ibn Zanjuwayh 323
'iddah 225
iḥrām 110
ijmā' 216, 358, 359
ijtihād 143, 216, 224, 226, 229, 359, 360
Imam al-Ḥaramayn 322
Imāmites 226
insān 184
insāniyyah 181, 182
Islam, House of 310, 323, 324
Islamic state 116, 117, 122, 323, 325, 328, 329, 330, 332, 356
istiḥsān 143, 216, 224, 226
istiṣḥāb 143
istiṣlāḥ 143, 226

Jacob, prophet 4, 265
James, William 16
Jesus, prophet 3, 4, 44, 51, 177, 191, 204, 247, 290, 309, 325
Jew 4, 67, 112, 241, 341, 350, 351, 354
jihād 155, 168, 170, 196, 225, 248, 290, 311, 327, 343
jizyah 349
Judaism 2, 67, 70, 123, 124, 137, 176

Khansā' bint Khaddām al-Anṣāriyyah 273
Khaybar, people of 228
Khazraj 323
Kufr, house of 324

Link, Henry 16

Makkah 83, 166, 168, 217, 238, 323, 344, 346, 353, 364
Malikī 226
Mani, philosophy of 261
manṭiqah al-'afw 142
Manuism 137
Marxism 35, 205
Marx, Karl 42
maṣāliḥ al-mursalah 216, 226
mashaqqah tajlib al-taysīr, al- 165
maṣūṣ 143
Māwardī, al- 322
Messenger of Allah 38, 40, 43, 51, 81, 90, 91, 93, 116, 121, 132, 142, 157, 163, 164, 168, 184, 189, 207, 213, 217, 220, 222, 223, 224, 228, 236, 239, 244, 246, 248, 262, 263, 266, 267, 269, 270, 271, 272, 273, 279, 280, 281, 282, 283, 284, 285, 295, 299, 303, 304, 311, 312, 313, 315, 318, 321, 322, 323, 324, 325, 326, 328, 331, 333, 336, 338, 339, 347, 353, 354, 357, 372, 374, 376, 377, 379, 384, 385, 386. *See also* Muḥammad (ṣ)
minhāj Allāh 175
mīthāq, al- 87
Moses, prophet 3, 4, 44, 46, 47, 61, 132, 191, 364
Mu'ādh ibn Jabal 103
mu'āsharah bi al-ma'rūf, al- 276
Mughīrah ibn Shu'bah, al- 271
Muḥammad (ṣ) vii, 3, 5, 43, 49, 51, 60, 67, 108, 132, 133, 174, 177, 178, 184, 190, 191, 216, 235, 246, 254, 310, 335, 339, 345, 347, 356, 372, 376, 383
Muslim, Imam 103
Muslim state 116, 322
Mustafa Kamal 319
Mu'tazilites 226

nās 184
nationalism 28, 52, 314, 315, 316

nawāfil 238
New Testament 191
Noah, prophet 3, 44, 49, 60, 74
Nuṣayriyyah 24

Paraclete 191
People of the Book 51, 63, 234, 236, 311, 331, 336, 347, 349, 355, 356
Pharaoh 46, 47, 61, 112
Plato 203
Plutarch 13, 18
polygeny 160
Psalms 44
qiṣāṣ 155
qiyās 143, 216, 226, 358, 359, 381, 385
Quraysh 119, 189, 221, 222, 353
Qurṭubī 277
rabbāniyyah 169, 171, 172, 173, 174, 178, 181, 182, 306
Ramadan 82, 83, 146, 163, 186, 217, 289
Raqāyak 15
Rashīd Riḍā 23, 26
religion and state 115, 325, 332
ri'āyah al-maqāṣid 143
rībah 282
Rib'ī bin 'Āmir 246, 335
Rightly Guided Caliphs 121, 122, 189, 218, 312, 342
Rustum 246
sad al-dharā'i' 143
Sa'd ibn Abī Waqqāṣ 267
ṣalāh 83, 109, 165, 185, 188, 225, 241, 368
Salamah ibn Akwa' 166
Ṣāliḥ, prophet 44, 49, 74, 257, 339
Salmān al-Fārisī 221, 314
Satan 73, 74, 120, 132, 195, 244, 297, 386
ṣawm 83, 109, 166, 186, 225
secularism 320, 325
sexual intimacy 277
Sharī'ah 76, 88, 126, 142, 143, 144, 145, 146, 148, 152, 155, 156, 157, 158, 159, 160, 161, 162, 165, 178, 199, 206, 212, 213, 216, 224, 225, 227, 229, 230, 231, 242, 245, 257, 275, 284, 300, 302, 310, 321, 322, 323, 330, 332, 348, 349
Shāṭibī, al- 375, 384
shūrā 144, 218
Sietec, Auguste 12
ṣirāṭ Allāh 175
Socrates 34
St Augustine 68
St Paul 177
Sunnah 372
  recording of 377

Ṭabarī 277
tawḥīd 171, 173, 235
tayammum 164

Thamūd 44, 339
theft 108, 117, 152, 153, 161, 189, 217, 299
Torah 3, 43, 44, 123, 129, 191, 364
Toynbee, Arnold 16
Trinity, concept of 44, 66

'Ulūm al-Ḥadīth 379
'Umar ibn 'Abd al-'Azīz 11, 231
'Umar ibn al-Khaṭṭāb 14, 189, 190, 342, 349, 350
'Umar Khayyām 11
'Umrah 288
Universal peace 343–347
'urf 143, 226
Usāmah ibn Zayd 189
'Uthmān 160, 327

Wahiduddin Khan 33

Zabūr (Psalms) 44
Zachariah, prophet 265
Ẓāhirites 145, 226
Ẓāhiriyyah 359
zakāh 83, 97, 109, 146, 153, 165, 166, 185, 188, 199, 210, 217, 225, 241, 289, 296, 298, 322, 350, 368
Zayd ibn Arqam 338
zinā 149
Zoroastrianism 3, 67, 195, 204